Dear John,

Happy !!

First published in Belgium in 2012

Rat-race to the Boardroom is self-published with the help of Lulu Enterprises Inc.

First edition. November 2012

Cover illustration licensed from Dreamstime.com.
Cover design: me, myself and I.

Illustrations:
14, 85, 206, 253: gratefully downloaded from www.freedigitalphotos.net.
44, 299: own picture
130: gratefully downloaded from British Airways

Any correspondence and enquiries with respect to this book should be sent only to: henry.w.derrick@gmail.com

Copyright © 2012 HWDConsult
ISBN 978-1-291-10475-2

All rights reserved. No part of this publication may be reproduced, stored in or introduced into a retrieval system or transmitted, in any form, or by any means without the prior written permission of the author. Any person who does any unauthorised act in relation to this publication may be liable to criminal prosecutions and civil claims for damages.

RAT-RACE TO THE BOARDROOM

HENRY W. DERRICK

Alasdair, An, André, Andrew, Anita, Bjoern†, Bob†, Bob, Chris, Claire, Clive†, Corinne, Dan, Daniel, Dirk, Dries, Eddy, Ellis, François, Gareth, George, Graham, Guus, Heidi, Herman, Hervé, Herwig, Hugo, Ian, Jane, Jeannine, Jo, Joanne, Jo-Anne, Joep, Johny, Jos, Kate, Kathryn, Khalid, Koos, Kris, Lea†, Leen, Liu, Luc, Luk, Marc, Marcel, Maria, Marleen, Maureen, Michael, Nathalie, Neil, Nicole, Pascal, Patrick, Patrik, Paul†, Paul, Peter, Rebecca, René, Richard, Rik, Rob, Robert†, Ronny, Rudy, Russell, Sabine, Sharon, Sharron, Smitte, Smurfke, Sonja, Tatjana, Theo, Thomas, Veke, Waleed, Winnie, Xavier, Yetunde, Zoltan.

Thank you.

Many, many thanks and kisses to Shirley.

Management summary.

Because that's what you want, isn't it? A short, succinct summary?
You don't really have time to read this in all its detail. Before the end of the weekend or before you land in Heathrow; you still have to read a lot of other stuff. Tomorrow you have a meeting on the premium brand pricing and you haven't gone through the 40-pager yet. I know it's on your iPad, so you can walk through it while Jack presents his strategy. You have full confidence in Jack. There is also your management meeting next week where you'll detail your team restructuring proposal. On this you feel less comfortable as the data you received Saturday evening from your Financial Controller don't seem to support the case. And don't forget – you still need to instruct your PA to change your plans as the meeting in Budapest needs to be cancelled. And you should also reply to Eve's draft notes on the Product Development meeting. And walk through the competency profile HR has kindly drafted for the new vacancy in your team. And wire over 20 Euros for the fundraising for Claudio's Brussels marathon. And buy the DVD of *The Hunger Games* for your daughter's birthday. And you are out of cigarettes.
And. And. And.

So, is there any free time in your busy life to read this book? You have been told it is great reading; but what's it about? Can anybody tell you?

Well, I can, with pleasure. Here is your management summary.
You are reading a story – in short, blogging chapters, and in the biography-style of a successful manager, flourishing in the corporate rat-race. It could be your story; your own business life experience.
From his early study years, through first work experiences and struggling to make money, towards him stepping into management roles, it includes some common and less common (sometimes kinky) business challenges like a hostile strike in France, fraud in the Middle-East, major acquisitions, the retirement of a remarkable CEO and the subsequent paradigm shift. Yes, "business buzzwords" is a chapter the author can't leave untouched. Similarly, because of living for so many years in the UK, the author doesn't shy away from sharing his views on the Brits. Some of you may want to skip that chapter.
He keeps rewardingly climbing the corporate ladder in blue chip organisations where he – just like you – meets some very interesting characters; very successful business leaders, managers with a distinctive talent for innovation as well as "puppet on a string" managers who do what they are told to do. He also comes across fraudulent managers and leaders who daily eat and drink the corporate governance manual, and consultants and advisors who work with you, as well as consultants who just invoice you.
On top of that, Henry shares some of his awkward business travel stories, including a police raid in Athens, hookers in Ukraine and full speed through Baku. And if you have ever been in a taxi in Istanbul, you'll easily recognise that story. The journey completes with Henry making some reflections on his work-life balance and on business life in general. While he is highly respected in his business, he realises he's only a part of the money-making machine and wonders if he's doing

the right things for himself. Self-reflection is the key theme in the final stage of his career journey.

All this comes with a sceptical but good-humoured take on some of today's corporate practices. Interleaved are some chapters containing detailed research related to climbing the corporate ladder, the risks of the ladder and of corporate life in general.

That's it, in a nutshell, as you asked.

This book doesn't pretend to be your coach or mentor; it's a novel, not a workbook. It could be, should you wish so, an opportunity for self-reflection. And that, for once, is not a business decision to be taken; this time it's about you.
And therefore, to even enjoy this book in depth, I advise you to pause from business distractions; all your important job stuff is somewhere stored on a hard disk, a server or a cloud. Leave it there for a short while and create some time to chill-out with this book in a relaxing environment; whether it's on your way back home in seat 4F (that's my preferred seat on a plane), a Sofitel hotel room in Paris, or the train to London. Even better, relax on your most comfortable sofa at home with a coffee or a good glass of Pinot Gris on the side table. And would you mind me advising you to put your smartphone in off-mode? I know that you have outspoken multi-skilling capabilities, but if you are at this very moment visiting one of your elder relatives in the Alzheimer care centre, honestly, please refrain from reading.

I realise that you – as a key player in the rat-race contest – may not be attracted by self-reflection. Why the hell should you? You are climbing successfully, you are enjoying it and you are making a nice living. You may prefer to once more walk through your corporate plan; that's going to be much more rewarding for your next bonus. Maybe. Or maybe not.

So instead of that "self-reflection", invented by the softies from HR you think, you could also use this book as an analytical tool; as a point of reference, a standard, a yardstick. Analysis and figures may be much more in your comfort zone; so benchmark yourselves with Henry, that senior Director in a FTSE50 company.
In terms of style...unconventional it is, that's for sure. It's a new style of writing that still needs to get a definition in the artistic world.
I have tried to be as close as possible to the reader, for whom ultimately this work is destined. In marketing terms – and I am not a Marketing Director at all – this would be called recognising customer needs or also customer awareness. I have checked with many members of the target audience, and what they confirmed is a need for easy/quick reading, management language and a bit of relaxing fun. Although the editor, the publisher, the bookshop and perhaps even the author may make a profit out of it, this book is there for the reader.
My desire to be as close as possible to the reader, has intentionally also created a specific language style. It is as if I am sitting next to you; in a meeting room, a pub or on a plane. As the author's mother tongue is Dutch, this work is not really in Shakespeare's language. Not at all. I have even insisted that the correctors did not modify some strange or less Anglo-Saxon constructions of sentences. Obviously, we hope to have corrected any spelling errors, but it should be clear that by the use of some specific vocabulary and less optimal grammar, this book is written by a non-native speaker. And that mirrors fully with the character of Henry, a Belgian/Dutch- –or Flemish should you wish so- speaking manager who builds his career in successful American and English companies.

I do realise that for the Brits, this may result in some strange feelings, but I am confident that for British managers who are working in an international environment, they may quickly have the feeling of listening to an overseas colleague, perhaps someone from Germany, France, The Netherlands, or Belgium. Not Italian, as then it would have been written even more staccato. And if you want to have the feeling of listening to a Spanish colleague who's speaking English, just replace any 'v' at the beginning of a word by a 'b'.

Even in this short introduction, you will have noticed that sometimes I talk about 'I' and sometimes about 'the author'. Yet again intentionally, as the author, Henry likes to leave it over to you to read this work as a novel or an autobiography. Or is it nothing more than the figment of a schizophrenic mind.

You will experience in reading this book, that Henry has worked for over 20 years in top-level jobs in US and UK companies and that part of his career was in Head Office corporate roles. From those roles, he has learned – amongst many other things – the importance of corporate governance, risk management and the mitigation of risks. This all turned him paranoia for litigation. Therefore, and not so common for a novel, you will find in the next section an elaborated and fun disclaimer. This also means that further on in this book, Deloitte may not be the Deloitte you know, Albert may never have worked at Coca Cola Enterprises and Marc Rich may not be a lawyer at E&O. It could be that Maurice Janot was never fired and still works in the Middle East. And Andy may not be CEO of Commonwealth Consumer Goods PLC, but Catering Manager at Red Bull. I leave it to you as to who the consulting firm McLinsey may be. And don't forget, this is a management novel; it is fiction. Written for easy reading in short chapters, a bit in blogging style.

Or is it Henry's autobiography?

And where I talk directly to you, dear reader, I have assumed that you, just like Henry, are a Gold member of the corporate rat-race Club. If that were not to be the case, then please accept hereby my sincere apologies. And congratulations.

Happy reading. Enjoy.

Me, Henry.

~ ~ ~ ~ ~ ~ ~ ~ ~

Contents

Disclaimer. To be read.		13
Chapter 1:	A drawing for success	15
Chapter 2:	The odours of some carefully distilled German liquids	25
Chapter 3:	Venus Grotto and Capitalism	34
Chapter 4:	Nothing urgent, André	45
Chapter 5:	Once I have received my bonus	54
Chapter 6:	The Dutch billionaire	63
Chapter 7:	Vous descendrez plus jamais	69
Chapter 8:	Again climbing the corporate ladder	86
The Facts 1:	**Predictors of success**	96
Chapter 9:	Management training in Prague	107
Chapter 10:	Not too bad	113
Chapter 11:	Mr X. – Fraud – Macedonia	124
Chapter 12:	Miles & More	131
Chapter 13:	Kiev turndown service	150
Chapter 14:	Con te partiro	159
Chapter 15:	McLinsey & Company	176
The Facts 2:	**Bullshit Bingo**	190
Chapter 16:	Family alienation	207
The Facts 3:	**Give it up, baby give it up...**	213
Chapter 17:	Twelve windows	220
Chapter 18:	Clifton Bridge	226
The Facts 4:	**Brain elasticity**	237
Chapter 19:	Into solution mode	250
Chapter 20:	The fat lady doesn't sing	254
Chapter 21:	The management basics	268
The Facts 5:	**The real management basics**	278
Chapter 22:	Athens, Georgia, USA	290
Chapter 23:	In good shape	300
Acknowledgements		303

Disclaimer. To be read.

Rat-race to the Boardroom is a work of fiction; sourced by the imaginative brain of the author.

Names, characters, businesses, places, events and incidents are either the products of the author's imagination or used in a fictitious manner. Any resemblance to actual persons, living or dead, businesses, running or bankrupt, or actual events is purely coincidental.

Any statements and views expressed on 'the Brits' should be seen as a generalising statement and may not apply to all Pound Sterling paid inhabitants of the islands west of continental Europe.

The information contained in the fiction chapters of this book should not be read as reliable and, while every effort has been made to ensure that the information is easy readable and sometimes amusing, less effort has been made to guarantee its accuracy. The author therefore disclaims any implied warranty or representation about its accuracy, completeness or appropriateness for any particular purpose.

Although the author has taken every care in preparing and writing the non-fiction chapters of this book, the current litigious world requires the author not to accept liability for any errors, omissions, misuse or misunderstandings on the part of any person who uses it. The author accepts no responsibility for any damage, injury or loss occasioned to any person or company as a result of relying on any material included, omitted or implied in the book.

Those persons who read this book – to whom the author is very grateful – assume full responsibility for the use of said information and understand and agree that the author of this book is not responsible or liable for any claim, loss or damage arising from the use of any information, nor for the actions that you may decide to take out of reading this novel.

Any reference to specific products, companies or services does not necessarily constitute or imply recommendation or endorsement by the author. While the author refers frequently to his smoking habits, this work should not be seen as an invite to the readers to take-up nor to quit tobacco consumption.

Rat-race to the Boardroom is not written as a guide to managers on how to react to the current pressures of business life; it does not advise to comply or to not comply with internal company regulations. This book is not written as a guide for the use of your Xerox copier, the London Heathrow eye-scanning machine, your colleague's stolen stapler or your office Sip Well water cooler. Nor does it advise on the use of your home Nespresso machine. You should follow your manufacturer's instructions for your specific type of equipment.

The content of this book does not substitute the local and national tax laws that may apply to you.

I reckon that's enough ass-covering.

Oh, and, objects in your rear-view mirror are closer than they appear.

CHAPTER 1

A drawing for success.

> *"But there are advantages to being elected President. The day after I was elected, I had my high school grades classified Top Secret." – <u>Ronald Reagan</u>*

I am told that I was a smart kid.

In the last year of the kindergarten in our local small village school nearby Mechelen, the classroom was overpopulated.

Ingrid, the teacher, was tall, drove a flashy red Triumph Spitfire and had been a strong contender in last year's Miss Antwerp contest. Our fathers adored Miss Ingrid. I don't think though that her beauty was the reason for us thirty ADHD-boys being packed like sardines into the smallest classroom of the school, suitable only for up to twenty-five kids. Probably our parents, five or six years ago, had been a bit overactive in reproducing the human race. Our parents were young kids themselves during the Second World War, and they had collectively decided to create a better world. So two, three, four kids was becoming the norm.

We are in the mid-sixties, so the most honourable people in the village are still the mayor, the notary with his blue-white two-doors coupé Studebaker, the priest and the head teacher. The mayor and the notary weren't bothered with the issue at school; they had other things to do as more and more households moved from the big neighbouring towns of Mechelen and Antwerp to our peaceful village; so a small issue on school desks and limited square metres in the classroom wasn't a money-making machine for them. Selling off many acres of agricultural land and turning these into plots for housing – that was the money. Thus, the problem was raised to the catholic priest who in turn would be 'networking' with the head teacher.

Filing a complaint in those days wasn't by completing form C12/4a, it wasn't by emailing the governing body of Catholic Schools in Belgium, nor was it by raising it at the next monthly meeting of the Parent Association. It wouldn't even be handled through my uncle and aunt who both were teachers at that very same school. Small village! No, no, there were even more powerful resources to tackle this. Most parents raised their concern through approaching the priest after the Sunday services; either by waiting for him outside the church or by offering him a beer after the Sunday ceremony in the local pub, 'The Good Shepherd'.

My parents never went to the pub and found the education of their son far too important to be raised in public at the entrance hall of the church. This was serious stuff and needed to be discussed in private; so the priest got invited for lunch. That must have been pork roast with a delicious creamy mushroom sauce and potato croquettes. Or alternatively, chicken with apricots and – obviously – self-cut French fries. Stop right here. Just for a second as I need to share with you my frustrations on the culinary English language. Why are the Belgium-invented fries called 'French' fries? Similarly, why does any sole that you eat in the UK seem to originate from Dover? Have you ever seen anything else than a Dover sole on the menu? A Brighton sole? A Calais sole?

Anyway, we started lunch that day with the most traditional but overly delicious tomato soup. Every birthday party, New Year's eve, even at my wedding party, only tomato soup could be served.

There may have been a bottle of wine at the table (probably a cheap Riesling) but most likely it was a good large bottle of dark Piedboeuf beer, brewed since the mid-nineteenth century in the south of Belgium and currently owned by – who else – Anheuser-Busch InBev. We most certainly concluded lunch with a coffee and my father will have offered the priest a good Cuban cigar. The priest will have declined the offer and lit a few of his own Bastos cigarettes. My father had loads of cigar boxes. And bottles of best whiskey and cognac. Also, the local farmers frequently brought us boxes of tomatoes, cauliflower, celery or leeks. Following the mayor, the notary, the priest and the head teacher, my father, the local tax inspector, was probably next in rank. Funny, isn't it, with a tax specialist at home, I will later in my career experience many tax issues. That will not be with the tax authorities as such, as we Belgians of course never experiment on tax avoidance – hey we are not Greeks, you know. But issues will arise with specialist tax consultants. 'Specialist' here refers mainly to their excessive fees, not their quality of service.

The priest said that he would first talk to the other five complaining parents and then "take it from there". One of the nicest English non-committal phrases, isn't it? But in French it's probably the same: "On verra ce qu'on fait alors". Clearly the priest didn't want to commit anything to my dad until he so-called had spoken to the other parents; in fact he meant he'll consult with Mr. Schelkens. The priest was probably one of the first adopters of the RACI-model; he knew who was Responsible, Accountable, needed to be Consulted and Informed. He could have made a very rewarding career in the consulting industry.

Every next Sunday my father was very nervous while leaving the church and hoping to catch-up with the priest…who mastered to avoid my dad extremely well.

One month later, in the early evening, Mr. Schelkens rang at the front door. Mr. Schelkens had been appointed head teacher of our school two years previously, in 1965. He was young, early thirties, a little thick and it was clear that he would be bald before the age of forty. My mother hated unexpected visitors but for the head teacher she had no other option but to let him enter the living room and offer him a cup of coffee. My father would be home in half an hour, so he'd had to wait, as in our catholic and conservative family, this issue was one for the pater familias to deal with. The waiting time was nicely broken by my sister –three years older than I –proudly sharing with Mr. Schelkens her maths homework. Today she had learned measuring her own height and that of her class friends. Tonight she would be measuring Mum, Dad and myself. But having the head teacher at home, what an opportunity to also get him in her measurement book!
"No Marleen", my mother had shouted from the kitchen. "You don't do that." At the same moment, my father entered the living room.

The head teacher advised my father that he recognised the problem and that he had decided to move some of the kids from the last year of kindergarten immediately to the class of the first year primary school.

There were three spare places in the first year class and three kids would be considered to be promoted to this class.

"I will leave the selection to Ingrid. She is best placed to make this assessment and then...we'll take it from there," Mr. Schelkens said.

Ingrid was very pragmatic and would make sure that this got sorted with a sense of urgency. She didn't need to call upon the Centre for Learning Advice, didn't need any psychometric testing, no ISO-certified Kids' IQ test looking for numerical, logical and linguistic ability, and no personality questionnaires. Ingrid would fall back on one of the most basic assessment techniques for kids of this age. So next Monday, all of us would have to make a pencil drawing, and based on that she would assess our readiness for promotion.

It was Monday and we had all just had a cup of hot chocolate milk. The task was clear, are living in an agricultural village.

"Today kids, we are all going to draw a vegetable. Choose whatever vegetable you like," Ingrid instructed.

The same day at 4pm, my mother was informed of her son Henry's first promotion ever. It didn't come with a company car or stock options; and also no retirement benefits. I graduated from kindergarten and could go at very young age to primary school!

My secret for success: I drew the best leek.

Since then, I also adore leek and potato soup.

Later on in his career, as you will read a bit further on, Henry enjoyed many more promotions. It was rarely the result of a great drawing however; sometimes he admits it was through pure luck, being the right man at the right time at the right place. Many of his upwards steps, in all modesty, were mainly driven by what he as a leader stands for. As he's not a great propagandist for leadership buzzwords, he would describe himself in very basic terms as follows: hard working, with a high level of integrity and of authenticity, direct communication, leading with passion and inspiring others.

It may sound a bit outdated, but he has always been very people-driven and his people skills have brought him to where he is today. Henry is perhaps not an analytical guru – OK he can add figures, something some of his bosses will contradict him on, but he's essentially a people man. Genuine interest in people has been his drive throughout his career; and that applied to his staff, bosses, business partners, and so on. Even to trade union leaders and tax officials. Now there is another thing, which initially may seem difficult to reconcile with his people interest, and that's his leitmotif: "Shareholder first". That supports his belief that those who invest and give source to the existence of the business should get priority attention. "First" however, also explicitly means that it's not just about shareholders; there are many other parties involved who also have the right to attention.

Henry's success story and his leadership style seem to tick many of the boxes of what Gary Burnison (CEO of Korn/Ferry International) recently described in *The Twelve Absolutes of Leadership*, a book, absolutely worth reading.

The next years at primary school went very smoothly; same for secondary school. However, my father made me study economics at the Saint Rombouts school in Mechelen, the most prestigious secondary school in town. The very catholic school was 'managed' by the priests; and as such it was a very normative and traditional school. And the more strict the regulations were, the more I saw opportunities for my rebellious alter-ego to develop. In fact, I liked that place very much, but hated economics. In hindsight, these were nice years. I learned a lot about music, beer, cigarettes and girls.

In reaction to the boring economics studies at secondary school, I later went on to study psychology at university in Antwerp. I probably wasn't really ready for this programme. My first exams in Antwerp for the major Applied Psychology lessons were a disaster. I had an 8/40 mark. So I did the exams again after lots more studying during the summer holidays. Part of that study though was in Antwerp's student bars. But it worked. The professor at the summer exam said that my knowledge of applied psychology had significantly improved.

I will never forget that summer exam. It was hot, very hot, that day in August. Only a few students had an audience with 'Pope' – his nickname – Van Calster. Some of my female short-skirted colleagues distracted me, massively. But then psychology is largely about observing the human kind – and that's what I did. Those were of course the testosterone-years. We had to wait in the Beethoven room before being called in for the first written part of the exam. We normally only went to that room twice a year; for the academic opening ceremony and at the end of the year for the results day. This very spacious room was very nicely decorated with ancient oak columns, folding chairs with red velvet, carved wood panelling and on the podium, a shiny black Steinway piano. There was no air conditioning in this room, the sunbeams were barely stopped by the stained glass windows and every minor movement was registered by the dark wooden floor.
Up until today it's still not known why she did that to me. Angelique first planted her C-cup in my neck to look outside the window and later she bent down in her short skirt to supposedly pick up a plastic folder from the wooden floor. It was even getting warmer in the room. Since that day I lost every contact with her; I am told that Angelique got a degree in languages and is currently working in a hotel in Paris.

"Excellent. Your knowledge of the study material has significantly improved," Professor Van Calster said.

He was a humoristic but also very sarcastic man; for this much improved performance, he gave me a 12/40. Oh, how I hated this man – and myself.

The last study year was very hectic. I started far too late on my thesis. And this time there was no Miss Ingrid and no room for a 'leek trick'. On top of that, I had decided to create for the thesis a masterpiece on the relationship between school and the business environment. On how does the industry work together with schools? On how college prepares for a successful career in business.
I surveyed hundreds of previous years' college students and approached around fifty local business leaders to get their views. Apart from some collaboration between technical schools and some small industrial local businesses, in fact there was little collaboration. My study confirmed that students, once graduated, had to start from scratch and were largely unprepared for the challenges ahead of them. Simultaneously, I also surveyed circa a hundred people who'd graduated two years ago and were looking to work in a field that was closely related to their major study subject. Only 30% responded positively and another 25% said that there was "a slight link". To demonstrate the non-existant relationship, I would have been better off handing over 150 blank pages. Only, because of professor Van Calster, it took me an extra year to graduate as a Master in Organisational Psychology and become accredited in psychometric testing.

But as I had to fund part of the studies myself, I learned to work for the money. Four years earlier, Rick had obtained the franchising of the local village public swimming pool. He was a certified life-guard and was there all day around the pool to ensure safety. In the evenings he and his much younger wife Jeanine managed the cafeteria of the pool where on Friday evenings it could be very busy. Rick had managed to turn this simple cafeteria into "the place to be" for a Friday evening party. Excellent snacks were prepared by Jeanine and these got so popular that they needed help at the bar. And so I came into place on Friday evenings. Sometimes these parties went on till 2 or 3 o'clock in the morning and nobody fancied cleaning up the place. So apart from bartender, I soon also became the cleaning manager and started on Saturday mornings at 6am as the pool opened again at 9am. I'll spare you the details on the cleaning of the washrooms. Strangely, at home I never touched a brush or mop, but here I just had to get it cleaned; but then it was all for the money. And that came in swiftly, because rather than spending money on drinks in the evening, I now got the drinks for free and got paid for the hard work. I also started doing some bookkeeping and accounting for Rick, and as his Key Account Manager, I lobbied with local organisations for them to have their parties at Rick's place.

It all brought me more commercial sense than the economy studies at secondary school did. And I was happy that I had decided to specialise in organisational psychology, rather than educational or clinical psychology. I had the strong belief that through the study of employees in a business environment, I would be able to make people perform stronger and business and employees thus, would benefit. That was in terms of timing a perfect choice as it was in the mid-eighties that businesses started to talk about people being "our most important asset".

By the way, good to see you listened to my advice. You found yourself a relaxing spot to read this book. Is this fly living on your garden terrace or somewhere on a sunny beach? At least, you are not in your sterile office.

Already during my studies I had started to prospect clients to help them with their 'people' issues. That was mainly to help local small and medium-sized organisations on their people resourcing issues. Soon I got a few assignments to recruit warehouse operators, banking employees and management assistants. It all made nice extra money.

And so it became clear to me. I would never become a head teacher, a notary and certainly wouldn't work for the government at the Inland Revenue department.

Nor would I ever professionally cultivate leek.

~ ~ ~ ~ ~ ~ ~ ~ ~

CHAPTER 2

The odours of some carefully distilled German liquids.

> *"I asked God for a bike, but I know God doesn't work that way. So I stole a bike and asked for forgiveness."* -<u>Unknown</u>

While studying in Antwerp, I was used to early wake-up calls. So the 7.22 train to Brussels for my first real job wasn't a problem at all. Less pleasant was the daily journey by bike to the Mechelen train-station and, especially in the rainy autumn, standing during the trip with soaked clothes in the second class carriage full of physically present but mentally absent civil servants. And even worse was their absolute collective need to read their oversized newspapers in this stuffed box departing the notorious Mechelen railway station – notorious, as during the Second World War, 28 trains left from the Mechelen Dossin Casern and deported 24,916 Jews and 351 gypsies; most of whom arrived at Auschwitz-Birkenau.

Frustrated but alive, we arrived at Brussels Central station at 7.47am. From there, it was just another 15-minute' walk to the office of my first employer in the Rue de la Loi. The company was a large player in the insurance business; it's currently part of the orange (so Dutch) lion bank.

On my first day at the insurance broker I was welcomed by Rob. He was my mentor, inductor, coach, facilitator, Socratic questioner, trainer, appraiser, etc. To keep it simple, he was my boss and he made me do 365 days, eight-hour day assessment centres and interviews for potential insurance salesmen.

Great experience, I loved it and I learned a lot from Rob. Unfortunately, the Belgian government only sponsored the youth employment for one year and so the year after, the cost of my sweat and efforts would have increased by 45%. That was too expensive to my employer thus my first job came to an end and a new 'cheap victim' started throwing psychometric tests to the future salesmen.

As said, I learned a lot and gained in-depth experience of batteries of intelligence, behaviour and personality tests. I played so much with the Stanford-Binet (it was Alfred Binet himself who introduced the term "Intelligence Quotient" in 1904), with the Wechsler, with the Reynolds Intellectual Assessment Scale, with the 16 personality factors by Cattell, with the MMPI, etc. I seasoned these tests so much that, when applying for my next jobs, I managed to complete all these tests towards the expected outcome.

Didn't I say earlier on that Henry was a man of high integrity? Well, nobody is perfect.

None of the tests required me to draw a vegetable.

Later on, this recruitment and selection approach luckily moved further away from its old source and initial purpose, i.e. selection for the US army. More and more modern techniques were developed. Today's assessment centres are slightly better predictors for success – but only slightly. There are too many companies who believe that these kind of so called 'analytical techniques' present a linear correlation with success. Mainly engineers and economists see it as too black and white. People can't be measured in the same way as reading the speed of electric current through a copper wire with a 0.8mm diameter. People are like share prices, they have their own values and behaviours but are also largely influenced by external factors. Or can you infallibly forecast next Tuesday's share price of Google Inc on the NASDAQ through analysing the last 200 days' moving average?

The validity and reliability of most psychometric instruments is still relatively low; the interpretation of the results by unskilled practitioners adds another big risk to the prediction of the desired outcome. And let's not forget, it's only just a snapshot. A few well prepared interviews, reference checks and a balanced – yes, subjective – gut feeling can give you more assurance on the success of your new employee.

My extensive experience with psychometrics however, gave me an entry ticket into some big companies such as IBM and VW for some short-term assignments.

But then it went downwards for me as I struggled to secure career-building opportunities. So I was jobless for almost half a year. This may sound strange, but I would advise everyone to be unemployed for some time. It gives you good knowledge on what that does to your emotions – not just to your wallet. When you are full of energy and have endless ambition and drive, but not one employer matches with you, you risk ending up in a vicious circle and it requires a high level of perseverance to survive. So I accepted a job outside of my real area of expertise and went for a five-month assignment to Germany. Well, not really Germany but a Belgian enclave in Germany where I was engaged as educational mentor at the college for the children of the Belgian military services in nearby Cologne.

There were seven of us in the office; Luc, Robert, Lisa, Claire and Luk – for ease of reference, called "Luk II", the Director Patrick Janssens and I. This was my first experience where collegiality in a work environment can also be called friendship. Although the office in the old castle was absolutely unattractive, there was an atmosphere of camaraderie.
Most of my colleagues lived in Germany in government sponsored housing, only Patrick Janssens lived during the weekends in Diest in Belgium. It was commonly known that every Monday he wouldn't be at work before lunchtime. So Monday morning was party time. With an agreed rotation system, one of us would be sitting in the first office, first floor, at the end of the stairs and would prevent – good naturedly but vigorously – any visitor access to the other offices. Two rings with the intercom was a sign for "intruder is on his way". The rest of us gathered in Luc's office where the window gave view to the parking lot, just for those rare occasions where Patrick didn't enjoy the Monday morning breakfast with his wife and arrived earlier than expected. We all had a clear task for that Monday morning. Luc was the duty officer keeping his eye on the parking; one had bought – of course from the

military duty free shop – two bottles of Martini Bianco, one the crisps and olives, and another one salted TUC biscuits and cheese. Director Janssens was a good man with a warm heart. Sometimes he let us go home on Friday lunchtime in recognition for the full week hard work.

While most of my colleagues lived in two or three-bedroom houses, I was stationed in a small studio in a large compound of the Belgian army called 'The General'; this place was the reserve of fixed-term workers. The average age of all of us residing there was probably 25 and all were single or had a partner at home in Belgium. So as you can imagine, this was just a continuation of student life. We had more beer, schnapps and Bacardi-coke than potatoes or steak. The only culinary pleasures I remember are soup (tomato of course) and ready-made spaghetti with meatballs. Our studios and the shared kitchen were an absolute mess. Of course, the army wouldn't be the army if there weren't strict rules and regulations, so there was always the risk of an unexpected inspection of the property. Therefore, again with a formal rotating system, each of us had cleaning duty once every month. And of course the army wouldn't be the army if that unannounced inspection would not have been leaked to us by an insider.

Thank you Sergeant Ronny for your insights and tips, we at 'The General' love you.

Now, the danger wasn't coming from the inside. It was that really unexpected visit from my wife Sonja – then my fiancée – on a Friday morning. Still today she keeps talking about how my place was stinking like hell. I thought it was just a mixture of good natural Virginia tobacco smoke, well-blended with the odours of some carefully distilled German liquids, the paprika fragrance from the Smiths crisps, the scent from yesterday's meatballs and perhaps a bit of human body aroma. Or was it the socks from yesterday? Wednesday, Tuesday and last

Monday? But we were young and in love and then much more is tolerated. Fortunately, the condom on the sink had disappeared before she arrived.

This was the life for us psychologists and pedagogues, responsible for the development of the kids of the Belgian military services. And we were paid for it.

Not only were we paid for it, we also could enjoy the benefits of the Officers' mess and of the military tax-free shop.
Every time I had to visit another Belgian army school in Germany, I tried to visit another tax-free shop. My chauffeur – you read this right – was always happy to do so as he saw some personal benefits in the small detour. Of course I had a chauffeur-driven car as with my role, I had 'Officer' status. For information, I have never served in the army as a soldier; I cheated a bit on the personality tests at the mandatory service assessments. I reckon my test evaluation file will say "Serious indications of Schizoid and Avoidant Personality Disorder. Not retained for service." Clearly no-one went back to these files when I was offered the job in Bergisch-Gladbach. Understandable as my file was somewhere in a cupboard at the Ministry of Defence while the job at the military school was managed by the personnel department of the Ministry of Education.

Apart from cigarettes and alcohol, I also bought at the Monchengladbach shop – I think that was the American army – a Blaupunkt car radio at a very small price. The thing was discounted as it was the last one on the shelf and on top of that it came without tax.
With my educational background in social science, I was of course an absolute technical nerd. Luckily I had built over the last few months a close relationship with Alain, a teacher of technical subjects at the school. Alain and I often "put the flowers outside the village centre".

(Oops, that's a fun but not so great Google translation from the Dutch saying – I think in English it's about "painting the town red"). Alain only needed a few minutes to get the radio installed in my red and rusty Fiat Ritmo and then we went to the pub for a few drinks. At my expense – in gratitude. Two days later, my brand new radio was stolen. And three weeks later, I noticed Alain had 'bought exactly the same car-radio.

Following the recession of the early 80s, in the US and in most of Europe, a period of sustained economic growth began in the mid-80s. At that time, not even the savviest economist predicted the world changing earthquake of Black Monday, 19th October 1987 when the Dow Jones decreased 22.6% on one day. Just like nobody predicted the other Black Monday of 8th August 2011 when US and other stock markets crashed again following the Standard and Poor's downgrading of the US debt position from AAA to AA+.

During the 1987 crash, I was working for the consulting firm CTA in Leuven, specialising in the recruitment and training of sales reps. This was yet another fixed-term contract to cover for the maternity leave of Annika, the daughter of the Dutch owner, Mr. Nilsen. For their search activities, CTA worked on the basis of no cure, no pay; so if we didn't deliver a suitable applicant, the client didn't pay anything. Mr. Nilsen had a slightly enlarged definition of this approach, he also thought that when clients didn't pay, he didn't need to pay his employees either.
In November 1987 I asked Mr. Nilsen about the future prospects of my employment at CTA; it was important for us to plan as in next July Sonja and I would be marrying. "Without doubt," he said, "I am very pleased and the business is booming. Make sure we get an invite to the wedding party." In the last week of the trial period prior to a promised permanent contract, he terminated my employment without notice.

We married in July 1988, only three weeks after I had started at ES Pharmaceuticals (ESP) as Personnel Supervisor. That was my first real step in the rewarding journey on climbing the corporate ladder.

It was clear now. Both my private life and professional career would evolve with great enjoyment and satisfaction. It was an absolute perfect match with my lovely wife; I was also confident that at ESP I would be finding great challenges and start building a truly rewarding career.

1988 was a great year for us; the same for George Bush. As President Ronald Reagan was unable to seek re-election, it was George H.W. Bush who became, in 1988, the 41st president of the United States. In France it was François Mitterand who won the presidential elections but he was forced to cohabit with the conservative party of Mr. Chirac.
And what happened in the air in 1988?
In September, the space shuttle Discovery got launched, the first one after the disastrous accident with Challenger. Late December, Pan Am flight 103, on its way from London Heathrow to JFK, was taken out of the air by a bomb explosion in the area of Lockerbie in Southern Scotland. All 243 passengers and 16 crew members died; while the crash killed another 11 people on the ground.
There was also the accident at the air show in Ramstein (Germany) where 67 people were killed.
Most remarkable however, was the safe landing of Aloha Airlines flight 243 from Hilo (Hawaii) to Honolulu. As the aircraft reached its normal flight altitude of 24,000 feet, a small section on the left side of the roof ruptured. The resulting explosive decompression tore off a large section of the roof, consisting of the entire top half of the aircraft extending from just behind the cockpit to the fore-wing area. Captain Robert Schornstheimer looked back and saw blue sky where the first class cabin's roof had been. The captain and the crew performed an

emergency landing at Kahului Airport, runway 2. Miraculously, the only casualty was flight attendant Lansing who was blown out of the plane when the roof zipped of the plane's body. *Miracle Landing*, the movie from 1990, pictures this unforgettable adventure very well. I just hope you are not reading this section while you are on a plane on your way to a next business meeting?

1988 – what a year. And I should have been worried about a few socks on the floor.

~ ~ ~ ~ ~ ~ ~ ~ ~

CHAPTER 3

Venus Grotto and Capitalism.

"Le capitalisme, c'est l'exploitation de l'homme par l'homme. Le communisme, c'est le contraire."
-Coluche

Strange isn't it? I love the stodgy and greasy German cuisine.

During school holidays, as well as during the initial periods of unemployment, I was acting as a tourist guide for a large travel company specialising in bus tours. Europabus was one of the strongest players in this segment. Their journeys were pre-arranged with hotels and restaurants booked by the back-office. As a tourist guide, it was expected that you knew everything about the journey and about the places to visit. Any historical data and stories, as well as recent key events were written on my travel cards. At this point in time, we are of course in an era without iPads and satnav. So this was not just a small job for fun, it required some prep work.

Most of these journeys brought me to Bavaria in Germany or to Tirol in Austria. Our passengers were generally more interested in Dirndls and in lots of wheat beer, Knödel, Kartoffelsalate, Leberkäse and Bauernwurst. That was helpful for me as it didn't matter whether the Ulm Cathedral – the tallest church in the world – was from the 14th or the 18th century. In fact, construction started in 1377 and the work was only completed in the late 19th century. Or whether the Oberammergauer Passion Play was established in 1634 to spare the residents from the bubonic plague or to protect them against an invasion from Napoleon. None of them knew that Napoleon Bonaparte was born in 1769. It also didn't matter whether a town hall or cathedral was renaissance, gothic, or rococo style. What matters was a few good jokes, the next stop, the food that night and the starting time for the dance party.
I adapted quickly to this lack of cultural interest and the prep work for other journeys became a quick fix.

Our bus driver for the journey in May 1988 was Bart, a good looking guy in his early thirties, recently divorced and a bit desperate. Well, he wasn't going to find a new girlfriend this journey as the average age of the women on the coach was around 60. I remember that one of our passengers told us one evening that she still had two one-way tickets for a boat journey to the US. The tickets were dated 10 April 1912 but fortunately she and her mother arrived too late in Southampton and so they missed the boarding of the *Titanic*.

But as I said, he was good looking and while parking the bus at Linderhof Castle, he decided not to join us for the visit of the castle.

"Why?" I asked him. "It's very nice inside and you should see the King's bed and the Venus Grotto in the gardens."

"I am just a bit tired and tomorrow we have a long drive home."

"But we are free this afternoon, you can rest till tonight."

"Come on," he said. "Didn't you see that Spanish bus arrive? And have you seen that gorgeous tourist guide? That driver is a lucky bastard – and look here at us, they have sent me you!"

The Spanish tourist guide was dressed in a fluorescent light green skirt, shiny high heel turquoise shoes, Dior sunglasses and matching wristwatch.

"I hope she's also very tired and needs some rest," Bart said. "I'll visit her Venus Grotto. And you, you make sure you don't return too early."

When I returned from a two and a half hour long visit – and while our clients were still at the castle's shop – I knocked carefully on the door of the bus. With an endless smile, Bart pushed a button on the dashboard to open the door. It was clear that I shouldn't ask any question; certainly not whether he slept well. I have a strong feeling that the Spanish tourist guide didn't join her touristas for the castle's visit either.

On our way back to the hotel Alpsee in Garmish-Partenkirchen, Bart whispered to me that I shouldn't organise anything for the clients tonight.

"Tonight, I invite you for a beer in another hotel, in the Hotel Edelweiss," he said.

I didn't fancy going out that night as I had thought to write a business plan on enhancing the profit opportunities of the castle. I saw plenty of profitable activities that could be added to the current offers. Clearly, this attraction was managed by civil servants who had zero commercial awareness. There wasn't even a bar or cafeteria; just a Coke branded fridge with cans at similar price as in the supermarket. But I got convinced by Bart to join him that night. So there wouldn't be a business plan but yet another night of drinking and joking. And we had great fun that evening, Bart, myself and Valeria – the Spanish tourist guide.

The early morning wake-up call was a bit painful; 5 o'clock. However, the management of the hotel Alpsee had arranged for an early morning breakfast. Just like large hotels the world over, at the entrance of the breakfast restaurant, a waitress welcomed me and asked for my room number. I believe it must have been in this hotel where I did it for the first time, but since then I keep doing it in every hotel; anywhere in the world. It's a fantastic game and an excellent assessment of the waitresses' assertively level.

"Can I have your room number, Sir?" the young girl asked. I noticed on her name tag that she's called Beate.

"Well Beate, that's a bit of an indiscrete question for a beautiful girl like you, isn't it?" I replied.

"Hmm," was her only reaction and the poor girl turned her eyes to the room list sheet to avoid any eye contact. I kept silent. After a while, she had found all the strengths to raise her head and to look me back in the eyes; but without saying a word.

"It's 126, darling. Derrick," I replied quickly so as to not pester her much longer.

"Enjoy your breakfast, Mister Derrick," she replied with relief in her smile.

Years later, I remember another clearly much more mature waitress in the Executive Lounge of a hotel in Shanghai who didn't want to play the game. Her reply was very effective, although I assume not according to the customer service guidelines.

"Can I have your room number, Sir?"

"Well Irene, that's a bit an indiscrete question for a beautiful girl like you, isn't it?" I replied.

"No number – no food," was her short and decisive reply.

In the same season, I did three more journeys with Bart; twice the same route to Bavaria and once the "Romantische Rhein"; an easy four-day journey to visit the Rhein-vineyards, wine paradise Rüdesheim and some medieval castles.

It must have been in the mid-nineties when on a Saturday evening I got a call from Bart. I had moved residence twice in the period and had no clue how he traced my phone number. He had started up his own business as a tour operator and travel agency and now had seven coaches and nine drivers working for him. The office and sales operations were handled by his wife and sister-in-law. So he got married again. He was in urgent need of a tourist guide to the Austrian Alps with a departure date of the following Monday. He would be the driver. It would have been great fun but I had in the meantime grown in professional life and was now in a good mid-management position. However, I had a quick look in my diary to see if I could take one week off. No, I couldn't. On Tuesday a meeting was planned with the trade unions on urgent overtime arrangements and on Thursday I would be interviewing two final candidates for the Purchasing Manager role. I would really have loved to accept the offer, but I had to decline. Business before pleasure!

Of course I didn't want to hang-up before asking if he had ever met Valeria again.

"Oh, I can't talk openly about that; my wife is sitting next to me. She is inputting the drivers' planning for the week after next," he said, but I sensed he was suppressing a smile.
"Oh."
"Or do you want her on the phone?"
"What?" I said.
"Yes, Valeria and I married five years ago," he replied.

My professional career had clearly brought me to a stage where I was never going to be a tourist guide again. Rather than having lots of joy and fun but also just living from a gratuity of around 25 Euros a day, I had chosen for another lifestyle with a different kind of fun, income level and satisfaction. The joy now came from successfully tackling all the hurdles on the way to the top of the corporate ladder.

A nice characteristic of the corporate ladder is that it is a one-way street; you can only move upwards. Many though fall off the ladder; half-way up or just before reaching the top; as there is only place for one on that very last step. Sometimes people get demoted although that's unfortunately generally seen as a bad move, and as such, those initiatives soon end up in a termination agreement rather than public disgrace. People very rarely take a voluntary downwards step; today called 'remotion'. I am convinced though that in the future –with statutory pension ages climbing faster up the age ladder than managers climbing the career stairway – we'll see more of that.

At that time, I think I was almost halfway through that corporate mountain climbing expedition; halfway to a seat in the boardroom. And I was in no doubt about making much more money than Bart did, however successful he may have been with his own business. And again, no doubt that I was even making more than double what my friends at the Belgian school in Germany had earnt.

My frequent reflections on my income compared to that of most of my friends, gave me general satisfaction. And that came without any shame; why would it?

Is it then that wrong to define career growth as personal fulfilment? Is it that wrong to put your career first? First before anything else? I was working hard, delivered everything that was expected and in return, the reward was great. Again, what's wrong with giving in full to your company? At the end, it's the company that delivers the wealth for buying that nice flat, for having luxurious holidays and for shopping weekends with Sonja in Milan and Paris.

Today though, my thoughts and the principles of capitalism are seriously questioned. That's mainly because of the massive banking crisis. But at that time and in the early stages of my rewarding career, I saw nothing wrong in the capitalist approach. Companies should be rewarded for their investments and workers for their efforts; all of this in a free market where people are free to decide where to work, to spend, to save, to invest, etc. What's wrong with that? Aiming for profit is a basic economic principle; nothing wrong with that. It's absolutely fair that business owners and investors who take a much higher risk than employees – who get their guaranteed weekly or monthly pay – get rewarded much better. And let's not go into the debate that the CEO or owner's pay should only be five times more than the company average, or 10 or 20. It's an absolute useless debate in a free market. Aiming for continuously increasing profits is also not wrong as long as these gains are achieved through decent ethical business practices. Unfortunately, that's where it sometimes goes wrong with a few business leaders. And that then regrettably results in most countries having an overwhelming list of corporate governance rules and laws. But let's be fair, there are also some dodgy employees who only read in their contract that the boss needs to pay them; no obligations from their side. And with no risks from their side, but very well supported by employment regulations, trade unions and human rights acts, these employees occasionally test this theory. That's not illogical, even typical for a socialist system where the power is not put with those who drive the economy but just with those who outnumber the others.

I think it's realistic to say that by this time, if you are an Indignado, you have set fire to this book. So be it, the Indignados and the 2011 Occupy Movement have already banned Henry from this planet. At one of those typical demonstrations in London, they were shouting their motto "we are the 99%"; so called indicating that 99% of the population are paying the price for the greed of a tiny minority. In hindsight very stupid, but Henry couldn't resist responding, "If that's so, than I am one of the 1%." Again, not very smart but he'd had enough of that culture of envy and propagandistic jealousy. On top of that, Henry is not even one of the multi-million earners; not at all. He's not and will never be in the ranks of Warren Buffet, Bill Gates, Carlos Slim, Mark Zuckerberg (oh what a disastrous IPO) or the German "Aldi"-Albrecht brothers. But I don't envy them; that's the difference. And what was the real value or worth of those millions to Theo Albrecht when he was hijacked in 1971 and when he died in 2010? The same can be said for Steve Jobs. There are other things in life much more important than money. So why envy those fortune makers?

Still today, I strongly believe that killing the capitalist system, and as such the free market, would just kill people's freedom. I am convinced that a system that would limit entrepreneurial freedom would be detrimental to the wealth of all people; the rich as well as the less fortunate. I am really afraid of the current left wing movements in Europe. I am not pleading to go back to the feudalism system – where capitalism so called originates from – but I am also not a Marxist; not at all. Do we honestly believe that a government controlled economy, de-privatised businesses, price-fixing and hundreds of additional regulations, will be to the benefit of us as consumers?

We may need to prepare for a European Spring; similar to the 2011 Arabic Spring. Not that I believe that our current leaders are demagogic dictators, but if they further attempt to take our freedom away and to give everyone an equal share of the cake – irrespective of their contribution – then why would our entrepreneurs still take commercial and financial risks? Why would they generate employment? Communism and socialism may work in small sized and homogenous groups; where all members share the same view and beliefs. Like in the cooperatives and kibbutzes. With today's globalisation, have we not started to live in a more diverse world; where we do not all share the same beliefs?

Apart from one: a desire for sustained freedom.

I would like to give another example of entrepreneurial freedom which, at that time, was very challenged in the media.

Xavier, a good friend of mine from the earlier study years, had become a teacher; his wife Rachel was a junior IS manager at Ontex. They both had a dream: buy and run a small boutique hotel in Vienna. Being both in their late twenties, they planned to materialise their dream in 10 years' time. They both resigned from their jobs and started a small business in the textile industry. It was a well thought through plan but not without serious financial risks. Working day and night, they abstained from many pleasures in life; they soon were running a good business. It was at very low profit margins, but their business was growing exponentially in terms of customers and staff numbers. For their investment and employment initiatives, they received several awards from local and national business circles. After eight years running their own company – with at that time 34 employees – their financial position was as such that they started to look out for acquiring a suitable property in Vienna. Simultaneously, they were looking for an acquirer of their business who would hopefully pay a good price and ideally also continue to invest in their start-up to make it grow further. Eighteen months later, they found a nice property in Vienna and had also attracted an Indian businessman who was seriously interested in buying their textile business. But for the Indian manager, the acquisition deal was clear; he was only interested in the two brands, a few machines and the customer portfolio. So the Belgian company had to be closed and Xavier and his wife would have to terminate all 34 staff; which they did. And although they offered enhanced redundancy terms, above industry practice, they were both slaughtered in the local press and labelled as ruthless capitalists.

So let's evaluate this in detail, objectively and without any emotions. Two hard working individuals take a serious financial risk to resign from their jobs and to start-up their own business. If this goes wrong, they both end up in unemployment without any jobseeker allowances. But they are willing to take this risk in their pursuit of a dream. For more than 10 years, they offer income to 34 households, pay massive taxes and contribute significantly to the social security system. At the end of this journey, and ahead of their next expedition, they are forced to make 34 people redundant; who all receive an above standard redundancy package.

Can anybody tell me why these two entrepreneurs needed to be massacred in the media; so hard that even today they are reluctant to come and visit their family in their home town?

~ ~ ~ ~ ~ ~ ~ ~ ~

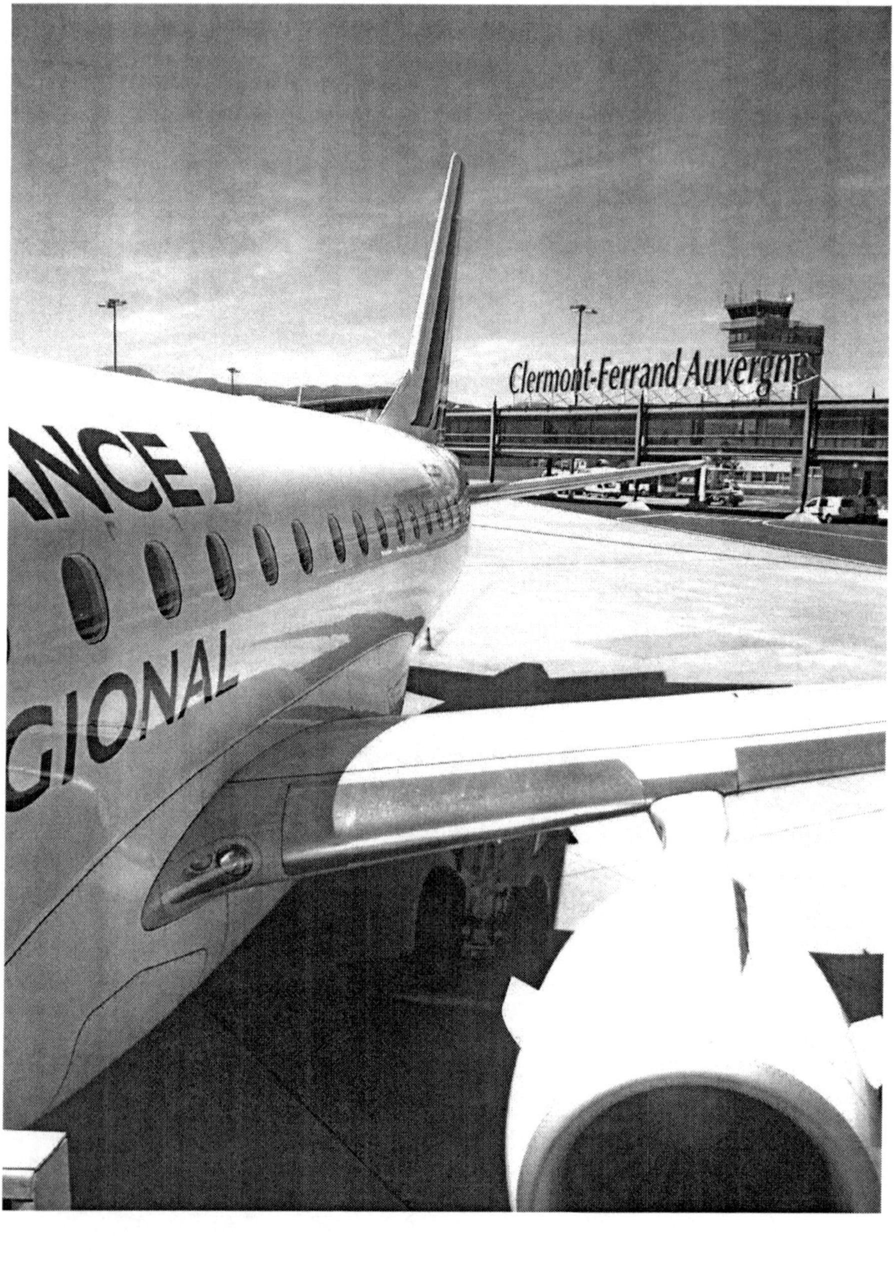
Clermont-Ferrand Auvergne
ANCE
GIONAL

CHAPTER 4

Nothing urgent, André.

"Common sense is not so common." - <u>Voltaire</u>

André Van Bever recruited me in that HR job for ES Pharmaceuticals in Lier, Belgium, a manufacturing subsidiary of ESPharm Inc., based in New Jersey. The division also holds an important European distribution operation; all together, there were at that time around 220 staff.

André himself was the Finance and Personnel Director and was getting sick and tired of all the discussions and demands from the local union leaders. So he established the role of Personnel Supervisor to create a buffer between him and 'the ants', as he called the trade unions.

André has an irascible temperament, is a bit bullish and doesn't shy away from open conflicts with the unions. He has his own strong views on the employee/employer relationship, mainly that, "staff are here to work and I am here to ensure there are funds to pay them; it's that simple".

With a slightly different approach – and somewhat more respect and willingness to listen to employee issues, I take over the discussions with the unions pretty early on. But what the unions don't know is the critical importance of André for our business. Not only had he negotiated a very favourable tax structure with the Belgian tax office – safeguarding employment for many years – he also has excellent networking with the top guys at ESPharmaceuticals Inc. in New Jersey. Given the favourable corporate tax structure, the Head Office brought many product lines and new technologies to our factory in Lier. Our low conversion cost, high efficiency and positive social climate drove these decisions and this resulted in doubling the headcount over a five-year period. Indeed, over the last 10 years no strikes were reported to the Head Office – that doesn't mean there weren't any – just that André managed to downplay any industrial action into a minor non-reportable event.

Indeed, most debates I had with the unions were – apart from the annual pay negotiations – relatively minor issues such as recruitment of temps and agency workers, providing extra breaks on hot summer days, overtime requests for Saturdays, etc.

But there were also major and very critical negotiations, like the one on the placement of the Coke vending machine. ☹ That was placed too far away for the girls from the packaging department and therefore needed to move closer to their working space and slightly further away from the warehouse. But then, the warehouse operators – mainly members of the socialist trade union – would complain, according to Maurice, the socialist union leader. That was a difficult one to mediate on. So I jokingly suggested we should raise this issue to the senior national trade union leaders and perhaps call them in to help us solve this life-threatening issue. Less sarcastic but determined, I said that the machine would not be moved and so they asked for extended breaks for the packaging department. Again, the answer was no.

I slowly started to feel sympathy with André's frustrations.

With the company having been established in the late seventies, our employee demographics started to change and we got more and more staff aged close to fifty. At that time, Belgium had set up systems of government and company sponsored early retirement schemes to stimulate youth employment. Well, Belgium wasn't alone on this and now in the early 21st century, all countries are struggling to abolish these short-sighted initiatives. Everywhere in Europe, these initiatives were set up under serious trade union pressures and by politicians who were blinded by supposed electoral benefits.

André and I were absolutely and strongly opposed to these schemes, and as long as there wasn't any law to impose us applying this practice, we wouldn't. And that was well-known in the company – that despite heavy debates, all who filed a request got a nil return.

Maurice, the socialist trade union leader, turned 49 years and six months on 12th May 1993. He filed for voluntary early retirement. Our answer on the same day was "no". The socialist union informed us of their intention for industrial action. As you do, we (André extremely reluctantly) invited them for further talks. No response from their side.

On Thursday 20th May, I got a call at 5.40 am from John Dillen, the shift supervisor from the quality control department.

"It's for today. They are standing at the entrance and seem to have the support from the catholic trade union. All red and green flags. They're not letting anybody in," John said.

"That's unacceptable. There are rules to be respected. There may be a freedom for strike but there is primarily a freedom to work," I replied. "Try to get all those that are willing to work together. Seek volunteers to drive them to the 'Old Egypt' pub. I think they open at 6am for the truck drivers; ask Rita to give them coffee and tea for free. We'll pay everything. Ask Willy and Jo to arrange the same for their teams. Can you later also go to the bakery shop and get croissants for all of them. I'll be there in 45 minutes; so around 6.30 am. I'll also call André and Bob."

"What's going on?" my wife asks, with her eyes still closed.

"Strike. The bastards," I replied before getting into the shower.

Once in my car, I realise I hadn't shaved and had forgotten a tie. So what. I called André but got no reply; Bob replied and he would also be there in half an hour. I also called chief officer Mark Gots, from the Lier police department. He was already aware; he was informed the night before by Tony Van Den Broeck, the national trade union leader for the chemical industry. Mark – with whom I thought I had a good relationship and whose annual police barbeque is massively sponsored by ESPharm – had not felt the need to pre-inform me. We'll have that discussion later.

While driving at full speed, I am trying to call André again, but I still get no reply. I notice in my rear view mirror, that a grey BMW 3 series is approaching me with full speed. It's not a police car, so who is that? When the car overtakes me, I see two uniformed police officers. They make it clear that they want me to stop the car. I lower speed and pull the car to the hard shoulder.

The two officers are very polite and listen to my story. I mentioned that I was just of the phone with their colleague from Lier. While one was looking at my driver license and insurance papers, the other one makes a call in his car. I assume he is checking my story with Mark Gots. When he returns, I get a five-minute lesson on safe driving and speeding and then they let me go without a speeding ticket. Next time ESPharm will probably also have to sponsor the Antwerp police department.

When I arrive at the plant – of course 20 minutes late due to the police intervention – I see Bob arguing with Tony in front of the entrance gate. I now see that the gate is still closed and even locked with a heavy chain. There are 20-30 people; our security guard is chatting to some of them. I call John Dillen who confirms there are around 20 people in the pub having coffee and croissants. He reckons 10 drove back home. At the end of the street, I see a police car with two officers parked just behind the young oak trees on the parking of the Fiat car dealer. They clearly have got the instruction to observe but not to intervene unless absolutely needed.

I see that Bob is losing his calm – and right he is as he is the Managing Director of the business employing in the meantime now almost 400 people. I advise him to go and visit those at the 'Old Egypt' who are willing to work.

"They also need your support, Bob," I say. "It's no fun for them either, Bob. Let me handle this circus. I'll call you when the gate is back open."

"No way. I want this gate opened and right now!" he shouted at me but even more into the direction of Tony Van Den Broeck. "And if that doesn't happen now, then I'll call the police to raise a formal complaint against Tony."

It was clear, and by the way, who was I but that young junior Personnel Supervisor? Bob was not going to leave. He indeed called the Lier police department and got the reply that they would send somebody as soon as possible. I invited Tony to my car. Before we even started to talk, I got a call from Mark Gots.

"Good morning again," I said.
"Bob van Putten called. Are you already at the factory? Bob wants to get us in and to file a formal complaint against Tony Van Den Broeck. Can't you try to calm him down?"
"Bob is our Managing Director, Mark, and if he wants you to intervene I think you have no option but to send your two shy guys that are parked at the Fiat dealer right now so that they can note the formal complaint. But thanks anyway for the call, Mark. A call yesterday evening would also have been appreciated."

Tony, sitting next to me in the front of the car, didn't like my response to Mark's call. He knew that Mark had to send his guys in now and knew for sure that Bob would insist in the police noting down the infractions. Also Mark very likely didn't like my approach. I realised too late that probably Mark saved me from the speeding ticket. I'd double our sponsoring next time.

I can't go further into detail here on what we both discussed in the car. Also Tony wouldn't appreciate these details being disclosed. The official version was that Tony agreed to stop the industrial action immediately and that I had agreed to hold constructive discussions with the trade unions on the early retirement debate at ESPharm. Informally, I would also try to convince Bob in the coming days to withdraw his complaint.

The gate opened around 8am.

Around lunchtime, I was still chatting with Maurice in my office when André arrived. Like always, he just entered my office without knocking on the door. He brought the smell of cigarettes and alcohol into my office.

"Hi Maurice, you're not complaining again about your pension I hope? You won't get it mate," he said. And then looking at me he said, "I had two missed calls from you early this morning. What was that about?"

"Nothing urgent, André; I'll tell you later," I said and André went satisfied to his office.

Maurice didn't get his early retirement at age 50. He left the company at age 50 and a half – with a golden handshake. I can't share more details. Bob van Putten retired one month later at age 62; without a golden handshake. He was succeeded by Patrick Linck. I did succeed Bob in the role of social judge at labour court as the representative for the employers.

André got more and more into alcohol and I got more and more into the picture at Head Office. They had noticed over the last few years that I had recruited some excellent junior management guys. They said that, "my investments on filling the talent pipeline were exemplary for our business". That sounded to me like, "get ready for your next step on the corporate ladder". I agree, humbly, that it's true that I recruited a lot of very talented young managers; many of them later on ended up in international roles in Switzerland and in the New Jersey Head Office. And I ended up as a centrefold in the bi-monthly corporate magazine; with an article headed, "The Belgian pipeline".

Patrick Linck arranged a few visits for me to the Group HR Department in New Jersey. At my first visit, first time ever over the Atlantic, I spent the weekend in Manhattan prior to going to the Head Office in NJ. On the Monday morning, I had arranged for a stretch limo to pick me up at the Crowne Plaza hotel on 49th street and to drive me to the office. The same day, it was brought to Patrick's attention that I had "an expensive travel style". Patrick got that info from the European Operations Director, who got it from the Global Quality Assurance Director, who got it from his personal assistant who got it from Melisa, the Mexican girl at reception desk. I never made that mistake again.

Anyway, after the second visit to the Head Office, it was by then 1994, I returned with an offer to go and run the ESPharm European People Development department, based in Basle, Switzerland. We had just moved house and like they say, the painting was really still wet on the walls. I politely declined the offer. The Americans didn't like that. Patrick did the utmost to convince me that it was a free choice "but with potential consequences".

One year later, Patrick accepted my resignation letter. It was time for me to move on. After eight years I had seen everything possible there on the industrial relations side and on building our structures for this very successful plant. I needed another challenge, perhaps one in an environment where things didn't go that well. Where there was massive profit pressure or where downsizing was needed.

And another twelve months later, André retired from ESPharm and relocated to Gibraltar. There, tobacco and alcohol are somewhat cheaper. But I am sure he's not out of business; I bet he is making good money with advising companies to set up a tax structure in Gibraltar. I hope he also found himself a new girlfriend. André had always been very clear that – although his wife was five years younger than he was – he would never sleep with a woman aged over forty. Not even with his wife. I remember that three days before she turned forty, André returned home after a hard day work and found that his house was emptied. Not a wife at home, but also no furniture, no paintings, no china, not anything was left, apart from the bottles of Johnny Walker black label. And top of the bill, also his bank accounts were emptied.

She had taken the initiative. On this, André's foresight had failed.

~ ~ ~ ~ ~ ~ ~ ~ ~ ~

CHAPTER 5

Once I have received my bonus.

"Knowledge is knowing that a tomato is a fruit;
Wisdom is not putting it in a fruit salad."
- Unknown

It was Mario Tishler, someone I first met at an INSEAD course, who approached me in September 1995 for the role of Human Resources Manager at "Les Papeteries SA" in Antwerp.

Les Papeteries SA was a production plant and Benelux sales office for paper tissues. The Group had other manufacturing plants in France and in the United Kingdom and another small office in Holland and in the USA.

After 25 years of very successful owner- and directorship by Jean Blancpain, he had sold this family enterprise to investment bankers

UBS. The success formula of Jean Blancpain was a very strong purchasing position for raw materials, a very devoted workforce and pricing flexibility. All of that delivered high margins. On top of that, Mr. Blancpain had excellent "informal contacts" with competitors; in terms of "I won't hurt you in Germany but you stay out of England", etc. European competition laws made that very profitable strategy later illegal.

In 1995, UBS paid an undisclosed amount to Mr. Blancpain to acquire his family business. The plan was to prepare the business for a listing on the European stock exchange or for resale in five years and to make over that period a 40%-50% profit. We'll come back to this later, but it's worthwhile noting here that in January 1997 the business was sold for circa 250 million Euros. It's also worth noting that Mr. Blancpain was a middle educated self-made man who started his career as a shoe sales man. At a business fair in Bordeaux, he met the initial owner and establisher of Les Papeteries. They kept in contact, he bought some shares for the owner to further invest in technology, a few years later bought another 10% of shares and yet another few years later, he was holding 51% of the shares.

Jean Blancpain passed away in 1999; leaving a fortune to his two sons who never worked for the company. I believe they never worked at all. One is currently living in Zurich, and commuting regularly to his Sunseeker yacht in Nice, and the other one runs a golf club at La Reunion.

Nothing wrong with capitalism, I would say.

UBS was going to modernise the business, bring more professionalism and bring in new technology to make production even more efficient. One of the three plants may have to be closed.

That sounded an attractive challenge for me to run the HR operations for the Antwerp division – mainly as the UBS management was Antwerp-based and therefore I already saw further opportunities.

I took up this opportunity in March 1996. Yet another remarkable year.

The world's most famous sheep "Dolly" was born in Scotland as the first mammal to be successfully cloned. Still in the UK, in August, Prince Charles and Diana, Princess of Wales, got formally divorced. It's also the year where Motorola launched StarTAC, the first ever clamshell/flip mobile phone. Still in electronics, the IBM Deep Bleu chess computer for the first time ever beat the reigning world champion Garry Kasparov. And would you believe that the first mass-production electric car dates from 1996. It was the General Motors EV1 that was brought on the market; but as only 800 cars reached interested drivers, the EV1 program was discontinued in 2002.

1996 was also the year of the exceptional mid-air collision of Saudi Arabian Airlines flight 763 with Kazakhstan Airlines flight 1907. All 349 people on board both flights were killed, making it one of the deadliest mid-air collisions in the history of aviation.

And for the softies, the '96 lucky tears news came from Binti Jua, the female gorilla from the Brookfield Zoo, Illinois. She is renowned for an incident that occurred on August 1996. A three-year old boy climbed the wall around her zoo enclosure and fell 18 feet onto the concrete floor, rendering him unconscious. Binti walked to the boy's side while helpless spectators screamed, afraid that the gorilla would harm the child. Binti picked up the child, cradling him with her right arm, gave him a few pats on the back, and carried him 20 metres to an access entrance, so that zoo personnel could retrieve him. Her 17-month-old own baby clutched her back throughout the incident. The boy spent four days in the hospital and recovered fully.

On Monday morning 4 March 1996, I went to the office to pick up my mobile, laptop, and company car and would prepare for my first working day on Wednesday. It only happened once in my career, but I was 24 hours late on my first working day. My wife saw the need to give birth to our son on that same Wednesday morning at 11.45 am. We named him André. And when he was a bit naughty and too demanding in his early childhood, I called him 'the ant'.

On Friday 8th March – so one day after I really started – Luc called me in the early afternoon. I had taken one day off to bring my wife and the newborn back home from hospital.

Luc Essen, the Belgium General Manager who recruited me, was himself headhunted by UBS management and joined 10 months prior to me. Previously, he was Plant Manager at P&G. He is a very intelligent manager an extremely fast thinker but indeed needed some support on the people management agenda.

Luc's call was – oh, we have been there before – on an upcoming social unrest in the packaging department. The operators, paid solely based on individual production volume, had been complaining to Robert Daloux (the previous Finance Director – now Project Manager) on the poor quality of the raw materials. According to them, with the poor paper quality, they could never achieve their production quota. It was proven that over the last three months their earnings were lower than the same period last year and that it was all due to the cheap materials Robert had bought from a new supplier.

In the local boardroom, Robert admitted there were quality issues. When this happened in the old days, Mr. Blancpain would have given the operators additional discretionary pay; but the Swiss management liked the pure pay for performance system, as I did; but no extreme system works. So I pleaded for a better balanced pay structure. That was much more difficult to sell to Robert and to the Swiss than to the operators and the unions. But I got it implemented with the support from "maths mastermind" Luc and with the great support from the employers federation of the paper industry.

Only a few weeks in business and I was already applauded by staff, unions, Swiss management – who liked the avoidance of social unrest – and the employer's federation. My God; why? What had I done? Nothing spectacular. Just listening and showing respect to all parties involved, using a bit of human sense and confidently putting my proposal; that's it. Nothing more.

It's surprising how sometimes managers have the best ideas but can't get them sold and how at other occasions minor achievements get over-rewarded. My next pay increase was 15%. Why? And 'old-style' Robert – who strongly and emotionally continued to oppose – was sidetracked.

The rest of my first years at Les Papeteries were largely what I was hoping to experience; managing the factory downsizing resulting from the new technology and getting more experience in the sales division.
Of course there were the odd and unexpected issues to be dealt with. Like the police raid in the cloakrooms as one of our mechanical operators was accused of dealing hard drugs. And the fire in the finished goods warehouse where one of the operators had allegedly been smoking. But also the solidarity of the packaging team when one of their colleagues had lost all her goods in a fire at home. The colleagues collected an amazing amount of furniture and clothes. We added three months' pay.

And then the annual complaints about the late payment of the holiday pay. The local union leaders argued heavily for immediate payment, but forgot that holiday payments in Belgium for blue collar workers are paid by the unions! Like the payment of jobseeker allowances; in Belgium it's outsourced to the unions. No surprise we lost all our respect in our political leaders. And no surprise that 70% of them have close ties with the unions. Through employing the trade union structures as an outsourced payment agent – on behalf of the government – it is estimated that the Belgian unions make around 180 million Euro annually.

For the sales division, I also recruited a number of top sales and marketing guys like Paul De Roeck. Paul was a remarkable sales manager, very hard working, really engaging with all his teams and with exceptional analytical skills. And Dudley Fields who, however, resigned after four years to go on a world tour with his wife and two daughters. At the end they only saw half of the world as he got hooked with his family in Arizona where he is currently running a small internet design firm.

I will never forget how Paul in December 1996 entered the offices dressed as the Christmas man. He made his tour through the factory, chatted with all the operators a few minutes and gave them a small present. It was amazing how much he knew about their private lives, their kids, their partners. Clearly my HR assistant Sabine must have been in the plot as she was the only one who knew everything about everyone.
He also walked through the offices, first to his own teams and then to the Suisse guys on the first floor.

"And for you, John," (our Swiss CEO), he said, "I have a brand new Jaguar XJS Convertible. But I can only order it once I have received my bonus on my bank account."

"That's a deal, Paul", John replied. "I'll wire over the 50 Euros this afternoon."

"Oh super, John; thanks for your personal contribution. Then I can even fill it up," Paul smartly replied. "Although the Matchbox version doesn't need any fuel, does it?"

Paul later moved on to British American Tobacco and to Unilever. I heard that while he was on a business trip to Morocco, he'd had a severe and career-ending stroke. While he is mentally OK, his left arm is fully paralysed. I understand nowadays he's finding joy and fulfilment in making aquarelle paintings.

In the second half of 1996, I got many – almost daily – requests for reports and presentations on the general business, on productivity, on social costs, on redundancy practices, etc. All the senior managers also needed to confirm their Christmas holiday plans, and holidays outside Europe were kindly asked to be rebooked to a destination closer to Antwerp. It was clear, the Suisse were preparing for a deal much earlier than initially planned. That was also confirmed by the urgent request to sign a special confidentiality agreement. The wording of some of these clauses revealed to me that the interested buyer was a publically listed company; most likely an American or an English multinational. Through the traditional grapevine – yes through the bankers – we also learned that a Dutch billionaire was showing interest.

That deal came in January 1997.

Before we move on to that next stage, I would like to pay tribute to another remarkable man. It was an honour and a pleasure to work closely with him. You may recall that I was recruited to "professionalise" Human Resources at Les Papeteries. There was however a Personnel Manager in place; his name Marcel Van Acker. When I joined, Marcel was aged 59 and had been working for the company and for Mr. Blancpain for over 30 years.

Of course you can't generalise, but many long-serving people like Marcel suffer and struggle a bit once they turn 50-ish. They normally have seen it all and as everything in business life is cyclic, they have seen it many times.

New bosses, new processes, abolishment of old processes but "please keep doing it", new reporting guidelines, new bosses leave, consultants come and consultants go, top-down and bottom-up, outsourcing and insourcing, rebranding of previous approaches, business process re-engineering, quality control becomes quality assurance, personnel management becomes human resources, listening to each other becomes the idea box and the idea box gets transformed into a satisfaction questionnaire which than gets canned and becomes an engagement survey, talking to each other is substituted by team feedback sessions and that evolves into a 360°, safety becomes OHSE, customer oriented becomes consumer centric, do what the boss asks to do becomes "alignment". And sometimes, leadership becomes …bullshit management.

Marcel had seen it all. And I am grateful for everything I learned from him; including his amazing skill to cope with change. He probably wasn't the most innovative manager; nor did he really introduce lots of change. That's why I was brought in, but I wouldn't have been successful without his genuine and candid feedback. He was the perfect sounding board.

Good old Marcel had gone beyond the point of frustration. He indeed had seen it all; managers come and managers go. And he created his own job satisfaction. He kept programming on his antique IBM AS400 – very useful stuff by the way – and was instrumental in the continuous improvement of the outsourced payroll. While he kept doing anything that he was asked by the senior management, he did on top of that everything that he believed was right for staff and the business. And frequently he did those critical things that we, senior leaders, do not even think about. And if you one day were to find in a vintage shop AS400 tapes labelled 'Les Papeteries: payroll month/year', then let me tell you a secret. Marcel was a fanatic tennis fan. So the password for any year is the surname of the winner of the women's' final at Wimbledon of that year. All capitals. So for the tape 'Les Papeteries-payroll 06/97', you need the password 'HINGIS' and for next year it's 'NOVOTNA'. Any tape from beyond 98 is not ours as in 1999 the AS400 retired; so did Marcel in May 2000.

Today you'll find him with his grand-kids in Benidorm or at home; cleaning his salt water aquarium.

I realise, Marcel, that I promised you'd get an invite for dinner once every year; and I also realise I've only kept my promise once. Unforgivable. Of course I can blame the workload, and yes I am now working abroad which makes it a bit more difficult. I am sorry, Marcel.

However. I have now also joined the rat race club; and that's time consuming. Thus these days, only opportunities to build my career make it into my diary. Only colleagues and business partners who potentially hold a key for future progress, end up in my diary. Only bosses, consultants, professors of INSEAD or Kellogg School of Management get my time. And headhunters, of course. Day and night.

I plead guilty.

~ ~ ~ ~ ~ ~ ~ ~ ~ ~

CHAPTER 6

The Dutch billionaire.

> *"You can be appointed a manager, but you are not a leader until your appointment is ratified in the hearts and minds of those who work with you."*
> *- John Adair*

Les Papeteries moved ownership in January 1997.

The new boss was a Dutch multimillionaire, named Koos van Groningen. He owns a plenitude of businesses in very diverse sectors: food, diamonds, shipping and real estate. His imperium also includes some top-notch restaurants in Amsterdam, Paris, Phoenix and Sydney, bakery shops all over Holland and two immense cattle breeding farms in Arizona. Not surprisingly, as he was Dutch, he also manufactured bicycles. Koos van Groningen sent Melvin Bos, his right hand man, as Chief Operating Officer to Les Papeteries. Melvin was a good boss; he listened very well and communicated directly; his instructions (we couldn't call it strategy nor visionary leadership) were clear. Indeed, Melvin lacked vision and was also very vague when explaining the rationale of his multimillionaire in acquiring Les Papeteries. We, the management, didn't see any synergy opportunities with the current activities of the imperium anywhere.

"This is not about synergies guys," Melvin always said. "This is diversification; nothing else."

Anyway, the van Groningen family, one of the top ten richest families in the Netherlands, had bought us and we all together had the appetite to make the future of Les Papeteries a success story.

Talking appetite, after the first management meeting in early February, Melvin invited us to one of the van Groningen restaurants in Amsterdam. This was not one of their top restaurants but in any case a memorable event. In the restaurant, you relax on beds with soft and massive pillows whilst you enjoy your Mediterranean food. The tapas I managed whilst lying down but honestly, for the tomato soup I had to sit up. As the restaurant also holds on the first floor a very popular but tremendously noisy night bar, we returned pretty early back to the hotel where Melvin had arranged a private bar. In a rather informal setting, he gave us an opportunity to ask all kind of questions about him and the new owners. All senior managers of Les Papeteries appreciated his open style and honesty very much in answering all our questions. I really liked his answer to the question of Jean-Luc Tarot, our French Plant Manager.

"Melvin, do you have a set of company values that you would like us to roll out in the divisions of Les Papeteries?"

"That's an excellent question, and the answer is no. We don't distribute massive posters or booklets with core company values. But it's important for you to know the leitmotif of the van Groningen family."

"And that is?" Jean-Luc impatiently asked.

"You will hear Koos saying many times – and by the way, he is serious about it – the following: 'If you make me rich, I'll make you rich.' That's his guiding principle, his corporate value, if you will."

I felt less comfortable though when further questions on the unclear synergies were popping up. This time, even twice that night, his answer didn't feel genuine; it felt like an overly prepared reply.

"This is not about synergies. This is diversification; nothing else. Next."

We should have known better. Quite frankly, still today I don't understand how we have missed the obvious. The Dutch have never been interested in our business, not in its totality. But for the van Groningen family, there was one hidden gem. Given that the Swiss owners didn't want to break up the business, they probably said to the Dutch family that they had to buy the entire business or nothing at all.

That gem was one of our patented production processes. Obviously, and given my very detailed confidentiality agreement, I need to be careful here on what I share with you. But what I can say, in general terms, is that it is about our patented process of producing very thin, almost cigarette paper thin, but strong and waterproof paper products. Funny that the Dutch family was so interested in this product; it was not even a core or high volume product for Les Papeteries.

In retrospect, we indeed should have known better. Both the trademark and patent lists, as well as the list of customers for Les Papeteries' thin paper product, were of great interest to Melvin in the first few months after acquisition. You may recall that Koos van

Groningen bought us in January 1997; in May of that same year, that specific patent had already changed ownership to a subsidiary of the van Groningen imperium. As well, the specific manufacturing equipment used for its production was moved to Utrecht in July 1997. We informed our customers that this product –internal code WPP3– had been taken out of our product range.

Late August that year, Melvin called for another urgent management meeting in Amsterdam. This time we wouldn't be meeting in the expensive Krasnapolsky; it would be in a cheap Novotel. Most likely the Mediterranean food would be replaced by a glass of milk and meat croquettes. It would be Koos van Groningen himself who would open the session in the morning. It would be the first time, and perhaps the last time, we would meet him in person.

I am enjoying a cigarette and having a chat with Luc Essen outside the hotel lobby; the meeting will start in half an hour. A large chauffeured Audi A8 stops in front of the lobby. White? That's not a colour for such an expensive car. It's van Groningen arriving; accompanied by Melvin. When white became the trend for luxurious cars – the 'new black' – fifteen years later, it became clear that boss van Groningen was a strong trendsetter.

The boss steps out of the car and is introduced to us by Melvin, who carries the boss' briefcase.

"Very nice to meet you Mr. van Groningen," I say, adding, "And not by bike today?"
"You are Henry, yeah? The HR Manager? Good to see you, Henry. No, I stopped going to work by bike since I replaced my HR Director's car with a bike. So, she is now riding my bike. Melvin, can you let me know tomorrow the details of the car policy of Les

Papeteries? And let's now go inside, gentlemen; we'll start the meeting soon."

Now, that's 1-0 for van Groningen. It was an open goal; I gave him a free penalty shot. He easily kicked the ball in the goal; that's extraordinary for the Dutch. But then his name is van Groningen and not Seedorf or Arjen Robben; both world famous for missing penalty shots. And I, I got at least a yellow card. Or was it red? We'll find out later. And you know, I fancied playfully scorning the billionaire; the business ethics he had demonstrated over the last months made it clear to me that this is not the business where I wanted to further build my career. Under the Swiss ownership, I had clear opportunities, but they did not exist in this configuration. Even if I had wanted it, the Dutch ladder didn't provide many openings for rewarding climbing.

Anyway, I am convinced that this meeting is about van Groningen telling us that he is going to put the business in the shop window again and that we'll have to start providing reports in preparation for the second due diligence exercise of the year. Luc and I even had a bet on the matter; I would get his 1000 Belgian Francs (now €25) if van Groningen announces today that he's planning to sell the business.

In the meeting room, things get very clear very quickly. Koos van Groningen takes the stand, sips first from his orange juice – "jus d'orange" as the Dutch like to call it – and kicks off the meeting with,

"Good morning gentlemen, we have important and good news for you all. But before we go into detail, Melvin will distribute you some documents. These are confidentiality agreements that I would like you to read, sign and return before we continue the meeting."

I look at Luc, point at his wallet in the back of his trousers and say, "You see, I was right. Show me the money."

During the meeting, it turns out that I wasn't right.

The message was not that he was planning the sell the business, the story was that he had already sold the business. Last week, Koos van Groningen had signed a private treaty with the Board of an English company. This company was in fact the second highest bidder when the Swiss UBS management had put the business up for sale. So they had already been in the due-diligence room and thus had all the relevant details of Les Papeteries.

As the English company is a publicly listed company, they however first had to go through an enormous process of preparing the materials to communicate to thousands of stake- and shareholders. This took some months of hard work for us to assist the English on this.

On November 21st, the deal was publicly announced to the London Stock Exchange and to the press. And I, I looked forward to returning to Anglo-Saxon business life.

~ ~ ~ ~ ~ ~ ~ ~ ~

CHAPTER 7

Vous descendrez plus jamais.

> *"Desire is the starting point of all achievement, not a hope, not a wish, but a keen pulsating desire which transcends everything."* -Napoleon Hill

"The English" had also seen it all in business life.

Different to Koos van Groningen, we were bombarded very quickly with corporate policies, values, mission statements, etc. but also with clear communication on substantial management bonus opportunities. These opportunities, though with challenging volume and profit targets, were very well documented and detailed. So this time we trusted this much more than the hollow leitmotif from van Groningen. I am still waiting for his Dutch Guilders in return for his wealth.

For CCG PLC – the name of the new owners – Les Papeteries was their first major international acquisition. CCG PLC stands for Commonwealth Consumer Goods; listed on the London Stock Exchange and today in the FTSE 50.
Commonwealth Consumer Goods is an English company, over one hundred years old, which is very profitable through focus on strong cost control, balanced product mix and investment in high margin fast moving products.

CCG appointed David Cornwall as the divisional Managing Director of this newly acquired business with establishments in the UK, France, Belgium, the Netherlands and USA. Apart from playing golf on the Channel Islands, David – a 55 year old electrical engineer – had never left England. Similar to the Swiss, he based himself in Antwerp; it must have been because of the great restaurants. David loved dinner at the Sir Anthony Van Dijck (rated then with two Michelin stars) and the Neuze Neuze. But he was also in for just a good portion of "moules frites".

David's entire career at CCG had been in manufacturing; now leading the paper tissues division including the sales and marketing aspects was a great career move. It was a great challenge for him and even more for the senior team of Les Papeteries.

It was great – and sometimes amusing – what we learned from him. CCG's financial year is October to September. We learned how to apply this flexibly. When in the last quarter of the financial year, the estimate for the full year's sales volumes looked to be above target, he shortened the year to 51 weeks; moving the extra week's surplus volume to next year, thus a 53-week year. And both years we would achieve targets and therefore get full bonus.

He also guided us to report product dimensions in inches, fuel consumption in gallons, and an invitation for a meeting in Antwerp at 1pm meant that the meeting started at 2pm. UTC+1. And to get more order on the factory work floor in Antwerp, he let the Technical Services Manager redesign the flow of goods and people. And yes, on the walking paths, the operators had to walk on the left side of course.

Some of the products in CCG's portfolio are claimed by some to be controversial. Indeed, CCG's large portfolio also includes condoms, tobacco products, energy drinks and alcohols. I'll never forget a dinner with David's wife in London. After the Shepard's pie with truffle sauce – what a disastrous combination and absolute attack to my gustatory papillae, she volunteered the following statement that I'll never forget:

"I don't mind David selling controversial products; it gives me a nice lifestyle. Especially in December when the bonus gets paid."

On the Human Resources side, he implemented English shift systems, all job adverts would now mention the job's salary and all employment contracts should refer to the laws of England and Wales. An instruction I of course didn't execute. The few times I could convince him to invest in management development, he would send over a consultant from Birmingham, or London or Nottingham. Even for safety training for the operators – who didn't speak English – we got a consultant in from Bristol.

"They are very good and they have done the same work for CCG in the Swindon factory."

"And they can deliver this in Flemish, David?"

"No they can't, but that's your problem. You just let them talk and the shift supervisor will simultaneously translate. And if they can't do this, then you'll do it."

David also introduced a new set of redundancy terms in the Antwerp factory; a copy-paste of the terms applied in the CCG factory in Birmingham.

"This country David, however small it may be, also has a set of employment rules. As a judge at labour court, I happen to know these rules. And your proposed terms are for some, more generous – which is not really a problem – but for others these terms are below the industry agreement. Our workforce has a Belgian contract, we are a Belgian employer and therefore we need to be in line with the local laws and practices."

"You need to understand that you are now part of an English company; whether you like it or not. And thus we'll implement consistent redundancy terms so that we don't discriminate amongst our workforce."

"I can and will not implement practices that are below legal standards David, I am sure you'll understand that. But no problem, I'll take the details up with George (the CCG Group HR Director) in Birmingham. I'll explain to him the details and we'll look at how to bring more consistency."

"Fine by me; talk to George, but in the meantime get ready to implement this also in Holland and France."

I learned quickly that in order to get David's respect, it was much better to strongly argue with him than to just obey to his sometimes absolute provocative nonsense. That was his way of assessing people's capabilities. But don't get me wrong, I also learned great things from

David; like having for lunch a BLT sandwich and crisps and starting dinner with a G&T. Double shot.
For those who have spent less time in Shakespeare's country, BLT stands for Bacon-Lettuce-Tomato and G&T of course stands for Gin and Tonic.

After two years, David moved on to another senior job in the Group and was succeeded by Graham Morris as Managing Director of the Papeteries division. With his excellent sales management track record and his high level empathy skills, Graham was of a much less autocratic style and got things done through giving his direct reports clear direction and lots of autonomy and accountability.

It was under Graham's leadership that the Group decided to close the French factory of les Papeteries. A brave decision as the factory with 60 employees in the small town of Saint Pierre, nearby Marseille, was the only employing company in the village. Over half of the adult population of Saint Pierre was working in our factory; so the closure would be a social and economic disaster for the village.

It was understood that this wasn't going to be easy and therefore George Leister, the Group HR Director with massive global industrial relations experience – that meant in Birmingham, in Liverpool, in Bristol and from his early career in Zimbabwe – was going to take the lead on this closure.

But George had never faced trade union leaders like those of the CFDT and even worse the 'communist' CGT. In my experience, in terms of toughness but also immaturity and socio-economic unrealistic demands, the ranking of the European trade unions is headed by France. Then followed by Spain, Belgium, Italy; and Germany and Poland somewhere in the mid rank. And somewhere at the bottom the

Netherlands and the British trade unions who, while defending workers' rights, also have economic reasonability. Thank you, Baroness Thatcher. And the blame for France goes with pleasure to Madame Martine Aubry who also invented the 35-hour working week in 2000. Since then, most major international companies only recognise France for its 65.8 million consumer population but if possible will never establish a manufacturing plant in France.

Graham and George, accompanied by my good friend Robert Daloux, the project manager that I frustrated through my review of the pay structures at my first days at Les Papeteries, had organised a special works council meeting. Robert was there mainly as he was French speaking and could therefore be helpful for the corridor talks. They had chosen a large business hotel in Marseille as a 'safe place'.

George opened the meeting.

"My name is George Leister, I am the Group HR Director of CCG. I have with me today Graham Morris, your divisional Managing Director and Robert Daloux, who is project manager of the paper tissue division and PDG of your company. On our right hand side is Isabelle who will help us with translations into French in case anything is unclear. And on the left hand is Laurence who will prepare minutes of the meeting. We are here to inform you of an important decision which we will explain to you in detail. We have arranged for lunch here in the hotel at 1 pm and expect the meeting to end around 4pm. The meeting will be in English; so will be the official minutes of the meeting."

The response from one of the members of the works council was quick, succinct and to the point.

"La réunion sera en Français, seulement le Français. Laurence, veuillez noter que la réunion s'est terminé à 11.03. Il est un peu tard pour retourner à l'usine donc on accepte bien l'invitation pour le lunch." (This is translated as follows; "The meeting will be in French; French only. Laurence, please note that the meeting ended at 11.03am. It's a bit late to return now to the factory so we gratefully accept your invite for lunch.") The members of the works council left the room and went to the pub next to the hotel.

Robert, as Président Directeur Géneral, replied with a high voice and in French, that they couldn't leave the room.
"This is an official meeting, and an important one. You better listen to what we have to say." But before he finished shouting, they all had left the room. George – who of course didn't understand a word of what was said, nor had he experienced ever that people were leaving a meeting without his permission – turned pale and asked Robert what was going on.

Later on, it became clear to the management team that the workforce very well knew that this was going to be about a closure and that the issue of the English language was for them an excellent argument to apply their first tactic of delay. And they had plenty – hundreds in fact – of similar and effective postponement tactics for the rest of the process.

Three days later, a crisis meeting was called in Antwerp with Graham, George, Robert and a French lawyer. George also invited me to this meeting; he was clearly looking for mainland expertise. In addition, the French plant manager Jean-Luc Tarot was invited. He had never been consulted or involved in the decision process to close his factory. He was only informed by Graham on the morning of the special works council meeting. Jean-Luc had lived for 12 years with his wife and three daughters in a company owned house, called le villa du Directeur, in Saint Pierre, next to the factory. He was very well integrated into the local village and being the plant manager of the only factory, he was a man of high importance. But Jean-Luc didn't show up in Antwerp. He faxed via his lawyer that for the safety of his family, he had resigned and left Saint Pierre and moved to another undisclosed place. Any further contact would have to be via his lawyer.

Jean-Luc's reaction surprised us but it made us even more aware of the seriousness and the risks of this process.

In that Antwerp meeting – and in the following days – we updated the critical path, further planned the process steps and agreed roles and responsibilities. Jean-Luc would be replaced – to keep the business running as far as possible – by Jean-François Beaufort, a crisis manager with over 20 years of experience in the UK; but French.
The management team would get process support from three guys from the Birmingham-based Grant Consulting, headed by Frederic Dermax; a Frenchman. He was going to play a key role in informal stakeholder management with top trade union leaders and with the French Department of Employment.
George would never return to Marseille or Saint Pierre but would coordinate all actions from Head Office. He would meet the most senior trade union officials if and when needed, but only in London or Paris.
The negotiation team would be Robert, Graham, Frederic and myself. Meetings with works council and trade unions would be in French and would take place in the meeting room of the old office block of the factory. For any travel that one of us would make to Saint Pierre, we would be accompanied by someone from Group security.

Two weeks after the very short Marseille meeting, the negotiation team went down to Saint Pierre. The next works council meeting took place in the meeting room of the old office block; first floor, on Tuesday afternoon at 2pm. With us were Isabelle and Laurence. I saw on the other side of the street our security guard walking along the pavement. For the rest it was very quiet in the village. This looked like such a nice romantic and peaceful Southern-France village. I thought we could play "jeu de boules" on the market square after the meeting.

The members of the works council entered the room on time and calm. Robert opened the meeting – in French of course – and brought the company's message of the intended closure. The employees listened calmly to our arguments and to the description of the legal process. We would start formal discussions on the rationale of the intention (the so called "Livre IV") in a few weeks' time. Then a few weeks later, this would be followed by the negotiations on the social measures (the so called "Livre III"), on redeployment and redundancy pay. We said that it was our intention to close the factory within six months.

Again, they reacted calmly and asked politely to adjourn the meeting so that they could meet amongst them. The meeting would restart at 4pm. But they added immediately that the meeting whatever was null and void as the invitation to the meeting was not signed by Jean-Luc Tarot, the formal president of the works council. Yet another tactic for delaying the process.

None of them returned by 4pm. Graham and I were enjoying a cigarette and decided we would wait another 15 minutes. Exactly at 4:15 we heard some voices downstairs in the large reception hall but no-one seemed to come upstairs. I opened the door to have a quick look and got the surprise of my professional live.

The large reception area downstairs, I guess around 100 square metres, is not only populated by the six members of the works council but also by another hundred people from Saint Pierre and probably neighbouring villages and supported by trade unions from other companies. They are armed with drums, trumpets and whistles. Once they see me, they start to produce a noise that made my eardrum feel as if I was standing on a landing strip right under a Boeing 747. Robert and Graham ran to the door to witness the demonstration and turned red and pale at the same time.

"F**k you", Graham says and returns to the meeting table and immediately calls our security guard; who doesn't pick up the call. I look outside but can't see him anywhere on the pavement. We call Group Security who also had not heard from him at 4pm. It was pre-agreed that he would call them every hour at the hour. We learned afterwards that eight men had surrounded him on the street and forced him to hand over his mobile. Three men had stayed with him all the time so that he wouldn't move.

The demonstrators downstairs continue to make a deafening noise. Each time they go quite, I open the door and look from the landing. Once they notice me, they started again. The demonstrators are also carrying a large banner: "Vous descendrez plus jamais"; freely translated as, "You'll never get out here."

It is around 7pm when Robert really has enough of this hostage-taking. Frederic discourages him but he whatever leaves the meeting room and walks slowly down the large stairs. I think he had only gone down three steps when around 10 men walk up the stairs to hinder him from going further. Without any touching or fighting, not even a word was exchanged, Robert got the message and returns back upstairs.

Only 10 minutes later, Laurence and Isabelle are preparing to go downstairs. We insist even more strongly to them to stay with us, but there is no way to convince them. Together they walk down the first three steps, and the next three, and the next three, and the next ones and are not once hindered. All the demonstrators are looking at them but don't say a word. We see Isabelle and Laurence walking out of the hall and going on the street. There they have a short chat with the two local police officers and then walk further into the direction of the village centre.

At 7.45 pm, again a lot of noise comes from downstairs in the hall, but it doesn't sound as hostile this time. Suddenly the door of the meeting room opens and we see Laurence and Isabelle entering the room; with a big smile on their faces. And with a basket of bread, some blue cheese and three bottles of red wine. And some crisps for Graham. And with two packs of Gauloises; they had noticed that Graham and I had run out of cigarettes. We welcome them with a big kiss.

We have never ever known how the girls managed to do this. Was it their charms or the weakness of the French for beautiful women, cheese and French wine? The Rocquefort cheese was delicious, but nevertheless we wanted to get out of this hijacked situation.

In the meantime, Frederic had been making many calls to his network in France. Also George had been working very hard from the Head Office. He has been talking to the British Chamber of Commerce in Marseille who in turn liaised with the Prefect. He made contact with the mayor of Saint Pierre and learned that he had instructed his own local police force not to intervene. So the Prefect had no choice but to send the Gendarmerie.

The Gendarmerie arrives with 10 men; four wait downstairs in the reception hall and six come to the meeting room. They advise us to pack all our stuff and to leave the building together with them. Once we leave the meeting room, the crowd downstairs starts shouting again and terrifying us with their drums and trumpets. With three gendarmes on our left side and three on the right side – so with us nicely protected in the middle – we walk down the stairs.

Halfway down the stairs, we suddenly hear – even louder than all the loud drums and whistles – a gunshot. The gendarmes order us immediately to go back to the meeting room. Two gendarmes stay posted at our door; the others go back downstairs. I really hope they will be capturing the perpetrator of the gunshot and bring this circus to an end.

After the gunshot, it became calmer downstairs.

At 1am, the gendarmes tell us that we now will go down. So we do. The reception hall is empty; there is no-one there. But what a mess, everywhere there are plastic forks and knives, plates and cups on the floor. Next to the door to the basement, there are two cartons of tomatoes and half-empty bowls of ketchup and mustard. I sense a strong smell of burning coal and herbs.

"The bastards, they had a barbeque party!" Graham mumbles while we leave through the front door.

No way was any local taxi company going to pick us up, so the gendarmes drove us in two Renault Master vans back to our hotel in Marseille. The security guard, who found his mobile in the desolated reception area, followed us in his rented car. On our way back, we first called Head Office to say we were too tired for a long call now and

would go straight to bed. The bar was closed so we all went to Graham's hotel room to kill his mini-bar.
And later on Robert's, Frederic's, Isabelle's and Laurence's mini-bars were emptied too.

In the following weeks, things calmed down. We went relatively fast through the process with the works council. Now we needed to start the negotiations with the trade unions. Robert had decided never to return to Saint Pierre so I was appointed PDG – or Managing Director – of one of the most rebellious factories in France. A factory declared dead.

Having read so many management books on empowerment and engagement, I decided to be as much as possible in Saint Pierre to be there for and with the staff; irrespective of the intended closure. We still had to go through a very difficult process but I felt that my management by walking around had a positive impact. Discussions and negotiations were becoming less hostile and, not unimportantly, there were very few days of strike. So we achieved a higher factory output than planned in the current circumstances. This was also largely thanks to Jean-Francois' excellent management style and to Frederic's work behind the scenes.

It's now Wednesday, the day before hopefully breakthrough negotiations with the unions. After a quick sandwich lunch with Graham, I decide to go for a walk on the footpath around the factory premises, bordered by a small river full of trout. At the bike park, I see Françis Brun, the local trade union leader for CGT, having his lunch on a wooden bench in the shade. It looks healthy food; a baguette with cheese and sliced tomato. He stands up and walks to me. Brun and I had had many serious arguments and he was also the one who has been most vocal in the workscouncil. And most hostile. I have always tried to understand his emotions as this intended closure was mainly hard for him. He was a fitter in the factory, his wife and his sister Elise both worked in the packaging department.

I tell Brun that I am going for a short walk.

"Je t'accompagne," he tells me while he stands up. He even volunteers to translate his saying. "I walk with you"; in not so bad English. What a nice gesture I think.

He leads me into the area of the parking lot and walks with me to his car; a white old and a bit rusty Peugeot. I am curious and wonder what he is going to show me. A propaganda banner, flags, leaflets announcing a strike? I had no idea. Perhaps he is just in a good mood – he's also a human being you know – and wants to show me some pictures of his family or some vegetables from his own garden. Or some bottles from his backyard's illegal distillery. Whatever it is, at least we are building some rapport and that's a major milestone on the day before a next key negotiations step.

Brun opens the boot of his car and shows me... a gun. Then he points the gun to my chest. In French he says:
"The gunshot in the reception area was from this machine. Today it's not loaded, but next time when we meet, I'll make sure it's loaded again. Get ready for a hot summer. Or a short one for you. You decide."

I decided not to report this accident to Head Office; they would have gone crazy, filed a civil complaint and closed the place without any further negotiations which would have been hard for all the other staff of the factory. CCG is very keen on the safety and security of his staff; it's a key value and the act of Mister Brun would have been seen as just one step to far in CCG's tolerance level. To be cautious though, I confidentially informed the head of the gendarmes but asked him not to intervene immediately.

We continued the negotiations during many months. The toughest negotiator turned out to be the mayor of Saint Pierre, who was also the brother-in-law of Françis Brun, and the husband of Elise.

At the end, we closed the factory six months later than initially planned. Head Office was however very pleased on how Graham and I handled this complex closure. Graham got promoted to a Regional Director job. Frederic continued to provide consulting services to us and joined the company five years later as the HR Director for all our businesses in France. Immediately after the Saint Pierre closure, George moved me to the Netherlands to combine the roles of HR Manager Netherlands with Regional HR Manager for the whole of Europe – excluding the UK of course. Our key market – at that time still good for 70% of global profit, could only be handled by a British HR Manager; not a "junior" Belgian. I was OK to get them out of the shit in Saint Pierre, but getting a role in the UK, that's another league.

I accepted the offer, although I was hoping to get a role in Head Office. Most managers with serious ambitions like to end up in the centre one day, don't they? That's where the career enhancing networking takes place, where you can really have an impact on global strategic decisions and where the pots of gold are. That's where you have direct access to the CEO, the CFO and all other Executives; that's where you can make your mark. That's where operational execution moves into real strategic intelligence. But George was very clear on that; the key roles in the centre are dedicated to the Brits. Every time I challenged George on this, he returned with his very empowering statement:

"As soon as I find somebody on Europe Mainland with brains, I'll get him over to the Centre."

Three operators of our Saint Pierre factory accepted redeployment in Antwerp, 35 found alternative employment in neighbouring places. The others ended up being unemployed or retired. Except for Elise and Françis who are now working in the Musée de Les Papeteries, developed in our factory buildings.

The villa, the factory, the old office block and all the land of our premises were sold to the community of Saint Pierre for a symbolic £1000.

Elise and the mayor – who got easily re-elected – are currently living in "le villa du Directeur". Françis Brun got a job in the trade union office in Marseille.

The last time when Graham and I went to Marseille, was to have a relaxing seafood dinner in restaurant "Les Miserables". That was with Laurence and Isabelle; in return for their cheese, wine and cigarettes offer a few months ago.

~ ~ ~ ~ ~ ~ ~ ~ ~

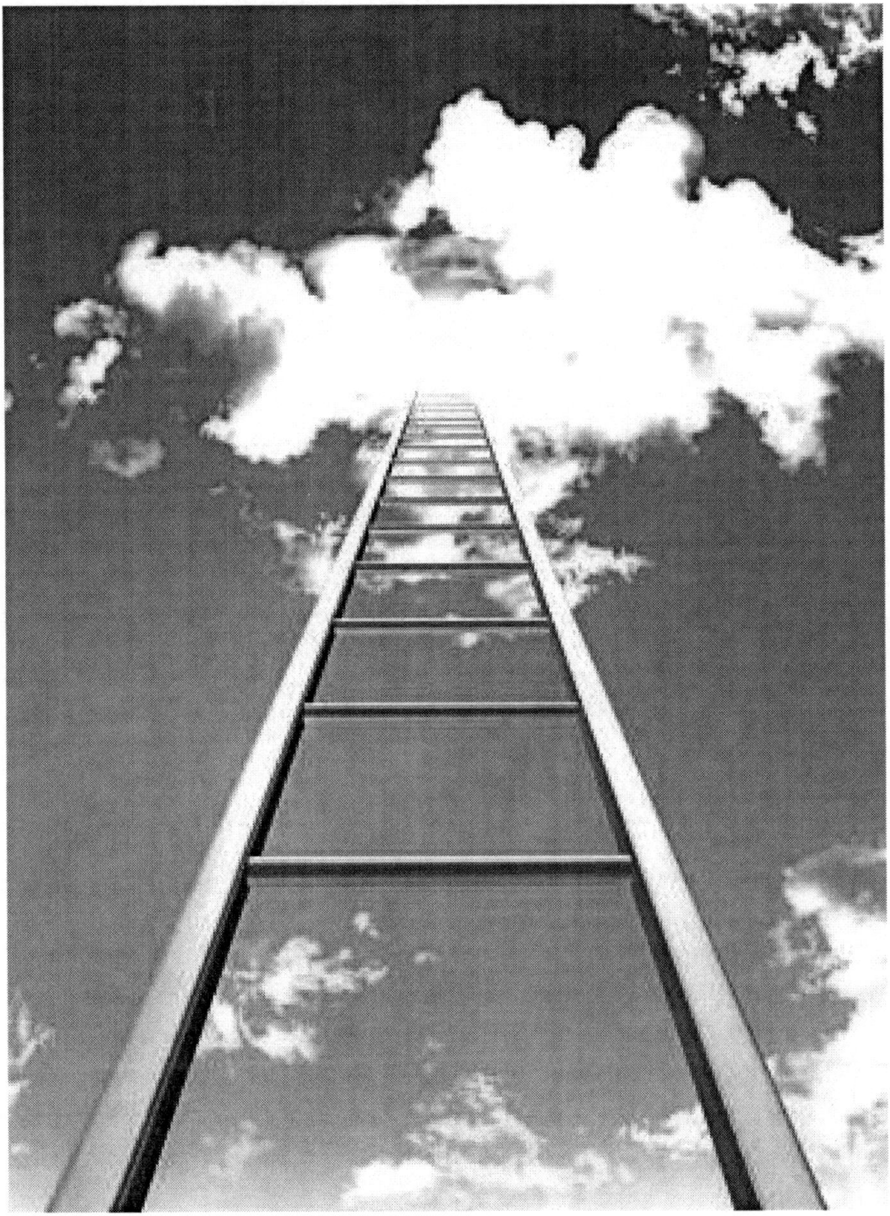

CHAPTER 8

Again climbing the corporate ladder.

> *"My main job was developing talent. I was a gardener providing water and other nourishment to our top 750 people. Of course, I had to pull out some weeds, too."*
> *– Jack Welch*

In my combined role of HR Manager Netherlands and Regional HR Manager Western Europe, I had to start with a big 'cleaning up' exercise. Many local senior managers had to be terminated. This all went together with the due diligence and preparation for yet another acquisition in 2002; the biggest one since CCG decided to go international. The target company was Smareem AG, a German company in the fast-moving sector with an extremely diverse product portfolio including sweets, crisps, coffee, alcohol, rolling tobacco, chocolates and chewing gum.

Lode, the General Manager for our CCG business in the Netherlands – and one of my new bosses – had to leave only six months after I started working for him. That decision from Head Office was entirely correct. Later, Lode started his own brand marketing consulting firm but wasn't successful. I have heard from his ex-PA that he is in a care home as he is suffering from early dementia. He must be in his late fifties now.

Next was our GM for Belgium. With his severance pay and some money that his wife inherited from her uncle – a successful business leader in the textile industry – he bought a vineyard in South Africa. He went bankrupt after six years and returned – divorced – back to Belgium where he is now running with his new girlfriend a newspaper shop somewhere in the Brussels area. His two sons stayed with mum in South Africa.

Another Dutchman, Guus, was put on the lead to manage the Benelux cluster. He became one of my new bosses and we worked very well together. I will never forget our management meetings in the Bilderberg Hotel in Tegelen near to the German border; these meetings were very constructive and with time for fun. Unfortunately, head office requested me to terminate Guus six months later at the completion of the acquisition of that big German company. That was a very questionable decision.

Next was the GM for France who was side-stepped into a more junior role in Business Development; and got terminated one year later. He is still unemployed. And also the GM for Spain got pre-retired.

To replace Lode, I attracted Mike Writers, our Australian GM, to run the Netherlands. Mike was a high potential and was willing to relocate to Rotterdam. Mike was a super manager and highly respected by his staff and superiors. But I shouldn't have done this. I should have learned my lessons from ES Pharmaceuticals where we also – for a short period – had an Australian leading the business. After two years, his wife gave him the choice to return back to Melbourne or to stay in the Netherlands, but that in any case would be without her. To all the Australian readers, I advise you to stay where you are. You live in such a nice country; Europe has nothing to offer to you. The same happened to Mike Writers and to another Australian senior manager who thought his future was in the UK. He returned – divorced – to Adelaide after four years in Birmingham.

Also, some more junior European managers had to free up space prior to the acquisition. When I search for these colleagues these days on LinkedIn, I only find half of them back in corporate life. Some of the others have made positive life-changing decisions. At least that's what they mail me. Jean-Pierre, previously Finance Manager, became a teacher helping children with learning difficulties, Patrick, ex-Benelux Logistics Supervisor, is renting out small yachts in Bordeaux, and Elly, previously Accounting Manager, is touring the world with Cirque de Soleil. Pol, Manager International Brands – and the only money-maker in the family – is now staying home to take care of his sick mother and his three kids; his wife started working at the local post office. He tells me he is enjoying his family more than ever, although the company car and the weekly lunches with marketing consultants have been replaced by a bike and one family Christmas dinner per year. Regular business class travel around the world is now substituted by two easyJet weekend-breaks per year.

In that period, I was nicknamed 'the butcher' and I know for a fact that when I called a European senior manager to inform him of my upcoming visit, for whatever reason, his next call was to his legal advisors.

It's strange. Normally the shelf life of a corporate butcher is very short; but I seem to have survived all my bosses. I have reported to 11 different senior managers at CCG, and today only one of them is still working for the company. Strange, isn't it?

Apart from the support from the financial brokers, Gary Mavis, the than CEO of the Commonwealth Consumer Group, decided that this massive acquisition would be managed without the involvement of any consultants.

"We have done this before, guys. We know what we have to do; you have the expertise. Let's go for it," he said to the acquisition and integration team.

For the first time, I am at the table of the acquirer.

It was good that all the due diligence to acquire Smareem AG went smoothly. At the end, Smareem had been in the hands of the family Smareem who after the successful leadership of five generations, had decided to put the business in the shop window. That was of course known by senior Smareem management, who were therefore also helpful in the provision of information. The CCG Board – advised by Citibank and Deutsche Bank – and the family Smareem, very soon came to a deal.

From an HR perspective, we had good information on the capabilities and the cost of the top Smareem managers. So 'the butcher' could start again as obviously there would be much duplication. However, it wasn't so dramatically given; Smareem had strong presence and had experienced managers in many Eastern European countries; a geographical area of weakness for CCG. Similarly, outside of Germany, Smareem had small operations and low market shares in most Western European countries. That geographical footprint and Smareem's strong expertise on brand management made the deal so important to us.

At the very top level of the business – not managed by me but by George and his newly recruited successor, Kathy – it was relatively easy. The acquirer keeps the CEO and the CFO. We also kept the Manufacturing Director, Corporate and Legal Affairs and the HR Director. So ex-Smareem management got the roles of Sales Director, Marketing Director and Supply Chain Director.

Now, Smareem AG wasn't a small business and their head office operations in Hamburg were much larger than ours in the UK. Their total sales volume was higher than CCG's, but our overall EBITDA was much higher. Also their headcount was in total 2,000 staff more than ours.

For the top structures in markets – my responsibility in Western Europe – it was relatively easy. In most markets, apart from Germany and Poland, we maintained the CCG top management structures. Don't forget we just restructured our businesses ahead of the acquisition.

In the early days of the preparation for the take-over (the Germans still call it a merger), I recruited a successor for my role in the Netherlands so that I could concentrate on Western Europe. Given George's interesting experience with continental unions in Saint Pierre, and somewhat afraid of the German works council, he appointed me as the Group Employee Relations Manager, reporting directly to him and

Bristol based. Paul McTann, a rising star and at that time in the role of Regional Director Western Europe, didn't want to let me go. So I again ended up combining two jobs; but I was ambitious and full of energy and self-confidence – and speedily climbing the CCG corporate ladder; with one leg in the head office – as one of the first non-Brits. Impressive isn't it! I am extremely proud of myself.

It was just a pity for my wife and son that I wouldn't see them that much. But I'd commute to the UK weekly so that I could spend a bit of time with them at home on weekends. And for the rest I'd compensate my absence with some nice family holidays to exotic destinations.

Yes! George found someone with a set of brains; on mainland Europe! And George got all my help he needed. Wherever there was a potential social conflict or an issue with a local management team, I got on a plane and extinguished the fire. The 'butcher' had been promoted to 'senior fire fighter'. I also had a significant impact on the establishment of the company's European Works Council and, together with my assistant Kate, we developed basic Employee Relations policies.

Simultaneously, I worked very well with Paul McTann. It was under his leadership that the integration of Smareem in Western Europe was completed ahead of planned timing while at the same time we delivered additional savings of circa 3 million Euros above target. In his entire career at CCG, Paul always over-delivered. It was therefore unfortunate that he became the victim of the biggest risk in corporate life. His corporate deficiency syndrome was fatal to Paul. His biological error was loyalty! Loyalty to his boss and to the company; that was his credo. But when his boss lost a strategic fight against the CEO, the boss had to leave. The very same day, also Paul McTann was terminated.

Then, George retired. His successor Kathy got the full responsibility in the role of Group HR Director. I would then report to her.

The same applied to Kathy as to me at Les Papeteries; she was brought in to modernise and professionalise the HR Department. In George's time, everything was based on trust; we didn't need 10-page long reports or documents. When I said to George, "Don't worry, the problem in the factory in South Germany is solved," then he didn't need more. He then reported to the CEO "problem solved," and the CEO trusted George, and George trusted me. Corporate life can be very easy; if you want it to be easy. That was the time when we respected each other, trusted each other. That was also the time when we communicated to each other; in straightforward language. No benign and obnoxious corporate jargon, no mumbo jumbo, no gibberish, no gobbledygook. That was the time that we didn't need 'bandwidth', 'value-add', 'six sigma' or a RACI-model; these were the days of 'let's do it'. No virtual teams; just teams.

The phase of working with George was probably the stage in my career that gave me highest enjoyment; sometimes despite his management style based on his Zimbabwean experience. OK, the big leader of the CCG tribe occasionally sent me into the jungle without any weapons and without satnav, but he trusted that I would come back with a game trophy. Again OK, I admit, sometimes I returned with a cockroach instead of the targeted elephant. And then we sat together in the dark clay shed of the tribal chief and George explained me – without a PowerPoint presentation – what went wrong in my planning and also how to trap the elephant. So I went back to the savannah. The trusted leader guided me to learn from my mistakes; that's key.

Teams work well when you have the right capabilities in the team and when the key principle is mutual trust and respect. Bryan Dyson, ex-CEO of Coca-Cola Enterprise, is so right in his famous saying:

"Don't forget, a person's greatest emotional need is to feel appreciated."

In all modesty, I think that Kathy also very quickly noticed my capabilities and work ethics. She though, wanted much more reporting. We came into an area where it's about what you write rather than what you do. She redefined the way of working and interacting in the corporate head office. It wasn't any more about the boys' club who knew and trusted each other for years; the HR governance now required endless policies, work process descriptions, etc. It was made clear by her that this company had been lacking real state-of-the-art HR strategy and practices. And I agreed with her, to be competitive in the market and to prepare for further acquisitions, we needed to bring in a more modernised strategy, new HR tools and practices.

And the strategy came; slowly. And our key success factor of CCG – respect and trust- disappeared; quickly. Not that I blamed Kathy for that; not at all. CCG just wanted to prepare for playing in the Premier League and in return we had to give up some of our successful DNA.

On a spring day in 2004, we had a meeting in London. Kathy offered to pick me up at my hotel in Bristol and to drive together to London. Why not? She's driving a nice Mercedes SLK – and we could discuss the issues about the private medical plan in Germany.

We didn't discuss the medical plan at all. After chatting about her dog and my wife's three cats, she came quickly to the point. So this wasn't a free ride.

Even before we passed Swindon, she had offered me the role of Global HR Director for all Sales & Marketing operations.

"I want to retire Dieter in half a year time. You can already start in the role next month as deputy so that you can prepare for your future HR structure. You will continue to work for me. I would like to know your response by tomorrow lunchtime. Mark Haus will leave the business and be replaced by Brat David. Also Gary Mavis is very supportive to your promotion."

So, I had 48 hours to decide; to decide to further climb the corporate ladder.

And although she said that I would continue reporting to her, I'd build a case soon to make me reporting to Brat, the top Executive for all Group Sales & Marketing Operations. Then I could introduce to the global business the concept of HR business partnering – and get out of the ivory tower concept. I have always hated 'groupies' who tell you what to do but have never seen the real world; I strongly believe in the powers of decentralised structures. But also, Brat is a member of the Board and Kathy isn't; reporting to a Board member of a top 50 FTSE company, I should see that reflected in my pay cheque.

Shortly after Swindon, still on the M4 to London, we get a flat tyre. With a conservative mindset, I thought, "Oh God, I am the only man in the car so I'll have to solve this." But luckily she called the AA and my tyre repair skills didn't need testing.

"And you also get yourself some help as soon as possible," she said. "You'll have a massive change agenda. The Smareem integration in Europe went fine but not in the other parts of the world. So that isn't completed yet and you'll have a lot of work on building a management pipeline in the East and in Asia. And on Asia, could you drop me a note by early next week on what you are going to do with the Taiwan Marketing Director role. This needs to be filled urgently."

It felt as if she didn't need my response anymore by tomorrow lunchtime. She had already decided that I was going to take up that role. And this time on my way to the savannah, I would get a satnav, a 40-pager PDF manual, a Blackberry to text her every hour to describe every tree we passed and a local assistant who will help me to find the elephants.

Things evolve and business practices evolve too. That's great; that's change. Today, when I go on a hunting mission, a private jet will drop me on a small strip in the savannah very close to tens of elephants. The native assistant is supplied with the newest state-of-the-art shotgun. We'll be very efficient; once we see the beast we just have to call the boss and seek permission to fire. Obviously that will also require the completion of two approval forms; one will be electronically signed by the PA of the CEO; in case he's not available. The other one will go to the Chairman of the Audit Committee, who luckily doesn't need to approve ahead of the killing; he's just checking that the forms are completed correctly. Once the form is returned, we shoot. No possibility to return with a cockroach. That's delivery from the first shot.

The same plane will also drop three accompanying consultants from McLinsey.

~ ~ ~ ~ ~ ~ ~ ~ ~ ~

THE FACTS 1

Predictors of success

Human beings have an inborn desire to be successful in life. That statement is commonly accepted. It is also commonly recognised that people hold differing definitions about what success really means for them. But overall, we share the aim for success in our private and professional lives. An individual's definition of success may also change over the years, impacted by external factors or just by internally changing desires. Obama wanted to be an architect; David Cameron was interested in art; so was Hitler but he was rejected at school. On 20 July 1969, Neil Armstrong set foot on the moon. His childhood dream was to be a fighter pilot. On the same day in 1969, Eddy Merckx won his first Tour de France. As a child, his dream had been to win the 'Le Tour' one day. Similarly, as a 13 year old boy, a Briton jumped on the train to Paris to watch the cycling on the Champs-Elysees. His dream was the same: to bring home the yellow jersey. And so Bradley Wiggins did in 2012.

There are also different timescales for achieving and defining success. If you are in an emergency room, you may define success as hic et nunc; it's now that you want to save the poor guy's life. But if you are an environmental scientist, you may define success by achieving a 20% reduction in CO_2 emissions in twenty years' time.

As children grow, their dreams become more tangible plans and as students, most of us hope to have a "great" job one day; again whatever "great" means. In most cases, we chose our major study subjects in view of what we desired to become in professional life. This was also influenced by the guidance we received from our parents and advisors. Today however, we see a trend developing in literature and research that emphasises requirements in addition to theoretical and intellectual capabilities. Even academics don't shy away from stating that the social skills acquired and developed in higher education become a prime competency influencing professional success.
Obviously, today there is also the enormous hurdle of pure lack of jobs. In the UK, the Office for National Statistics data shows that graduate

unemployment nearly doubled during the recent recession; resulting in one in five university leavers not finding a job. The average youth unemployment rate in the Euro-zone in April 2012 was 21%; with both Greece and Spain having over 50% of their under-25s being out of a job. High unemployment also massively impacts the likelihood of finding a job aligned to your area of study. A survey conducted by the UK's Chartered Institute for Personnel Development (CIPD) in 2010 revealed that 60% of the surveyed UK graduates who were lucky enough to find a job were working in an area unrelated to the degree they had studied. In the Alumni newspaper from Leuven University, a somewhat similar study was published in May 2012. Here 60% of the respondents indicated that their study degree was seen as a requirement for the job they are currently fulfilling. It being a "requirement" does however not mean that they work in an area related to their study degree. And the University confessed that most of the respondents were working at the University and as such the results are somewhat "inflated". So we can assume the CIPD figures get somewhat confirmed.

With significant levels of unemployment and with a high number of people not working in an area connected to their area of study, what is it then that's needed to develop a successful career in business?

Unsurprisingly, there are a large number of opinions and significant research into this question. In this chapter, I have put forward those views that in my personal experience, deliver the highest returns for someone building their career in a commercial environment.

Before digging deeper, I would like to refer to empirical research by the Center for Advanced Human resources Studies from Cornell University (1). In their 1994 study, the authors define and differentiate career success in terms of objective and subjective elements. As objective elements to measure career success, they list pay and the number of career promotions and ascendency; whereas the subjective elements are defined as job and career satisfaction. In their findings, they conclude that that technical skills, degree subject studied and quality of education received have a clear impact on the financial aspects of career success. In contrast, the subjective element of job satisfaction is more heavily impacted by social and motivation variables, and also by elements more related to the organisation (company) than to the individual's own background.

Returning then to the issue of what are the key drivers for career success. An overarching requirement is well explained by Ram Charan in his book *"What the CEO wants you to know"*. (2) To be straightforward and to keep it simple –that's what Ram Sharan likes – it's all about understanding your business. Whether you are working in marketing, manufacturing, internal audit or sales development; it is all about **commercial awareness** or business acumen. In today's world, it has become an absolute requirement to understand the building blocks of your organisation and to see the relationships between these blocks. This includes getting to grips with how your business makes profit. Ram Sharan underlines that this is more than just knowing that you buy items at a cost of, say 10 and sell them at, say 30. It's also about having a deep understanding of the return on your assets and other financial measurements, an understanding of your route-to-market, your customers and so on.

I know that the traditional "Finance for non-finance managers" is seen as a bit outdated, but it's still a very good start. However, you need more. Business acumen is not about learning the words from the textbook; it is about seeing the links between the different drivers. With progression up the career ladder and gaining business understanding, comes an in depth comprehension of competitors and the industry as a whole. It's the understanding of why, for example, competitor A goes for direct distribution, why B has a lower margin and why competitor C is stronger on innovation.

Next to an in depth business understanding, the development and application of **social skills** is another factor to influencing success in career growth. This includes motivation, drive, willingness to accept projects outside of your technical scope, self-marketing and networking. Career progression opportunities are rarely volunteered to the backbones in an organisation; you have to stand out from the crowd. That's about visibility; about being positively noticed in meetings. I have seen many people ending up on a succession planning list purely and simply because of having said the right words in a high level meeting or having done an excellent presentation to more senior managers. Although many organisations put more and more efforts into career planning, promoting someone to the next level up is still a somewhat subjective and impulsive decision. No need to say that therefore visibility at work related social events is also a strongly delivering tool for career progression.
Key to networking and self-marketing activities is the demonstration of self-confidence. Research has shown that being confident about your

capabilities for a particular role correlates with success in carrying it out. It's a self-fulfilling prophecy.

A little bit of selfishness, although counterproductive when you get to the top of the corporate ladder, is tolerated in the initial career building phase. Beware though – exaggerated and arrogant narcissism is never tolerated.

Extroversion and a good dose of assertiveness are the building blocks of social competencies. In a 2011 study, the Academy of Finland researched the social competencies of university students and the predictive impact on their professional social behaviour. (3)

"Our findings indicate that social optimism during university studies translates into a high level of work engagement up to 10–15 years after the study-to-work transition. On the other hand, pessimism and social avoidance seem to increase the likelihood of work burnout and exhaustion during the 10–15 years after the studies".

Linked to confidence and to social optimism is another factor that drives career success; one that you might not really expect to see on this list. It's **happiness**. Research has demonstrated that happy people perform better and that they earn more money. That correlation is supported by a range of research. I hear some of you reacting that this is no surprise; that although the say goes that money doesn't make you happy; a good salary will of course make people feel happier. True, but here comes the surprise, the chicken or the egg debate. A study from the University of California (4) supports the idea that happiness is also the cause of workplace success; that it is even an important precursor and determinant of career success. Research also shows that high involvement and commitment from happy managers does not go unnoticed by their superiors. As such, happy managers also receive more financial rewards and career opportunities than less happy people. While "happiness" has not been a business term in the past, it's good to see that these days many companies are starting to work more and more on the happiness levels of their staff. I expect in the years to come to not only see awards for the "Best Employer of the year" but also nominations for the "Happiest Company of the Year".

On the next driver for success I can be brief; it's **delivery in the current job**. It is so obvious, but unfortunately it is sometimes forgotten by over-ambitious career freaks. Sometimes companies with modern, enhanced talent development processes are not really helpful to some of their future leaders. I have seen many companies putting so much emphasis on the individual's potential in their career building guidelines, that the individual may be tempted to work too much on their development and neglect the primary requirement to deliver in the current role That's a risky strategy because even though some promotions are decided impulsively, line managers will always assess current performance before considering future potential.

There are a few more key competencies that can predict and enhance success, like language skills, cross-cultural openness and overall flexibility. The latter, I would like to call: **openness for change**. This is a really critical one.

Globalisation, increased competition, economic crisis, new regulations and an ongoing pressure for profit enhancement mean that companies are always on the hunt for ways of doing things differently. Change management systems are the white blood cells of a company;

continuously defending its interests against internal weaknesses and external attacks. Openness to consider change and even initiating change are critical drivers for personal success in business life. Career growth ends where the capacity to cope with change stops. Resistance to change is commonly seen as either a misunderstanding of the need to do things differently or as an indirect expression of fear. That fear runs contrary to the requirement to demonstrate self-confidence, which has been listed earlier as a key driver. Of course, reluctance to change is also seen as being fundamentally incompatible with a desire to develop your career by changing role or gaining promotion.

I have experienced that over the last few years, the above drivers for success have found their ways into many assessment centres. The same goes for another key driver on which I will elaborate further in this book: a **genuine interest in people**. This though comes with a health warning; something that surprised me through my own research conducted during 2012. I have analysed in depth over 250 "management" job adverts in media across some European countries. The purpose of this study was to find details of what activities are listed in job adverts as being the key elements of a managerial job. Hereby, I was expecting "people management" to be a key activity.

Two upfront comments:
- I have analysed only those job adverts where it can be assumed, out of the role title, that the role holds some people management responsibilities. Role titles considered included Manager, Head, Director, VP and their comparators in French, Dutch and German.
- In the advert, I have analysed the job content section, rather than the section covering requirements or experience.

The somewhat surprising key outcome of this research is that only 53% of the advertised "managerial" jobs feature people management responsibility. A few conclusions can be made from this observation:

- There is still a form of job title inflation to attract people to (and keep them in) the business. This is particularly observed in sales related roles. In other words, the job title implies that the role is more senior than it actually is.
- "Management" is frequently seen purely in terms of people management but "managing" can also mean responsibility for an activity, rather than a group of people. Observed examples in this area include Risk Manager, Business Development Director Key Account Manager. Obviously these roles can include people responsibilities on top of the accountability to manage an activity.
- In some adverts, the people aspect is just not detailed, although probably present, as it is probably not seen as a key element of the job.

Of the 53% of the job adverts out of our sample that do refer to people management responsibilities, the following job components were observed:

- 74% : general team management descriptors (e.g. leading a team of 3 accountants, taking full responsibility for managing the team)

- 54% : specialist / function specific descriptors (e.g. organises all regulatory activities for the vaccines portfolio, collects all customer's technical requirements)
- 36% : team development and coaching descriptors (e.g. create an environment for your team to develop their competencies, you are responsible for the coaching, development and support of your team)
- 27% : team performance tasking and control (e.g. monitoring the weekly sales performance of the team, implementing and controlling performance standards for the technical service team)
- 24 % : reporting requirements (e.g. to provide monthly market share data to the Marketing Director, provision of accurate data and reports on the project progress)
- 22% : financial planning and budgeting (e.g. budget monitoring and commercial awareness, development of the logistics budget in the regional network)

In general, successfully developing a career in a business environment means that your scope of control gets broadened. It tends to grow from limited responsibility for a clearly defined task, to accountability for a number of activities, then to overall managerial responsibility for a series of activities. Then it moves from strategy input to strategy setting and to the leadership of a team, a department, and ultimately the overall business. Although we have seen that a large number of roles titled "managerial" may not carry responsibility for people management, for most successful managers, somewhere in their career they will have "people" responsibility. For this, a genuine interest in people is considered a key trait.

Furthermore, management literature defines the following skills and competencies as necessary to enable successful navigation through company structures: commercial awareness, social skills, grounded positivism and happiness, job performance and flexibility.

~ ~ ~ ~ ~ ~ ~ ~ ~

CHAPTER 9

Management training in Prague.

> *"Some people ask the secret of our long marriage. We take time to go to a restaurant two times a week. A little candlelight, dinner, soft music and dancing. She goes Tuesdays, I go Fridays."* - Henny Youngman

The taxi to the airport was well on time but the flight SN2812 from Prague to Brussels was delayed for half an hour. We only started boarding the AVROjet 85 at 5.05 pm.

Once on board, I throw my trolley in the overhead cupboards and place myself in the bleu leader seat 4F. There's no-one in 4D or 4E, great; I have plenty of space for my legs.

"Ladies and gentlemen, the Captain has turned on the Fasten Seat Belt sign. If you haven't already done so, please stow your carry-on luggage underneath the seat in front of you or in an overhead bin. Please take your seat and fasten your seat belt. And also make sure your seat back and folding trays are in their full upright position. At this time, we request that all mobile phones and radios be turned off for the full duration of the flight, as these items might interfere with the navigational and communication equipment on this aircraft. We request that all other electronic devices be turned off. We remind you that this is a non-smoking flight. Smoking is prohibited on the entire aircraft, including the lavatories. If you have any questions about our flight today, please don't hesitate to ask one of our flight attendants. Thank you."

I feel so tired that I'll probably fall asleep before take-off. I should have gone earlier to bed last night; and the night before. But it's always the same at those events, you need to socialise in the bar with your colleagues and with the facilitators.

"Ladies and gentleman, also from the cockpit a warm welcome. My name is Fons Vleugels, I am your Captain, and the First Officer here next to me in the cockpit is Diana Toms. You have already met Tracey in the cabin who is there for your wellbeing and for your safety. We are now number three for departure so we'll be taking off in five to six minutes. We do apologise for this late departure which is due to the late arrival of the incoming plane."

Now, you always get the same story. You never hear them saying that they themselves arrived late; it's always brought as if it was someone else's fault.
I had a similar experience at the check-in of the Prague Hilton Hotel and Conference Centre. Although I had ordered a smoking room, the

girl at reception desk offered me a non-smoking room. I was told that the travel agency must have booked a wrong room. No way, our agency knows very well I only want smoking rooms. Again another example of sophisticated external causal attribution – as it's called so nicely in clinical psychology.

"Cabin crew, please take your seats for landing."

We landed safely in Brussels and while driving home, I reflect on the added value of management development training in general. Most professional consultants and trainers realise these days that also their cost and return needs to be measured. Their advice will be to agree during the session a number of company performance indicators and to come back in twelve months' time for another three-day session where we will be assessing our delivery against the agreed performance targets. If that assessment is positive, then of course the credit is to the trainers. If it isn't, then they'll work with us to further improve our capabilities, and enhance their income. For me, that still doesn't measure their impact. My personal measurement system on the added value of management training is very simple. After the training, I tell my wife what I have done and learned. Her reaction is my thermometer.

I arrived home shortly before 8pm on that Friday evening. My wife and son were in the kitchen.

"Hi darling. Good to have you back home safely. How was Prague?"

"Oh, apart from the journey from and to the airport, I haven't seen Prague. We were locked away all the time in the overheated meeting rooms of the hotel. But I think Prague looks nice."

"And the training?"

"That was super, really fantastic. You know I have been to a lot of these trainings but this one was really different. Very interactive and a couple of really good sessions. Although we did a bit of work on the corporate plan, it was largely about ourselves, team engagement and our way of working."

"And?"

"Yeah, really good. The facilitators made us analyse the interdepartmental interactions. We than did a SWOT on our internal collaboration practices and created a strategic alignment chart which we discussed in workgroups and then of course 'aligned' it to our corporate values and behaviours. We linked the chart with our corporate capabilities framework; that mirrored very well. This morning, we even added the customer engagement dimension to it; a very synergetic outcome. The CEO is going to use this all to write the Group's charter for success."

"Interesting. The soup is ready."

"Really great. I have also volunteered to join the virtual innovation workgroup that will create an innovation pipeline for the next generation category. In the next three years, we can invest double of last year while the expected category contribution needs to grow by a factor of 1.5. We'll use sensory teams, value-based brand reputation, new techniques for brand gap analysis. We'll have quick scans and focus groups in key markets where we'll also do lifestyle research. With social media we'll target the 'i-generation'. A professor from Rotterdam Erasmus University will guide us and we'll meet twice a year in Vienna."

"Vienna. Soup is cold now; it's tomato soup."

"We have also agreed for our internal reporting to apply the 'traffic light system'; highlighted in green is OK or good progress, amber requires some attention and red needs immediate action. ASAP. That makes reading the reports much easier. But the best part of the meeting without any doubt was a threehour session with Ram Sharan. Of Indian origin, Ram found his way to top executive guys in big, very big enterprises. He is now one of the top 25 leadership gurus in the world and author and co-author of many best-selling management books. I probably had too high expectations from his session, and the initial return I thought was a bit low. But in hindsight, that's unfair to say as I got one great lesson out of his lecture. That lesson is to not unnecessarily complicate business; keep it simple and never forget the basics of management. I'll try to adopt that approach as much as possible in any future projects."

"Chicken is on the table, darling. You'll have to put your soup in the microwave."

"Yes, I am there in a second. I just need to look quickly at the engagement scores of my team and analyse their scoring against the axes with the key themes. The company average was 61, the industry benchmark was 65 but my team's score was only 59. My team members seem to hint that I am somewhat invisible and not accessible to them. I really don't understand this. They only need to call my PA to schedule an appointment and I'll try to see them in that same week. I know that I travel a lot but I always listen to their messages on my voicemail. I have done so many courses on employee motivation. I really don't get it; they require so much attention and need to be stroked for the smallest achievements. I don't think there is anyone in the company who engages more with his team than I do! I am very disappointed in my team."

One hour later.

"Mister Engagement, I am putting your son to bed. You could perhaps say hello and at the same time goodnight. And by the way, his name is André and I am your wife, Sonja."

I got the message and didn't do any more work during that weekend.

At least not till Sunday lunchtime. I absolutely wanted to review those engagement scores again.

> "59 versus the average of 61; that's not good."

It looked like I had already forgotten Ram's key messages.

~ ~ ~ ~ ~ ~ ~ ~ ~

CHAPTER 10

Not too bad.

> *"I had the patriotic conviction that, given great leadership of the sort I heard from Winston Churchill in the radio broadcasts to which we listened, there was almost nothing that the British people could not do". -* <u>Margaret Thatcher</u>

Most of us find hardly any time to read books, whether it's on our iPad in the airport lounge or in a hotel room or whether it's an old-fashioned hardcopy on the beach. And if we do read something, then as a member of the rat-race club, it's one of the newest management books. Probably the book will be full of the newest buzzwords so that we can show off in the next management meeting on new strategies and techniques. And our colleagues will be impressed on our knowledge and vision; even if it doesn't make any sense what we're saying.

That's where management these days is closer to the art of acting than to anything else. Indeed, it isn't about what you do or what you say; it's about how you say it. Whatever the meaningless words are that you throw up, just produce your message with a high dose of shameless persuasiveness. Like one of the Belgian prime ministers did when visiting Clinton in the White House. I first need to learn you a bit of Flemish for you to get this. In Flemish, horses is 'paarden', pronounced 'pardon'. And breeding is 'fok'; pronounced just like that word that you shouldn't pronounce.

"So Jean-Luc, what do you do in your free-time," Clinton asks at pre-dinner drinks. It's an informal event and our Prime Minister is joined by the Ambassador, 20 business leaders and 10 journalists.

"Oh Bill, nice to ask. I know you like crossword puzzles; I don't. I fok horses," Jean-Luc replied with an arrogant smile of self-complacency. Clinton reacts a bit surprised.

"Pardon?"

"Yes, paarden," our intelligent Belgian authority replies eloquently while looking into the CNBC cameras.

Ok, forget this poor joke; back to reading books and the time you are lacking for this relaxing activity. If you want to read something interesting and funny, and mainly for those doing business in the United Kingdom, I can advise you on an excellent book.

By the way, the inhabitants of that European island that 'rules the waves', might consider skipping this chapter. In any case, the disclaimer at the beginning of this book certainly also applies to this chapter; I don't want to end up in court against all the Brits.

The book is called: *Watching the English. The Hidden Rules of English Behaviour* by Kate Fox. As this book is about the English in general, I thought it could be useful to reflect here more particularly on the English in business. At the end, I have been working for over 10 years in the head office of a UK PLC. So I should know a bit of it. It should be noted that most of the below specifically applies to overall Anglo-Saxon corporate life; not just the English. And yes, I realise it generalises and stereotypes. Just like popular survey results can do; like this one taken from the *Ricoh Process Efficiency Index*. According to their statistics, one in five British adults doesn't know that a dairy cow is female. This one I read in the BA *Business Life* magazine on a plane. The least you can say on the British is that they don't shy away from self-mockery.

Here it comes, my Top 10 of do's and don'ts in building a corporate career in an English business environment.

FIRST TALK ABOUT THE WEATHER
You'll find that too in the above mentioned book. It applies to general contacts but also to business contacts. You'll have experienced that your taxi driver picking you up at the airport will only talk about the weather and bad traffic. Once you'll arrive at the UK office, you'll talk about the weather. It's that simple; then you let the other party decide what to talk about. Most likely you'll be asked how your journey was. Even if it was a disaster and you have been in a traffic jam for hours, don't be too negative. Just say: "Oh not too bad; thanks for asking".

DEMONSTRATE A POSITIVE MINDSET
When asked how you are, you'll be feeling good. Or again: "Not too bad. Thank you"; even if you feel absolutely shit, have a strong cold and saw your flight being delayed for three hours. Don't comment on the negatives; just keep them for yourself. It is proven, by the way, that happy and positive-minded people are more successful in building their career. And that applies anywhere in the world. From Sydney to Moscow and from San Francisco to Tokyo.

Now in England, and certainly with respect to yourself and your achievements in professional life, don't be modest. Be extremely proud about your career, your current job and show off on what you have delivered. And a small tweaking of the truth is not a sin. Strange, but Anglo-Saxon managers will rather buy a positive colouring of the truth that the negatively sounding plain truth. If you want to climb the English ladder, than you better be very self-assured on your capabilities; up to the level of light arrogance. The Dutch are very good on this; as are the Spaniards. The Germans and the French are too factual for this critical game playing. And the Belgians with their modesty and underdog-culture, they play the game absolutely wrong. But the Brits don't; they are always outwardly positive and very assured of their skills and capabilities. Ask them about their language skills and they'll tell you proudly how well they speak French and Spanish; because they learned to order a pint in Paris or in Madrid.

DRESS CODE
One of the most controversial inventions is 'smart casual'. According to Wikipedia:
> "Smart casual (as distinct from business casual) is a loosely defined dress code, casual, yet 'smart' (i.e. 'neat') enough to conform to the particular standards of certain Western social groups. As 'smart casual' is not formally defined, the lines between it and the other casual styles (see Western dress code) are often blurred. For example, some may use the term smart casual interchangeably with business casual."

Now that's clear.
You better make sure you first ask somebody in the office what 'smart casual' means in your business context. Everybody seems to have their own definition.
And then, what to do when you get an invite for a tuxedo event; also called 'black-tie party'? But nobody wears a tie! All the Brits have a

tuxedo – in mainland Europe it's rather called a 'smoking' jacket, in their wardrobe. That serves for those two-three evenings a year that they will really get drunk. And for the women it's clear. Take those high heel shoes – we know you can't walk on them but we find it funny and sexy, and join the party in your most shiny long dress. And, it's the tits that will make or break your career tonight. It's cleavage time!

In the office, don't make the same mistake as I did in my early days; being oblivious of corporate fashion. A Walt Disney tie is a 'don't do'! I once went to the office in a nice white shirt with a yellow tie decorated with maroon small teddy bears. At least five people said to me that day, "Nice tie, Henry." That really means: 'Don't do.' And when I was wearing my new cashmere green vest, my boss said, "Oh, is it already carnival in Belgium?"

Keep it simple. Well-polished shoes, a two-piece suit, white shirt, cufflinks and one of your most old-fashioned ties. Double nod. However again, make sure you get informed on time as since 2011 there is a kind of dress-code revolution in men's fashion in England. The 20th century habit of upper and middle class business men wearing a black bowler hat and umbrella is long since. But also, wearing a designer made tie, a white formal shirt with cufflinks; it's all getting out of practice. Find me an investment banker or broker on the square mile in London with a tie; and I'll give you a reward of half of his bonus.

Now, as we are in England, the legal disclaimer – once again – specifically also applies to that commitment. So forget the half a million pounds.

GET DRUNK

Don't forget; you are in the country that invented the binge-drinking. It's part of the game. If you go straight to bed after dinner, you'd better forget your career. It does help when leaders hear colleagues saying, "I was with Henry in the bar till 3am." It's even better to be there with the leaders themselves. Of course you'll be asked the morning after how you're feeling. You know the answer: "Not too bad." And before you got drunk, make sure you said a few sensible things about the Premier League. Praise English football. Always. And Chelsea really deserved to beat Bayern Munchen in the 2012 Champions League. ☹

DON'T BE 'IN THE FACE'
The English are never direct; you'll need to master the art of reading between the lines. That's their biggest difference to the American business leaders.

When you need to assess a business presentation or even more likely when someone from Head Office proposes a change that is absolute nonsense, then you only have one comment: "Interesting." Never be negative to anyone publicly in a meeting; in fact not even in a private face-to-face meeting. Or a "121" as it's so nicely called. If you have a negative message for someone or if you disagree strongly; don't say it literally. Let him/her come to exactly that conclusion that you had in mind but haven't verbalised. As I did when CCG was going to roll out – by English law – regulated management contracts all over the world to standardise terms and conditions. I just asked what we would do if a manager would claim in court local terms on top of the English terms. I asked if they saw a risk for dual contracts. And I asked how they would ensure English law to a Taiwanese manager who had never been or worked in the UK. We quickly came to another approach without me having to say, "You are f***ing nuts."

NEVER SAY "I DON'T KNOW"
As you keep successfully climbing and you are on your way to getting a seat in the boardroom; you of course have no weaknesses.
If you are asked something in a business meeting and you really don't know the answer, then you'd better say, "Let me come back to you on

this." Or even better to show your leadership is to reply with, "I'll ask Martin to drop you a note on this tonight." Or a trick that also works very well is, "We'll come back to that later in the presentation" and during the next break you'll call the office and get the correct answer. At your next slide after the break – even if it's absolutely not related to the question, you then say, "Linked to what we have here on the slide on our market share growth, let me come back to your earlier question, …". Don't give the full answer at once, provoke a further detailed question and kill the question by showing off with your detailed (only just gained) knowledge.

And if the difficult question is asked by a more junior colleague, then it's even easier. Than it is, "That question is not too bad, Jon, but let's continue now with our core discussion. We can eventually tackle your point at a later time."

PRETEND TO BE ALTRUISTIC BUT REMEMBER: LIFE IS ONLY ABOUT ME, MYSELF, AND I.

From time to time, throw into your meetings how important you find the safety and the wellbeing of your staff. And how much you work and have worked for charities. Talk about the monies your office collected for the tsunami in Thailand, the earthquake in Haiti; talk about you playing football for charity donations to the local children's hospital.

But never forget, you played that football game in freezing weather conditions only because the other members of the Lions club invited you. And the Lions club is where you do your networking; for your benefit not for the kids in hospital. So next time when the Head Office in the UK participates in a charity event, without any hesitation you should join the event. Even if you have never played football or done the 10 miles or even if you have never cleaned the streets of Liverpool, just join the charity team. You'll be there together with the CEO or COO or any of the other big shots. And that's why you are doing it. And rest assured; I am confident your boss won't comment on you putting your travel costs to Liverpool on your company credit card.

HUMOUR

When you see the signs in Heathrow with "Welcome to the United Kingdom", you should read welcome to the country of Mr Bean, Tommy Cooper, John Cleese and Monty Python. The world of "mind the bicycle, Richard" and of "the Madonna with the big boobies". And the land of "always look on the bright side of life".

The best thing to bring – it's still very popular although it's now more than 60 years old, is jokes about the Germans in the Second World War. This for instance is a killer:

"A little boy and his father are listening to the Fuhrer's speech on the radio as Germany declares war on the USA. The boy asks his father where the USA is. The father takes down a globe and runs his hand across the USA, saying, 'All of this area of North America, son.'

The boy looks at the globe and asks, 'and where is the British Empire?' The father indicates Britain, Canada, South Africa, Australia, New Zealand, and India on the globe.

'I see,' says the boy. 'And where is Russia?' The father showed him the sprawling mass of the USSR on the globe. The boy's eyebrows furrowed with concentration.

'And where is Germany?' he asks. His father points at the area of central Europe where the Reich is located.

The boy looks very concerned and says, 'Dad, has Hitler seen this?'

One dinner party and a few of these jokes and you're one step higher on the ladder. For the German readers, I would advise to joke about the French. The English have still very mixed feelings on the French. They adore the French wine and food and also loved to buy French plots and old stone houses cheaply – because of the strong Sterling in the first years of the new century – mostly in Brittany. And if the English start to joke about your nation; don't react defensively. Just say, "That joke is not too bad."

Of course you know that the UK is the most powerful nation in the world; in the universe. So "Welcome to the United Kingdom" also reads "Welcome to rule Britannia, Britannia rules the waves." And you show respect to this 'ruling' power. You recognise their mastering position in politics, economics, education, military power, management, culture, science, etc. Therefore, you will never joke about the Monarch of the Commonwealths, her red-haired naked grandson, the Tudors, the Falklands, the *News of the World* phone-hacking scandal, nor about a British member of parliament who puts the renting of sex video-tapes on her expense note.

You will always respect the English supremacy. There isn't anything beyond England – except for the Commonwealth. An example; When CCG was rolling out their global car policy, it was written that in any country in the world, only Vauxhall cars could be ordered. Some managers in Russia, China and France who had received from me a preview of the draft policy, started looking for Vauxhall dealers in their country and couldn't find any.

FORGET ABOUT BUSINESS GIFTS
That's a saving isn't it? Thanks to Kenneth Clarke who introduced the new Bribery Act in July 2011.
Alasdair, one of my International HR Managers was invited by another CCG senior manager to join an English cricket game playing against the West Indies in Surrey. Ticket value was around £55. The week after the game, my PA asked me to approve in the system Alasdair's accepting that invite. Although this was an internal invite, so not even from a supplier, for us to be compliant with the new bribery act, this event

needed to be documented, listed and approved. I am confident Lord Alan Sugar will agree with me on this; the current paranoid system of corporate governance rules and regulations is the fatal poison pill for business growth.

So make your life easy, the Dutch are going to like this –and the Scots – don't waste money on business gifts. The receiving individual may be jailed under the bribery act. Now, that also creates opportunities; if you so wish. If you want to have a go at someone from your UK business network, than just invite him for a lunch (Kentucky Fried Chicken is fine; doesn't need to be at the Fat Duck restaurant), and afterwards declare that you invited him intentionally to get a business favour. He is now 'at risk' based on the new bribery act.

And don't forget, this also applies to subsidiaries of a UK business outside the UK. Of course English law applies abroad; everywhere in the world. Rule Britannia, Britannia rules the waves. Or is that "Britannia rules the world"?

I am impatiently and eagerly waiting for Burkina-Faso and the Sultanate of Brunei Darussalam to impose their laws on British sole. Or even better, the regulations coming out of Brussels. You will have noticed that BBC and other UK media always talk about 'Brussels' rather than 'Europe'.

OBSERVING AND COPYING

You have already learned to get drunk, to never say what you want to say, to dress appropriately to English norms, to bring black humour into the boardroom; so you are well on your way to be fully integrated.

Keep doing so. The last key to professional success in the UK is to observe senior managers' behaviour and to copy carefully. Now, don't exaggerate on this, like my friend Marc did in an interview in London. When the interviewer was crossing the arms, Marc did so too a few seconds later. He had read about this in a book on non-verbal behaviour. But when the interviewer was poking his nose, Marc continued the mirroring exercise. That was wrong, Marc.

Observing and copying is a subtle game of creating emotional rapport; it's about creating a warm environment with mutual understanding. It's to give them the feeling that you are one of them; that you are part of the club. It's not a cold Xerox copy machine.

And one more; for free:

BLACK PEPPER?
Yes please, black pepper.

~ ~ ~ ~ ~ ~ ~ ~ ~

CHAPTER 11

Mr. X. – Fraud – Macedonia

> *"Never forget that only dead fish swim with the stream."* -Malcolm Muggeridge

Hundreds of mails had been sent on this subject. Initially most of these had me on the copy line, but over the last weeks many of these were sent to me directly. I created a special Outlook subfolder, otherwise my inbox was going to explode.

Credit to the Group Security Department, I received in the meeting two weeks ago a large hard copy folder entitled; "X. – Fraud – Macedonia – 2006".

Obviously the real folder carried the surname of the person in casu, but here and for the rest of this story, I will refer to "Mr. X" to minimise any litigation risks. By this time you now must really think that I am paranoid. Perhaps I am; or perhaps I have worked too long in a corporate centre.

The company had been investigating Mr. X following some concerns from the Regional Director on his country performance figures. In the centre, we also at the same time got an anonymous letter from a whistleblower. This letter provided us more details of alleged fraud by Mr. X mainly through conspired falsification of documents by two named key customers.

The internal investigation brought to light that one of those named customers was not a customer at all of CCG Macedonia. The other one was on our account list and a separate investigation in 2001 into that account had revealed that the owners – two brothers – did not have the highest standards on corporate governance. One of them was at that time even on the CIA watch list. For obvious reasons they will also not be named in this chapter. Their credit levels, payments and shipments were continuously monitored by the Centre, but at the end, nothing fraudulent could be proven. We however, reduced our sales to them by 30% in the assumption that this would reflect their fair local market share.

The current investigation had proven that the physical shipments to the notorious brothers over the last eight months had again been at the level from before the reduction by 30%. This was however reflected nowhere in the reporting of CCG Macedonia. Since late in the previous year, a new account appeared on the books and that account seemed to buy the balancing difference. Their monthly payments had always been accurate and on time. This company however did not seem to be registered at the Chamber of Commerce. To the government authorities, this company was unknown.

Although we had strict rules on vetting new customers, Mr. X had clearly neglected his duties in this regard. He had however, on files in the accounting department, signed the standard vetting form and in there are clearly falsified statutes of the company.

Last month, Mr. X had been interviewed by members of our Group Security and Group Legal Department. Mr X denied any knowledge of the file and confirmed he received all the legal documents by mail from the owners. He named the owners but declared he had never met them. He was also asked how he could justify the private purchase of a VW Touareg and a Porsche in February this year (estimated to cost together around €150,000) and in March the acquisition of two sea-view villas at large plots bordering the Black Sea (yet another half a million Euros). He said this was all private stuff but volunteered to declare that these monies all came from the heritage of his father-in-law. But he refused to give us insight into this heritage.

In the meeting two weeks ago at Head Office, I agreed that Mr. X should be dismissed immediately. As always, that would be left over to me. I made a few calls to legal advisors and finally also to Max Richter, the Regional HR Manager for the region.

Max is an extremely trustworthy manager with a high level of 'German accuracy'. He is a very seasoned HR professional and knows what 'confidential' means. So I updated him in full and asked him to check the final details with our legal advisor. Given I had only met Mr. X once at a management conference, Max offered to join me. I gratefully accepted as I was sure he would be a great help in the meeting and for any after-work.

Given the potential relationship between Mr. X and 'the notorious brothers', Carl Fallon, Head of Security (we all call him John Cleese as he could really be the twin brother), offered me fully-fledged security in Skopje.

"Great Carl, but make sure your security guard has four mobile phones with him this time," I said a bit jokingly.

"No worries, Henry. The same guy from Marseille will be there but this time we have secured a specialist local team of bodyguards in addition to him."

"Carl please, don't exaggerate. It's just Max and I going. And until we knock on his door nobody knows that we'll be there. I don't mind one man being posted at reception of the Skopje office and us having an emergency number. I'll book the limo from the hotel to drive us to the office, so nobody from the office needs to pick us up."

"Leave it with me, Henry. My guys will be very low-profile but professional. Nobody will notice them. It's for your safety, mate. Leave it with me."

He then suddenly got a call from one of his assistants; so we left it there. While I walk out of the meeting room, I hear Carl saying with a high, loud and irritated voice – so loud that it was clearly intended for us to hear what he was saying – "Yes Manuel; what is it?"

So he knows about the internal John Cleese jokes.

On the plane to Skopje I started to become a bit worried that I had not really finished my conversation with Carl, so I was unsure on the arrangements. But Max, who had been there many times, reassured me that if there was nobody from security and if we didn't find a decent taxi; he would call the hotel to pick us up. They would be there 25 minutes later.

At the airport and once through security, we immediately see the company's security guard; the one from Marseille a few years ago. We shake hands. I ask him a bit jokingly how many mobiles he has with him. His answer is "seven" and I don't have the feeling he is joking. And while answering me, he very inconspicuously puts a tiny little mobile in the left pocket of my jacket.

"That's number one. In case of urgency, just push the green button. You don't need to say anything but we'll be there in less than thirty seconds."

"Who is we?" I ask.

He doesn't respond but guides us to the exit of the airport arrival hall. Just in front of the exit we see – what Carl described as 'low-profile' – our welcoming committee.

Five bodyguards are standing next to each other in a nice row in front of a black car. The security guys are all fully dressed in black, with black sunglasses, black shiny leather shoes, black socks, black shirt and – what else – black ties. Today it is around 30° Celsius in Skopje. And each of them have a white (why not black?) earpiece in their left ear. With a white thin wire and 'push to talk' button; the wire from the headset disappears to somewhere in the inside of their jackets.
Two guys open the sliding doors of the Mercedes Viano minivan and guide us into the car. The leather seats are – yes, black; the windows are one-way screens and guaranteed bulletproof. Disappointment 1: no minibar. The company's security guy joins us together with one local 'Kevin Costner'. Another local guy jumps in the front of the car on the passenger seat and one of his colleagues takes the driver seat. The two other guys keep standing on each side of the car. Once the driver starts the engine, I hear the doors locking automatically. Then the two guys outside run away and jump in the car (black) behind us. They will follow us all the way to the office. The local guy who joined us in the back of the Mercedes, talks to his wristwatch which seems to be connected to something by a white wire.

"All clear. Let's go," he says and we depart. Disappointment 2: no screeching tyres.

It all went so fast that I don't remember the details, but I reckon that outside the airport, around 20-30 people were watching this event and were probably wondering what political heavyweight had landed.

Thanks Carl for the low-profile security. Next time we'll define that together.

Oh, and by the way, the meeting with Mr. X went without any issues. He of course disagreed with all the arguments that we brought to the table but after less than one hour, he walked quietly and peacefully out of his office. We have never heard from him or seen him since. Except once. That was the day after the meeting when Max and I went back to the airport – by hotel taxi. While checking in for our flight to Vienna, Max saw a few rows further ahead, Mr. X, accompanied by two other guys, checking in at the Bulgaria Air business class counter for a flight to Bucharest.

"If those guys are the notorious brothers, then they are not going to get through security," Max said.

Twenty minutes later, we accidently sat next to them at the table in the lounge. Mr. X acknowledged our presence with a little smile and then turned back to the two guys.

Max agreed not to stay much longer in the lounge. We finished our Skopsko beer and walked to the gate.

~ ~ ~ ~ ~ ~ ~ ~ ~ ~

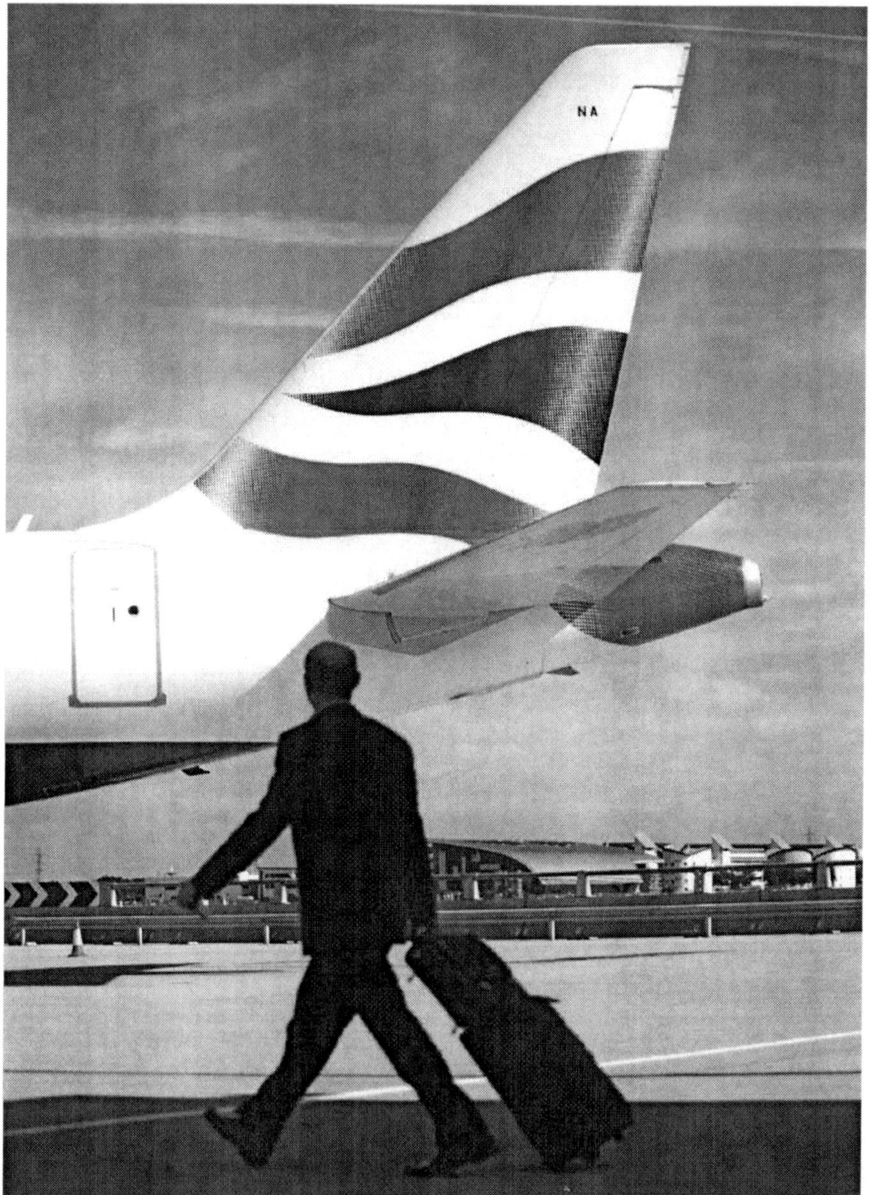
NA

CHAPTER 12

Miles & More

"I dislike feeling at home when I am abroad."
- George Bernard Shaw

I am not really sure but as far as I recall, that Skopje visit must have been in April or May 2006; probably it was May. Yes it was, as only a few days after the visit and at the end of a wrap-up meeting on the case of Mr X, Graham Hill called me to come and see him in his office for an urgent and confidential discussion.

Graham is a Regional Director and we both reported to Brat. Yes, I managed to cut that reporting line to Kathy pretty soon after my appointment in the new role in 2004. As I said before, it's never bad for your career or CV to have a direct reporting line to a Board Director of a FTSE50 company.

In the meeting with Graham, he started immediately to talk about Brat; in fact I think he started the conversation by saying, "This is strictly confidential. Only Gary (the CEO) knows that we are having this conversation. Brat doesn't and shouldn't in any case."

Graham shared with me that effective from 1 June, he would be appointed to the Board and he would take over the role of Brat. He did not directly mention what would happen to Brat but to me that was clear. It would be Gary in the coming days having a one-to-one with Brat and saying:
"Bye-bye Brat. Here's some money, please sign these confidentiality clauses, this waiver agreement and then, good luck, mate."

I massively appreciated Graham's trust in me to share this hot and reportable info in the early stage. It was the beginning of a very respectful and rewarding relationship. Although Graham was seen as a bit 'old school' – but that was probably mainly because he started at CCG at the very bottom of the steps and didn't really come with a master after master degree from a top business school, he was very successful in running the global sales operations. He knew his strengths and he knew extremely well whose input he needed and when to compensate for the 'W' in his SWOT. Similarly, he also knew my weaknesses and therefore didn't trust any figure I presented to him unless it was checked and double-checked by Russ, our Head of Finance. But what we certainly had common, and which is extremely rare in business, is the strong belief that the profit comes and is driven by the people in the field. That is a very remarkable strategy for someone who sits in the Head Office at the board table.
It was the beginning of a six-year long excellent working relationship; Graham later on retired in 2011 at age 65.

Our approach to decentralised business leadership, resulted in Graham, Russ and I frequently visiting the markets. On long-haul flights, that was Graham and I in business class while astute Russ many times managed to get an upgrade to first class. No surprise; he also coordinated the commercial contacts with the airlines and with the global travel agency. After take-off he then teasingly came to tell us how great the Johnny Walker Blue label was. Much, much better than the Black label. And of course served by the most beautiful Singapore Airlines girl on the plane.

These market visits were not just for meetings with senior local management but included also many regular field visits and contacts with sales and marketing staff. And so we collected a lot of plastic in our wallet.

I am Silver on BA Executive Club (that's where Russ has around 2mio miles on his account!), Senator on Miles & More, Silver on Air France/KLM, Platinum on Marriott, Platinum on PriorityClub, Platinum on Sofitel. On top of that, I carry the Gold on Hyatt, Gold on Golden Circle, Blue on Hilton, membership on SPG and Premier Advantage on Marina Bay Sands. And there is more plastic in the wallet; VISA Gold, AmexCo Silver, Thalys Ticketless, International SOS and the MEDI-Assistance card. And of course my plastic ID-card. And the business card from MySingaporeTailor.com.

And what about you? Is your designer branded wallet even more colourful? And what is it? Dolce & Gabbana or S.T. Dupont? Mine is a cheap Marc Jacobs.

I have memberships in many more hospitality clubs. I am not a member, just to be clear to you, of the 'Mile high club'. (http://www.milehighclub.com). I am just too tall for those claustrophobic toilets on a plane. Although, on reflection, the business class washrooms of the A380 should do I think.

According to my travel map on Miles & More, my most Northern airport is Moscow and most Southern is Singapore. I think that the most Eastern will be Taipei and most Western must be San Francisco. On my – however incomplete – travel map on Tripadvisor, I have slept in over 120 different towns and I have added comments on around 50 hotels and/or restaurants. Most of those comments are praise; I hate the current trend whereby the typical easyJet customer in his/her comments tries to kill the efforts of generally hard working hotel owners and staff. I am sure you keep your eyes open while on business travel and will notice that running a hotel is not fun; and generally low margin. In large business chain hotels, the profit threshold is set at an overall annual occupation of 30%; in most smaller and privately owned hotels that's at 50%. But as said, I really shiver when I hear or read the stories on Tripadvisor of travellers paying for a 1-star service and expecting lobster for breakfast.

My most famous visited restaurants, I can tell you that's not an impressive list at all. Honestly, invite me to an Italian place for a pasta or pizza and I am a happy man. Or a nice veal escalope with pasta and tomato sauce. Yes, and please with a Nastro Azzurro beer. Really, I am not that overly fond of the Michelin or Gault&Millau or AA Rosette type of places. Nor do I like the overly crowded and modern lounge-type restaurants; perhaps I am getting a bit older.

You probably won't know but recently a new top-notch hospitality industry award ratings scheme has been established. Very recently; in fact only five minutes ago. It's called the Henry W Derrick award and if you are interested; here are the 2012 winners:

Best bed: Marriott Hotels, globally
Best bathroom: South Lodge Hotel, West Sussex, UK
Best breakfast: Louis C Jacob Hotel, Hamburg, Germany
Best hotel restaurant: Les Ambassadeurs, Hotel de Crillon, Paris, France
Best work desks: Crowne Plaza, globally
Best hotel swimming pool: Marina Bay Sands, Singapore
Best hotel outside dining restaurant: FAI, the Palace – The Old Town Hotel, Dubai
Best customer service: Shangri-La, Singapore
Best bar: Ritz Carlton Sharq Village, Doha, Qatar
Best room service menu: Sheraton Park Tower, London, UK

Back now to some specific hotel experiences.

I think it was 2009 when I stayed in a luxurious place nearby London; I reckon I paid around £200 a night. The very old stone house building is hosting a 30-bedroom hotel. This three-storey property is all decorated with furniture from the late 19th century, with large dark paintings in gold painted frames, everywhere old oak doors and all ceilings have massive rounded oak beams. There are wooden floors in all the bedrooms on the first and second floor; the ground floor is paved with very old terracotta tiles. It's owned by a very successful businessman in the electronics industry and it's managed by his wife and his sister-in-law. Both women clearly run this place for enjoyment. Rather than going out for shopping every day in Oxford Street, they both seem to find satisfaction in running this hotel. Not to their fault at all, but here I had one of my most annoying experiences. Waking up in the morning and feeling that your bed is wet, is not what you expect when you are more than three years old.
Even if I was still half asleep, it only took me a few seconds to notice that water – not a bit but lots – was falling from the ceiling straight onto my bed and soaking the sheets at the end of the bed. More large

and frequent drops were also falling down on the white carpet on the left hand side of the bed. I immediately called reception and the desk manager himself knocked on my door only a few minutes later. That was just enough time to put on a shirt and some trousers; I never travel with pajamas. We both quickly came to the conclusion that something was wrong in the bedroom above my room. The issue: the guest in that room was filling his bathtub, went back to bed and fell asleep. The bathtub had no overflow. Through the wooden floor and oak beams, my bedroom had turned into a shower room.

Almost of the same magnitude of frustration, was the false fire alarm at 1am at night in a hotel in Berlin. It was early January and freezing cold, but the management insisted all visitors and staff to evacuate the building. My room was on the top floor, the ninth floor. And as you know, in case of fire, you 'don't use the elevators'.

I am convinced that you'll categorise the next event without any doubt into the section 'this can't be true'. Well, that would be wrong; the below is regrettably a very true and factual description.

It is March 2009 and I am in Athens for two days. The hotel that is booked for me is a good, comfortable place that defines itself as the best place in Athens for business and leisure. Apart from meeting rooms and business centre, it also offers a very nice outside pool, tennis courts, jacuzzi, steam bath, and dance bar in the basement of the 120-room property. After a first night's sleep and a long day of meetings and interviews in our Athens office, I return back to my room for a quick shower. Later, I'll be picked up for dinner with the local HR Manager. In the corridor of the fourth floor, two men are chatting not so far from the door of my room. Once I am in the room, I notice the room hasn't been cleaned; on the contrary, my room is an absolute mess. Pillows on the floor, sheets taken off the mattress, towels thrown on the bathroom floor. Even the two modern paintings of the Parthenon are taken of the wall and put on the small working desk. I wonder what's going on here. After a few seconds, I realise that my trolley with clothes, some files and personal belongings has disappeared. My small Ralph Lauren toiletries bag has also disappeared from the bathroom. What the hell is going on here?

Rather than calling reception, I decide to go to the lobby and talk directly to the hotel management. I had experienced that the English language skills of some staff was far from good; and my Greek language knowledge is nowhere. When leaving my room, I see the two 'chatting men' observing me when I walk to the elevators. They can probably read in my eyes that I am furious, definitively on the war path. Arriving at the hotel lobby and waiting for the manager, I call Ketty, the Greek General Manager to briefly explain what I just experienced and to cancel the dinner for tonight. While I call her, I notice in the large mirror next to the reception desk, that the two 'chatting men' are now also in the lobby and are definitely monitoring me. With a magic inspiration of imagination, I think by myself that if these guys are private detectives, they are absolutely incompetent. And for the same weird and imaginative reasons, I just hope these guys don't belong to the troops of the Macedonian notorious brothers. Is this revenge time?

The hotel's general manager invites me in his small, windowless private office and while I take a seat, the two incompetent 'detectives' enter the room. They present themselves but I don't understand a word of what they are saying, apart from the words 'Athens' and 'police'. Fortunately the hotel manager is very fluent in English, even with a Scottish accent, and directly takes up the role of interpreter. He brings the following story.

"This morning, the police raided room 409 – that's next door to your room 408, and found a significant volume of hard drugs. The two Belgian tourists in that room are now at the police office for interrogation. Both rooms are family rooms and have a connecting door. According to the police, they noticed during their search that this connecting door was not locked. As such, they have also searched your room and want to interrogate you. You will need to follow these two gentlemen immediately to their office. Your private belongings are already at the police office. For your hotel stay Mr. Derrick, we will charge your VISA card for a two-night stay."

"I don't think so," I reply but then immediately realise that this is the least of my concerns.

At 4 o'clock in the morning – I had been continuously interrogated by several police officers, and refused to make any call – the two 'chatting men' enter the small office where I had been put since 2 o'clock. This office is say two by three metres, obviously bars behind the small window, on the grey-painted wall a map of Athens and comes with a metal desk and green metal chair. On the desk, a white plastic ashtray, branded Davidoff. A small light bulb hangs high on the ceiling. The guys enter the room and offer me a can of Pepsi; since my arrest I had also been offered two glasses of water, two cups of strong coffee and two bananas. The overnight catering facilities at Athens main police office are better than in some hotels. It suddenly appears that the taller of the two guys speaks though a bit of English and he tells me – very apologetically – the story. My understanding of that broken English story (hey, that reminds you of Marianne Faithfull's song, doesn't it?) is that during the search of room 409, a police officer had ordered a member of the hotel staff to unlock the connecting door. That same officer was called for another duty and left the hotel before the search was completed. This critical event though, in the commotion of the raid, was not reported to the senior officers. Only when tonight a junior police guy typed the handwritten interrogation report of the hotel's staff member, it was noticed that the connecting door was unlocked and therefore there was no substance to assume that I was involved in this drug affair. Having accidently the same nationality as the dealers, was not enough substance to put me in jail. And so a 'minor mistake' was corrected. My personal belongings are returned.

Outside the police office, I stop the first taxi and ask him to bring me to a nearby Marriott; at that time not even knowing there is one in Athens.
You will now understand why – from that day onwards – I now always travel with a small wooden door stopper in my suitcase; just to ensure connecting doors can't be opened.

There is also the scary drive in Istanbul; it is my first visit to our newly established business in Turkey. For whatever reason; there is no chauffeur-driven car arranged for me so I take a taxi at the Ataturk airport to the office. The office is somewhere in the centre and with the very little English the driver talks, I understand it's a journey of around 45 minutes, up to one hour as in Istanbul traffic, 'you never know'. There are indeed some traffic jams so it may take a bit longer. After half an hour drive, the driver picks up his mobile phone; he clearly gets some news that makes him extremely angry. He starts to shout – I assume in Turkish – to everyone on the road and to me, but I don't understand a word of it. I think that most of what he is shouting is dirty swearing. It's also clear that he wants to take the next exit of what seems to be a kind of ring road. While he continues to swear, he now drives on the hard shoulder, heavily gesticulating to other car drivers. Once of the main road, I ask him at least 10 times what he's doing and insist that he drops me off now; he either replies in Turkish or doesn't reply at all. To him it's clear, he has another urgent mission, other than bringing me to the office. He drives so wild that I am even getting sick in the back of the car. All of a sudden, I realise that this may be my saving. So I start to exaggerate a bit and he realises that very soon – now after nearly one and a half hours in his car, he is at risk of me throwing up in his car. And then he breaks heavily, shouts at me, in Turkish, I don't give a shit, and I leave the car.

Another remarkable journey was the drive back from our visit to some shops in the outskirts of Baku, Azerbaijan. It was early afternoon and it was very quiet on the road. My two colleagues were in the company car of the Sales Director; I was accompanied by the Security Manager who drove me in his own private car. On a kind of motorway towards Baku, there was a police control. I guess that almost half of the cars – selected randomly – were guided towards the right-hand hard shoulder and into a sort of parking alongside the motorway. When Aleksey, the Security Manager, notices the stoppage a few hundred metres in front of us, he moves our car to the left lane and rather than slowing down, he accelerates. This gets noticed immediately by two policemen who sit on their motorbike on the middle lane. They get off their bike and make it clear to Aleksey that he needs to sort into the right lane. While we drive by the two policemen – still on the left lane and at a speed of circa 70 km/hour, Aleksey gesticulates to the policemen that they should have a look at the back of his car, at his car registration number. I turn back in the car to see what the police guys are doing. One is jumping on his motorbike but the other one stops him to drive away; of course I can't hear what he is saying. Aleksey tells me that based on his registration number, police can see that he has – these are his words – "top level military contacts". With a smile he adds,

"It's a pity that he didn't jump on his bike to make me stop. It would have been his last day as a policeman."

Once we are back in the office in the underground parking, he says,

"Wait a second before you get out of the car, I want to show you something."

"OK, what?"

"You see this button here. In a regular Mercedes, this is to open the back right windows. Not on this car. Have a look at the back window."

While he pushes the button, at the back of the car between the back seats and the back window, a small plastic construction raises slowly. He pushes once more on the same button and the blue and white light bulbs start to flash intensely. To me, these really look like police flashlights. Strange, in a private car of our Security Manager.

"It's a heritage from my previous job at the military intelligence services. It's a shame that I had to remove those behind the front window. "

Allow me to go back for a second to the profit margins in the hotel sector. Not surprisingly with my Marriott Platinum membership, I have spent many nights at Marriott; I reckon it must be close to 1000 nights in total. And I have seen Marriott coming under profit pressure due to things like 9/11, banking crisis, etc. What Marriott has done over the last say 10 years may not have been noticeable for the occasional visitor, but it's very remarkable though for the frequent traveller. Marriott has massively focused on the cost structure so to stabilise or even reduce the nightly rates. CCG's nightly rate today in one of the Marriott hotels is less than five years ago! But, of course this comes with a 'but'. Gradually, the offer of that hotel to the visitor has changed. The top class restaurant has closed; dinner is now in the breakfast room. The large bar has closed, that's now in a smaller room nearby the lobby. Haddock and 'at your choice' omelets and pancakes have disappeared from the breakfast menu. In the room, you get fewer and thinner towels. Also the mini-bar is disappearing as it seems to be loss-making. No, no says Mr. Marriott himself; it's "because we like to avoid alcohol abuse". Similarly, he's planning to ban pay-per-view in room movies. Some of the channels he is offering don't seem to align to the Marriott values. Bollocks; it's just another loss-making instrument. I wonder if the Marriott Book of Mormon is also going to disappear in every nightstand. One of the other values they are proud of is of their non-smoking policy. That's logical, as Mr. Marriott – God himself – stands for "no alcohol, no sex and no tobacco". He probably should add, "Just money". And that's why – I know this for sure – there are at least three Marriott hotels in the US and Europe who have corporate deals with large tobacco companies. And generously offer these guests smoking rooms. Now, it needs to be said, they have made a fantastic investment with the Marriott beds. Honestly, in my view the highest comfort standard in the world.

However, Marriott is not the only one who is on a cost-cutting journey. I know about a Hilton in Europe where in low season or in periods of low occupancy, one or even two of the four elevators is purposely put 'out of order'. I asked management why it takes them that long to fix the problem. "It's an issue with spare parts" was the answer. From the bartender, I know the real story; it saves them a few thousand Euros per annum.

A hotel in Frankfurt used to offer for many years the services of chauffeur-driven cars; this was purely from a customer service perspective. Now they have opened a tender process and the winner of the tender will have to agree a 10% profit sharing on the total turnover at the hotel's front door.

In a Knightsbridge boutique hotel, I used to get, as a thank you for my loyalty, an upgrade to the Oxford suite; a lovely room with freestanding bathtub, walk in shower, Chesterfield couch and a lovely terrace with sun loungers (I have never enjoyed those terrace chairs; this is London, you know). Since last year, I don't get the upgrade anymore. After having seduced me a few times; they now hope for me to book the suite. I challenged them on that and asked them why the offer isn't made when the room is free. Digging deeper, I learn that given the size of the room, it takes them fifteen minutes' more cleaning time than compared to a regular room.

I always enjoyed the early morning swim in the outdoor pool in a hotel in Madrid; since last year, this business hotel's pool only opens at 4pm. It saves them the cost of one employee.

Although it is not intended, this section seems to have digressed towards mooning over my travel experiences. In that respect, I should add a few stories on my experiences at airports. But that on its own may warrant a fully dedicated book of complaints and funny stories. An option I may consider.

But there is one though for this book.

It was a short flight from London Heathrow to Brussels. It was a 50-minute flight; so not a lot could go wrong. It was the 22nd or 23rd of December, my last flight back home before Christmas holidays. I think the BA flight was scheduled to depart at around 5pm; which would bring me home – considering time difference – around 7pm at Brussels airport and really 'home-home' at around 8pm. I was scheduled for 5pm so boarding would be at 4:30pm. And so it is; we all board nicely on time.
    "Boarding completed," gets announced just after I returned the hot towel and turned off my mobile.

We now will be pushed back from the stand and the safety briefing should start any minute. But none of that seems to happen. It doesn't make me nervous though, as it happens frequently that on this flight we leave LHR late. Officially they schedule one-hour flight time but in reality I guess we'll only be 40 minutes in the air; so no reason to worry.

And indeed, 10-15 minutes later the Captain informs us that we won't be pushed back yet; that we'll have to wait a little bit longer at the stand but that safety briefing will start in a minute. After the safety briefing, we get the Captain again.

"Ladies and Gentlemen, once again a warm welcome on our flight to Brussels. We will be pushed back in five minutes as we have to clear this gate for another incoming plane. We will be pushed to a holding area closer to the runway where we'll wait for the OK from the tower for take-off. The reason for this delay is the bad weather situation in Brussels. The weather for our flight route is OK but half an hour ago Brussels airport got heavy snowfall coming from the East. At the moment, this hinders take-off and landing at the airport. I will be monitoring the situation for you and I'll keep you updated as soon as we know more. Once we are at our holding position, I'll turn off the fasten seatbelts sign so you can use your mobile phone from that point onwards."

We are only 15 minutes at that holding position and the fasten seatbelts sign is turned on again. The cabin crew stops serving the extra glass of water in business class. Simultaneously, we'll get the good news from the Captain.

"Ladies and Gentlemen, good news from the tower; we can take off in 10. It is forecasted that by the time we are nearer to Brussels, the snow showers will have moved south of Brussels. Cabin crew, please prepare for take-off."

I quickly call my wife again to say we'll only be 20 minutes late. She always picks me up at the airport so that I don't waste another half hour walking through the Brussels airport car park. What a darling.

My body is so used to that Friday home-flight that it always forces me to fall asleep after an intense work week. When I wake up, I notice on my Tissot dual time watch – a necessity for a frequent traveller – that it's around 8pm Brussels time. And we are still in the air which means that we have been flying now for around one and a half hours. For a 40-minute journey? I notice some other passengers behaving a bit nervously. Just when I want to ask the guy next to me if he knows more, the Captain is there with another announcement. I hope it's to prepare for landing.

"Ladies and Gentlemen, as you may have noticed, we have now circled twice over Brussels waiting for authorisation to land. Unfortunately, there isn't enough Northern wind and Brussels is still heavily hindered by snowstorms. There is also not an unlimited amount of fuel on this plane, so we'll circle one more time and if the airport isn't cleared by that time, we will unfortunately need to divert to another airport. I will keep you all informed as soon as we know more."

At 9:15 pm, we touch down. While we are taxiing to the gate, the Captain tells us he's waiting for further instructions from BA which he will receive in half an hour time. Despite the hindrance and frustrations, it needs to be said, the Captain's communication efforts are remarkable. Perhaps except for his last announcement; although here, he deserves a special reward for having the guts to leave his safe cockpit, come into the cabin and look us straight in the eyes while bringing the bad news. As said, only praise for the man, except for his next first phrase, which in my view had a certain level of –hopefully unintended – sarcasm.

I make a quick call to my wife who is still waiting for me, the poor girl.

"Finally," she says. "It's an absolute disaster here, I had to drive into the parking as I couldn't stay that long in the kiss & ride area. I am in Parking 2 on the fourth floor. Call me again when you leave the building. It may take us two hours to get home; the motorway seems to have come to a full standstill."

"Eh, yes honey I am just landed. It may take me a while to get to Parking 2. I am still on the plane. We are just landed in … Schiphol."
"What?!"

"Yes, Amsterdam airport. There indeed seem to be many problems at Brussels airport. Is there lots of snow? Don't wait for me there; just drive back home and I'll call you when I know more. Assuming we are later flying back to Brussels, I'll take a taxi there to get home but that's probably going to be very late. I'll let you go, they are making a new announcement here on the plane."
Here is the Captain:

"Ladies and Gentlemen, this plane is going to take-off at 10.45pm; that's in almost one hour. Destination: London Heathrow. It will carry no luggage and no passengers; only the crew will return back home. For you, the BA Customer Service teams here at Schiphol and in London are working very hard on finding a solution. It is confirmed that Brussels airport is now fully closed for all air traffic and isn't expected to re-open before tomorrow late morning. The Head of Customer Service here in Schiphol will be with us in 30 minutes and will be ready to give you all further instructions. As you can see yourself through the windows, in the meantime snow has also arrived here in Amsterdam and this seems to start disturbing road traffic. We will need to wait for confirmation but I expect that BA will arrange overnight accommodation for you and will work all night long to ensure transportation for you for tomorrow morning back to Brussels."

Dirk, the man next to me in seat 4D, was in London all week; he is working there for Carta Mundi. Quickly chatting to each other, it's clear that also Dirk doesn't fancy yet another night away from home. We both stand up and go to the front of the cabin. We are telling the Captain that we don't want to wait to see what BA is putting together. We insist on leaving the plane now as we both, being very experienced travellers, are convinced that we can get home tonight. We'll go for the Thalys train and we know there is a train station in the basement of Schiphol airport. At least we'll sleep at home tonight.

We only have carry-on luggage, but nevertheless to our surprise, the Captain agrees. It comes of course with the message that this is all on our own responsibility and that we will not be able to claim anything back from BA. I then expected we first had to sign a waiver agreement 10 pages long, but no, nothing of that. BA is less bureaucratic than I thought. While we both disembark, we see four or five other passengers taking the same initiative.

On the bridge to the gate, we meet the Head of Customer Service who promptly advises us not to leave the group. She has arranged for hotel accommodation in Hoofddorp, very nearby to the airport. Three busses are on their way to pick us up. We decline the offer and run to the railway station. Knowing that the Thalys only takes pre-booked passengers, we run around to find a Thalys kiosk.

And there we are told that the last Thalys train is cancelled, due to bad weather conditions.

Pretty soon, we find out that most of the trains are cancelled that night and there isn't one going to Brussels.

Dirk suggests trying a cab; that's going to be expensive but why not give it a try? We ask five cabdrivers and none wants to do the journey to Brussels; not even to Antwerp as a half-way solution. While Dirk decides to keep trying, he promised to drive his daughter to music lessons in Leuven tomorrow morning, I am getting tired and decide to stay overnight in Amsterdam. Having been outside on the street now, I guess that on these snowy roads, the journey back home may also take several hours. We quickly share mobile numbers and agree to keep each other informed.

Of course for me, the BA offer for a free stay in a Hoofddorp hotel is gone now. I try the Sheraton at the airport but they are already fully booked. That's no surprise as it seems that all flights into Brussels have been diverted to Amsterdam. Although we are now close to midnight, I manage to get my PA Nathalie on the phone. She's trying to get something arranged through the travel agency. Impatient as I am, I don't wait for her solution and jump in a taxi to Amsterdam centre. I know there is a Marriott and with my Platinum card, I expect them to do the utmost to give me a room. I call Nathalie again to ask for the phone number of the Marriott. She gets a bit puzzled and asks if I still want her to go on with finding another hotel. I say "yes, we try all routes."

I call the Marriott immediately and yes, they have their very last room for me. It's €299 a night though; excluding breakfast. For the first time in my career, I accept the reservation of a non-smoking room. I tell them that I'll be there in 15 minutes. One second later I get a call from Nathalie.

"We have found you a room for one night in a hotel in Hoofddorp. It's €139 a night, breakfast included. We need to confirm reservation in the next 15 minutes. Shall I?

"No thanks Nathalie. I have just booked the Marriott. I'll explain to you next week. Thanks anyway."

She probably now hates me, but I just wanted to have a bed as soon as possible. And something to eat; I haven't had any food since the quick lunch in London.

While I check in at the Marriott, I get a text message from Dirk.

"Found one but traffic is very slow. Hope to be in Antwerp by 2am. And what a rip-off, he's charging €330. The Dutch bastard."

It's after midnight and the restaurant in the hotel is closed, I am too tired to go and find a restaurant nearby. My dinner for tonight comes out of the minibar – hey, this one still has a minibar. I enjoy the Mars and KitKat chocolate bars and search on the Internet for the timetable for a train tomorrow morning.

At 9.20am on Saturday morning, I am on the train from Amsterdam to Antwerp. There my wife will pick me up at 11am. Honestly, at 9.40am, the train comes to a standstill. A full standstill. This time, the message is:
> "Due to a technical problem….".

I even don't want to hear the rest. Nor do you, I guess.

On that Saturday, I was home at 2 pm; it should have been Friday at 7pm.

Not that I hope that you, frequent travellers, experience the same pain, I am sure that this all may sound familiar to you. To those readers who never or very rarely travel for business, I hope you will now stop envying us for all the so-called 'tourism at the company's expenses.' Yes, I agree, we go to many places but apart from seeing airport lounges, offices, meeting rooms, hotel rooms and apart from dinner obligations; we do not 'tourist' a lot.

OK, one more; it's a very short one. I regularly fly with Brussels Airlines on one of their many Avro jets. You know, that ugly and relatively small plane, four engines and the wings overarching the body of the plane. Once I had a Captain welcoming us on this machine with the following words; it was clear he also didn't like the look of the plane.
> "Ladies and gentlemen, welcome on this flight to Toulouse. The flight time is one hour and 10 minutes. Let me reassure you, although the plane may look like a chicken, it flies like an eagle."

~ ~ ~ ~ ~ ~ ~ ~ ~ ~

CHAPTER 13

Kiev turndown service.

> *"Behind every successful man is his woman. Behind the fall of a successful man is usually another woman."*
> -<u>Unknown</u>

The meeting with Valeriano Escrivas on their local sales development programme had run over by more than half an hour, so I ended up in the Madrid evening rush hour traffic. I had planned to work a bit in the airport lounge and to make some calls to the office, but none of that happened; the taxi dropped me at the new terminal of Madrid Barajas Airport just half an hour prior to the gate closing time.

Luckily, I made most of my urgent calls during the taxi journey. My wife was the only person I couldn't reach and it would be too late to call her once I landed in Kiev. That rarely happens. Sonja and I call each other every day, mostly late in the evening when I am in a hotel somewhere in Europe.

We landed on time in Kiev at 11:05 pm and getting through customs and security went surprisingly smoothly. The company driver – I asked for his first name three times but still couldn't pronounce it and therefore also forgot it – was waiting for me in the arrival hall. We walked to his dirty old dark blue Skoda in the parking lot and he dropped my hand luggage in the boot. I was ready for yet again another car journey of approximately one hour from the airport to the city centre. It's the same here in Kiev as it is in Moscow and Baku and many other places in Eastern Europe: very long straight motorways or dual carriageways through a desolated landscape from the airport to the centre.

I must say I was a bit disappointed by the welcome at the airport. In the good old days, during and just after the acquisition of this business, I was either picked up by the General Manager or the HR Manager, Tatjana, and one of their drivers. I remember that on my first-ever visit to Kiev, I was welcomed at the gate by the company security manager, who then got me very speedily, via a special channel, through customs and immigration services. Then the journey continued together with the GM, in a clean Mercedes with dark windows and with a small fridge holding two cans of Pepsi or water. Have we been too cost-obsessive over the years? Have we squeezed them too hard? Why did I become less VIP over the years? Well, I know. I was here to discuss with the General Manager his early retirement and he felt it was far too early. So it was clear why he wasn't there and why there was no invite for a late night dinner or drinks.

I had five missed calls during the flight; that's OK. One was of course my wife, one from Kathy, one from my boss and one from someone in the Business Development department. It was now 10 o'clock in the UK and as I didn't fancy returning the call of my boss so late in the evening, I decided to drop him an email tonight from the hotel. I knew what he needed. I also had a number of emails on my Blackberry that required some lengthy replies. The other call was from the General Manager in the US. A quick look at my build-in world time-zones map that I have stored somewhere on my mental hard-disc, taught me that it was early afternoon at the US east coast. So I returned the call but should not have done that.

Jonathan Blox, the GM for our US business, had once again had a bad day and his only reason for calling was to complain about the changed exchange rate of Pound Sterling versus US Dollars, which had had a so-called a massive impact on his local purchasing power. Unfortunately, I had to listen to his moaning; even if I had already decided not to compensate anything. But I had to be polite as he was appointed by and a close friend of the CEO. I personally would never have appointed him in this critical role; I would even have terminated him years ago when we had a strong case on harassment against him. But even there the CEO intervened in his favour.

I arrived shortly after midnight at Hotel Ukraine at 84 Institutska Street. I had never stayed there before. The night shift reception desk manager checked me in.

"Oh welcome, Mister Derrick. I see your reservation has been made by CCG Kiev. I'll upgrade you to a nice room. I'll give you room 408 with a nice king-size bed. You are here for two nights, is that correct?"

"Yes, it is."

I am such a fortunate business traveller, you know. It happens so frequently that they spontaneously offer me a nice room on check-in. Am I that charming? Are there also ugly rooms? And who gets these?

Well, I got one in Kiev. Tonight, I am definitely the lucky winner of the most dreadful hotel room in town. What do I say; in the whole country. Definitely; at least for the places branded 'business hotel'.

While I start up my laptop, I have a look around the room and through the window. The view is nothing more than to the back wall of another hotel building. Downstairs is a dirty courtyard between the two buildings where I see in the light of the parking, two hotel staff talking to each other; very closely to each other. I am not sure if this is still 'talking'. Next to them are three overloaded dustbins, visited by four skinny wild cats.

The room is spacious but has honestly nothing more than a bed, a small chair and a small old metal table as work desk. On that same table a miniature TV. No paintings or mirrors on the wall, no flowers, no room service menu. And nowhere a cupboard. The air conditioning unit blows at a freezing level; no matter how many knobs I turn, there is no change. The bathroom is very basic but clean. Next time I don't leave the hotel booking over to the General Manager; we'll do it from my office. It promises to be tough negotiations tomorrow on his leaving terms.

The discussions with Sergey however, went very well. Although he had hoped that I would pay him severance covering the remaining four years till age 60, he got more reasonable during the meeting. And it looked that his wife was the great push behind him stopping his daily routine as soon as possible and spending much more time with her and the grandchildren. We swiftly came to an agreement that he would leave in six months. That was key for the business. Not that we had any problems with Sergey, he was very devoted to the local business – a bit less to the centre. Our key issue was that a German high potential manager needed to get experience abroad; so poor Sergey needed to free up space, as a thank you for his 23 years' strong performance. He should just have stroked the centre a bit more and he would have made it till retirement age.

He invited me for an early dinner that night on a boat, together with Tatjana. She remembered that last time I had enjoyed the Borsch so much that I couldn't even order any other starter. For the main course, Sergey advised cabbage rolls (golubtsi) with veal. That was "succulent", as the French so nicely say. We ended with coffee and a local digestive. Tatjana's driver brought me back to the hotel around 10:00 pm and he would pick me up tomorrow morning at 7:15 am to drive me back to Kiev Borispol airport.

The man behind reception desk was the same guy who checked me in last night. I take the opportunity – with a sarcastic smile – to wish him a good night.

> "I'll go to my upgraded room. Have a good night."

> "Have a good sleep, Mr Derrick."

Impressive for this type of hotel; the pronunciation of my name was a bit strange but at least he remembered my name.

I was only in my room for half an hour, and somebody knocks on my door. I open the door and see a woman in her early 20s, fantastic shoulder-long dark brown hair, well powdered and very, very sexy red Botox lips. She could have been a L'Oreal model, or a top mannequin for Chanel. She also looked very like some of the girls from the Nightflight in Moscow or from the Club Napoleon in Paris. But no, she's not that type of girl. No, she isn't. Her name tag 'Sylviana. Trainee', made it clear that she is working in the hotel. She's probably a chambermaid.

"Do you like turn down service for tonight, Mr Derrick", she said with a soft and playful voice. Strange, she pronounced my name in exactly the same way as the guy at reception desk.

I normally never ask for turn down service. On the contrary I generally have the 'do not disturb' card on my door but for whatever reason I must have forgotten it this night. For whatever same strange reason, I reply, "Yes, why not. Go ahead."

A man is a man; and I thought there was nothing wrong with observing her – from that one chair in the room – while she was doing her job. And oh, she had a beautiful body. Why was she working here in this middle class hotel and not at L'Oreal? She bent down very slowly while making up the bed; turning the sheets very slowly. She then turned her head to me and her eyes pierced straight into my eyes. I felt like she had caught me looking at her. She then went to the other side of the bed and did the same, softly – almost massaging –the sheets.

"So now it's ready for two passengers; the journey can start," she said while walking slowly – step by step – towards me and without losing eye contact. My eyes seem to be pulled towards her long slim and nicely tanned legs.

"Yes, it looks like it is ready for two," I replied, a bit hesitant.

Yeah, come on, what else should I have said? Pure factual, she turned down both sides of the bed and had fluffed both pillows. So factually and mathematically it was ready for two. Before I realised what was happening, she was standing behind me and had her hands softly massaging my neck.

"Whenever you are ready, Mr Derrick", she whispered in my right ear.

I am so grateful to her that on the morning after, I bought her a present in the hotel's tourist shop.

Dear reader, before you get it completely wrong, 'her' here means Nathalie, my PA who called me exactly at the time that Sylviana's hands were leaving my neck and moved slowly downwards. So the present is for Nathalie, not for Sylviana. Thanks Nathalie. Thanks Vodafone and thanks Blackberry.

Of course I would have stopped Sylviana myself; immediately. What else do you think? My name isn't DSK and I am not working for the International Monetary Fund. This is not the Sofitel in Manhattan and this room is certainly not worth the US$ 3,000 that DSK paid. Room only.

But Nathalie's timing was perfect.

"Do I get you at a good time boss? We have a few things to discuss. Can I start with my issues on your next week's travel plans?"

"Yes, eh. Of course eh. No probs. Just eh, wait a second. Stay on the line. I am all yours in a sec; stay on the phone."

"You are sure? You seem to be busy. Shall I call a bit later?"

"No, no. Definitely not. Just stay on the phone. I am back with you in a second. I just need to sign the bill for the room service guy."

I put the Blackberry on the bed, take five Euros out of my wallet and give the money to Sylviana.

"For the turn-down service," I say very silently and show her the way to the door.

Her sexy smile suddenly disappears. She walks out of the room. Through the peephole in the door, I see her knocking on the door of room 409, opposite mine.

"Hi Nathalie. I am back and all ears."

Nathalie and I walk through all the current issues; we were probably 45 minutes on the phone.

"Ok thanks," Nathalie says. "Your room service dinner must be very cold by now. I am sorry."

"No problems Nathalie. We'll talk tomorrow. Have a good night," I reply and we end the call.

What an evening. I am very thirsty now. I need a gin and tonic. And given this middle class hotel doesn't offer a minibar in the room, I leave the room to go to the bar.

Not even five seconds later, I see Sylviana leaving room 409. While I am waiting at the elevator, she walks to me and asks with a very naughty look,

"Phone call finished?"

I don't reply and we both together step into the elevator. We don't say a word. Her hair is wet. She must have had a shower after the turndown service in 409. I don't understand that, hotels shouldn't allow staff to have a shower in the guest rooms. There should be dedicated shower rooms for the staff.

Still together in the elevator, she takes off the name tag "Sylviana. Trainee" and drops a business card in the upper pocket of my jacket. All without words. Once on the ground floor, I walk to the bar and she walks to the main entrance. Before leaving the hotel, she turns back and smiles at me and at the guy behind reception desk. I see him thinking and suppressing a smile.

In the bar, I take Sylviana's business card out of my pocket; I see the print of red lips and a phone number. I tear the card into small pieces and drop it in the ashtray. Do you think she made more money in 409 than in 408?

~ ~ ~ ~ ~ ~ ~ ~ ~

CHAPTER 14

Con te partiro.

> *"The conscious mind may be compared to a fountain playing in the sun and falling back into the great subterranean pool of subconscious from which it rises."*
> -<u>Sigmund Freud</u>

In March 2008, the European Commission approved CCG's acquisition of one of its main competitors, the French Aldessa SA. This major player was the last hunting trophy that our CEO Gary Mavis absolutely wanted on his red oak office cabinet; the last one before he retired.

It was an awkward offer process.

We were in competition against a private equity group. Despite the European competition laws, José Relvaras sat on the Board of the private equity group. This same José Relvaras is a non-executive Director of Aldessa. I have of course no evidence of anyone practicing insider information, but we ended up paying 20% over our initial offer. Was it José who beefed up the final offer or was it the personal greed of Gary Mavis? No-one will ever know. In any case, the traditional cost-cutting in the integration phase had to be significant. With my endless ambition to continue climbing the corporate ladder, I was smart enough to stay out of the manufacturing integration and out of the closure of three factories in France. Delivering strong performance in projects outside your direct scope of responsibility is one of the best career-enhancing tools. Staying out of risky projects is an even better strategy. Also, my colleagues understood pretty early the risks involved in the French restructuring and so we re-hired Frederic Dermax as an integration consultant, mainly on the manufacturing side. Frederic was the consultant who helped me in 2000 with the closure of the factory in Saint Pierre. I did not want to become a hostage of the CGT union once again. But even more importantly, I would have enough struggles on my desk in combining all the sales structures in all European countries into one aligned force.

Gert Spanjaard – a slightly strange name, but then all Dutch people got that habit from their rebellious anti-Napoleon history, joined us as an in-house consultant. He was focussing on the sales integration and came with strong experience from Heineken, Sanofi and BearingPoint. He joined us as an independent consultant with a strong resume and proven track record on aligning and restructuring field forces to corporate strategy. Gert was very hands-on and made very good progress on the integration activities in the Netherlands, in Poland and in France. In Greece, although he spent much time in Athens, things progressed more slowly. After six months, I advised him to conclude Greece as soon as possible as we were seeing the first signs of losing market share. With his experience, Gert understood this very well and offered to even spend his weekends over there to try to speed things up. He emphasised though that it would take at least another six months given the complexity of labour legislation in Greece. We were at risk of ending up in our new structure with only the poor performing salesmen and he was constantly working with the local HR Manager on defining ways out of this risky situation. Amynta Galatas, the HR Manager for Greece was gorgeous, slender, very sexy – and all other adjectives describing a very beautiful young woman applied to her. And let us not forget – well I will never forget – her piercing icy blue eyes.

She had very short communication lines with me. Amynta worked with me on a Group policies project in 2007 and that brought her frequently to the Head Office, where she was soon spotted by other senior managers. Even by some Board Executives.

I was told that she was very 'willing' after normal working hours, but I never tested that rumour. Soon I got evidence that Gert's frequent travel and weekends to Rome were for other reasons than the integration project. As an experienced manager, he should have known better; you don't compete with other very senior managers – certainly not when it's about catching the most beautiful fish.

From the boardroom, I got the request – in very clear wording – to make Gert leave the same day.

That was very unfortunate timing for me as at the same time, a corporate governance bomb exploded in our Middle East business. Mega kilotons!

It is Tuesday morning; 9:00 am CET and we are in the Marriott Bath Road, Heathrow. Present are the CEO, CFO, Kathy the Group HR Director, the Group Legal Director and Conrad, the Region Director for the Middle & Near East. I am presented by the CFO to an army of eight lawyers from E&O LLP.

Don Curlis, the CFO, opens the meeting, asks the lawyers to once again present themselves and then gives a very short overview of the issue.

In short, we are informed of an alleged fraud of circa £30 million and a risk for revenue loss over the coming years of circa £50 million. There are potentially eight senior and middle managers involved.

And this ends up on my desk at the same time as me losing Gert and me having to lead the sales force integrations in Europe all by myself. First thing I write on my notepad is 'call Philiep from Korn Ferry for an interim Manager'.

In his overview, Don uses the word 'alleged' so frequently that I in fact start to wonder if we have anything tangible. Marc Rich, senior partner at E&O, is more firm in his wording. He talks about 'irrefutable presumption', about 'double-checked evidence' and about 'confirmed witness statements'. E&O has been on the case for three months; they really must have done their work very secretly as normally any issue in the Middle East is brought to my attention pretty quickly. But this time, I didn't know anything up till today. Nor did Conrad Mather, the Region Director.

At the end of the meeting, we agree an action list and a critical path for the next few weeks. Gary Mavis proposes that I lead with the advisors from E&O all the employment related issues. There we go; it's now on my desk.

In the follow-up meetings and investigations, we come to the conclusion that the General Manager, Maurice Janot, will have to leave the business. I am personally unclear on the so-called proven fraud allegations but there is more than sufficient material to terminate him without pay for all the proven malpractices, poor management judgements and the absolute absence of any internal management control system. And the fraud aspects can be further investigated after termination. We will also need to investigate any potential conspiracy in the Dubai office, and as soon as possible interrogate all other employees in the office. Simultaneously, our internal audit department will see if any of these allegations have any links to our Near East office in Beirut.

Maurice Janot is 47, is dual nationality (French/Canadian) and has worked for us in Dubai since 2005. I remember he was one of the first high level recruits I hired in my Global HR role. Prior to CCG, he was four years with Campbell Soup and before that, eight years with British American Tobacco.
He now has over 20 years of experience in senior roles in the Middle and Near East. This gives him a very strong network in the distribution sector, in local administrations and I know for fact that he is also very close to many governmental decision makers; including the entourage of some Sheiks even. With his nicely tanned skin, dark black hair, his thin chin curtain beard, his most expensive shoes and his ever-shiny golden Rolex watch; he even looks like a modern Sheik. But, he doesn't need a Ghutra with cane Igal to be locally appreciated. He is Mr. Maurice, the respectful business leader.

I remember that two years ago, when we considered giving him the full responsibility for the Middle and Near East, for whatever reason I couldn't fly directly into Dubai so we booked a flight to Abu Dhabi. Maurice would arrange for me to be picked up there and to be driven to Dubai. Once landed in Abu Dhabi, indeed a driver waited for me. He however, dropped me only a few miles further at a private airfield where a helicopter from Aerogulf Services was waiting for me. Before stepping into the helicopter, I called Maurice and said that this was unexpected and also unacceptable as it must cost a fortune. He convinced me it didn't cost a penny as he had won a flight at the Dubai mall and given he didn't fancy whirlybirds; he offered this journey to me. Free of charge; no cost to him and no cost to the company. Once we landed in Dubai near the cargo area of the International airport, another car was waiting for me and drove me to the Toro Toro restaurant in the Grosvenor House. Here, we discussed the potential restructuring in the Middle and Near East. Of course, Maurice was very well prepared and described to me in detail his strong network in the Near East. Although we had not asked him at all to prepare for a structure review, he presented to me his future structure proposal while I was struggling to finish the lobster in a creamy mushroom sauce; a not so successful dish I must say. But then I was so tired that I didn't really fancy any food. The coffee, the sweet honey dessert cookies, the Montecristo cigar, the cognac and Maurice not talking business but good jokes, was the best part of the evening. After dinner, I had a few more drinks in the vibrant Embassy bar with Guido, the Starwood Vice President for the Middle East. He's a Belgian guy and a close friend of one of my uncles.

Back to the investigation. I branded the employment related part 'Project Dessert Storm' – yes 'dessert' and not 'desert'. With the support from Honoré Delfosse, The Regional HR Manager for the Middle & Near East, I get prepared to go into action. We develop a plan and agree to go the week after next to Dubai to terminate Maurice and to confront the other employees with our findings. The lawyers from the Abu Dhabi E&O office will prepare the paperwork and it will be me and Conrad Mather, The Regional Director, who will face Maurice.

This time, I was able to get the direct flight from Heathrow to Dubai; Conrad would fly in from Paris. Our meeting with Maurice is planned for tomorrow Wednesday at 2pm. Maurice had got the message that Honoré and Conrad would meet him to further discuss the Middle & Near East structure proposal; there was no mentioning of me being in Dubai. The three of us were staying in the Palace The Old Town hotel, just opposite the Burj Khalifa that was opened earlier in the year. I had suggested that the three of us meet at 9:00 pm for a quick bite and for some further preparations. Tomorrow morning we'd meet with the legal advisors and in the afternoon it would be action time.

Honoré and I are having a drink at the bar; it's now 9:15 pm. We have both called Conrad twice, but none of us managed to get him on the phone. I try once again but once more not successful. When Honoré calls Conrad's secretary, we don't learn anymore. According to her, he should have landed in Dubai this morning but since she hasn't heard from him. She checked his flight and it is confirmed that his flight landed on time very early this morning; that was around 7 am.
That is very strange, very strange indeed. Conrad is always contactable, wherever he travels.
It's now 9:45 pm and I agree with Honoré that we are not going to wait further; we both will keep trying to get Conrad on the phone in the coming hours. And in a worst case scenario, it will be Honoré and I facing Maurice tomorrow. We agree to have a breakfast meeting at 8:00 am.

In my room, I make myself a good cup of coffee and go to the room terrace to get some fresh air. And a cigarillo. The metal outdoor chairs and footrest come with thick yellow cotton cushions. I relax myself, enjoy the fresh air, overlook the artificial lake in between the mall and the hotel, sip from my coffee and light my cigarillo. Although I'll have an unpleasant task to do tomorrow, I do enjoy this moment of rest. In fact I am happy Conrad didn't show up tonight; now I have at least some time for myself; I'll sit here for an hour doing nothing; just relaxing. The reading I'll do later in bed.
But the peace, the warmth and the silence all of a sudden get interrupted by another hotel guest somewhere nearby my room switching on his radio at full volume. That's what I thought. Only a few seconds later, the dark manmade lake lights up. This music doesn't

come from a guestroom; that's clear now. And then I get it; I have seen it before on YouTube but never admired it real life. I am here, on my private terrace, about to enjoy one of the most spectacular Dubai events: The Dubai Fountains. It's right in front of me, no-one around me. This feels very VIP. The fountains are amazingly well choreographed and synchronised with the light projectors and with the music from Andrea Bocelli's Con te partiro. This is world class, so much that I forget the soft cushions, forget the coffee and the cigarillo. For a moment, I am not on this world; I am in heaven.

Until, in the middle of this angelic performance, I get a call. But I don't want calls now. In a fraction of a second, I slide the terrace door open and throw my phone on to the bed. I had though a quick glimpse on the screen and noticed it was Kathy calling me. So I run back to catch the 'still flying' phone and while it lands on the oversized bed, I take the call. Bye-Bye Heaven.

"Hi Kathy. How are you?"

"I am OK, Henry. And how are you? You had a good flight to Dubai?"

"Yes, that was OK; not too bad."

"I am just calling you Henry to let you know some more findings from today on the Dubai fraud issue so that you are fully up to speed. You are meeting Maurice tomorrow, right?"

"Eh yes. Yes, eh, indeed."

"Oh, am I catching you in the middle of something? Is this a bad time to talk?"

While Kathy is talking, I see on the screen that I get another incoming call; this one is from Conrad.

"No please go ahead; it's fine."

"I just wanted to let you know that earlier this afternoon I called Conrad and instructed him to get himself on the next plane to London. We want to meet him and discuss further issues in a face to face with him tomorrow morning in Heathrow. I realise he was expected to be with you tomorrow for the termination of Maurice but I am sure you can handle that together with one of the lawyers. I can't say more at the moment on this, Henry."

"Well that sounds serious, Kathy."

"As said, I can't say more at the moment. You also need to know that I have asked Conrad not to talk to anyone before his tomorrow's meeting with me and Gary."

She doesn't take the invite to share a bit more and we agree we'll call each other tomorrow at 2pm UK time. In fact I don't need more details; it's super clear that when you are asked to jump on a plane for an unplanned meeting with the Group HR Director and the CEO, than it's trouble time.

After the call, I go immediately back to the terrace but the exquisite performance is over. So that part of heaven is ruined for me.

Only a few minutes later, I get another call. It's Conrad.

"Henry man, what's going on?"

"Conrad. I should ask you. Honoré and I called you several times today. Where are you? What's going on?
In the background, I hear the noise of heavily blowing air-conditioning and I think I also hear the voice of a steward performing a safety briefing.

"I am in Dubai but on a plane on my way back to London Heathrow."

"But Conrad, you should be with us tomorrow for the meeting with Maurice. And we had…"

"Henry, I need to interrupt you; they're asking me to stop this call. But what's happening; quickly tell me. Are they going to fire me too?

"How do you mean?"

"Come on; what do you know?"

"Fire you Conrad? How do you mean?

"I let you go. I'll call you back first thing when landed in London. But you'll need to tell me everything you know. We have been friends a long time, remember."

I then hear Conrad, very arrogantly, shouting, "Yes I am finished!" to a probably very persevering stewardess. He is not in a good shape and not in a good place. Conrad, who is a very successful but less diplomatic leader, is now really flopping like a fish on a line. He acts like his days in corporate life are counted.

Hoping this call ends the day, I'll prepare myself another coffee and decide to have a last cigarillo on the terrace. And then, there is still the reading to be done; I think I'll skip that for the flight back to Brussels.

Relaxing on my private terrace, I start to wonder what the real meaning of the word 'relaxing' is, I get four more calls. One from Honoré – who was called by Conrad when I was on the phone with Kathy, one from my PA and one from our company Medical Doctor who wanted to get my feedback on the proposal to financially support a charity that is setting up an ambulance service in Dakar. Yet another report I have not yet read.

And the last call is from the secretary of Maurice, asking to schedule a phone call for tomorrow at any time most suitable for me. This is strange, very strange. Not only is it now in Dubai after midnight, Maurice never ever used his secretary to schedule a call or an appointment. Maurice is the type of guy who just calls whenever he

needs something. This is clear; Maurice must know more and probably he knows that I am in Dubai. I am responding to his secretary that I am travelling at the moment and that tomorrow will not be suitable for a call.
I just start to wonder where Conrad was all day. He landed this morning in Dubai and only left a short while ago; he was at least 15-16 hours in Dubai and all that time he was not contactable by phone. I know he likes to play golf in Dubai but I have that strange feeling he didn't today. Has he been seeing Maurice today? I can't believe it as that would be very close to conspiracy.

Very strange things are happening here. I have always been very supportive to Conrad and, although he could be a bit controversial and bullish to his team, I have always trusted his integrity. How wrong was I?
I go to bed with the thought that I have – yet no evidence of Conrad being involved in the fraud. I am a strong believer of innocence until proven guilty. Or do Kathy and Gary have the deciding proof? Whatever, we'll tackle firstly Maurice tomorrow and then we'll see what comes out of the woodwork.

In the morning, the meeting with the legal advisors and with Honoré runs smoothly. In the absence of Conrad, I decide I'll take the full lead in the meeting and Honoré will act as a witness and support where needed. The meeting with Maurice is planned to be short; we'll tell him our decision, he can then shortly reply or try to defend his position, and that's it. Full stop; no pity. On Maurice there is plenty of evidence that warrants his immediate termination; on Conrad I haven't seen any evidence at all.

Given however Maurice's high profile in the Dubai business world and to minimise all risks, we have once again ensured security for Honoré and myself. One security guard is posted in the hallway to the meeting room in the Palace The Old Town hotel. We rented the hotel's boardroom which has large floor-to-ceiling windows overlooking the lush gardens. That's were the second security guy is posted on a bench with direct view into the room.

I feel safe and relaxed; in my mind and based on the additional info from this morning's meeting with the lawyers, we have more than sufficient material. By dismissing Maurice, we are taking the right decision.

The meeting room has a large mahogany table, 12 light brown leather seats and against the wall, two heavy wooden dressers. On one of these cupboards stands a silver plate with two bottles of sparkling and two of still water and another plate with cups and coffee supply. Nothing fancy, just as I had instructed. The rent of the 'naked' room was already pretty expensive but I just didn't want this meeting to take place in Maurice's office.

Exactly one hour before the meeting, and as agreed, one of the security guys informs the Security Manager of the hotel with the message that our visitor will be Mr Maurice. Nothing more, no further details except that we have also posted two company hired security guys on their premises.

At 1:30 pm, so half an hour before the meeting, to my absolute surprise, four members of hotel staff enter the room and start bringing lots of food into the board room. I react immediately and tell them this is not ordered and will not be paid for. We get two plates of Danish pastries on the dresser with the water and coffee supply. On the other dresser, a plate of fresh fruit salad is placed, a small bowl of fresh yoghurt and eight portions of Actimel. In the middle of the mahogany table a Persian bronze teapot and six glasses are put on a glass oval plate with what looks to be like golden ornaments. On both sides of this tea offer, a small arrangement of artificial flowers is posted. Artificial? In a four or five-star hotel?

We also get two white and blue Wedgwood ashtrays; that I appreciate.

This all takes less than five minutes and the guys disappear without saying a word. I can only see two reasons for this happening. Either Maurice owns part of the hotel which I doubt because he never invited me here. Or, yes, call me paranoid, this is a trap and somewhere they have installed hidden wireless microphones. Or even cameras? Honoré and I do a quick check but we can't find anything. Nevertheless, it was a great idea from Honoré to turn all the plates and to move some of these to the cupboards. During the meeting, however long it takes, Honoré will keep his smartphone on the table and download some large files in the hope this may cause radio interference.

At five to two, we get a call from reception informing us Mr Maurice has arrived "for his meeting with Mr Honoré Delfosse and Mr Henry Derrick". I assume they are calling us while he is standing in front of the reception desk operator and as such Maurice will hear that I am in the meeting and not Conrad.

With the board meeting room only 20 steps at the left from the lobby, Maurice enters the room half a minute later, before Honoré could pick him up at reception as was agreed with reception desk. Both Honoré and I walk to Maurice and we shake hands. I explain to him briefly that Conrad won't be here and that also the content of the meeting will not be about structure changes in the Middle and Near East. I invite him to take a seat at the table and Honoré gives him a glass of tea.

At the table, he takes out of his white cotton suit a nice Mont Blanc pen and puts it on the left side of the hotel's writing pack in front of him. On the right side of the block-note, he puts his white iPhone and earpiece and next to that he puts another pen. For this pen, I don't recognise the brand; all I can see is that it is black and very large.

Everything is nicely aligned with the leather cover of the writing pack. That second pen is very large. I my mind, I convince myself that I am not getting paranoid. This is too obvious; the large pen is fully pointing at me opposite the table. I am sure it's a recording device and I decide to play the game together with Maurice. Because of the 'hindering sunlight', I invite Honoré to swap seats with me. I am curious to see what happens with the black pen; and yes miraculously it follows the move. Checkmate.

I have always hated to work with scripted notes for this kind of meetings as I have continuously – and still do today – strongly believe in the human touch when someone gets dismissed. But now, I am fully confident that our investigators have done a good job because the behaviour from Maurice doesn't please me at all. So this time, I decide to follow the script meticulously. With one exception.

"Maurice, do you have any recording devices with you here in the meeting room? And if so, are any of these activated?"

"No. Should I? he replies.

"Thanks. I take note that you have confirmed not to have any activated recording devices here with you."

"What is this guys? What is this all about? Maurice asks while staring at me and Honoré.

"Let's move on. Maurice, we are here today to inform you of the company's decision to terminate your employment contract with CCG with immediate effect. I have here a letter with me that details and confirms this decision. You can read this letter in a minute and afterwards you will have some time to comment should you wish to. Then, Honoré will explain to you the legal consequences of this termination."

Maurice reads the letter and mentions three or four times that this all is an absolute mistake and a scandal. He tells us he has always been open to Conrad and the Head Office about some less respectful but critical customers; that he has always administered all accounting activities in a very detailed and open way. He mentions that never, since he was appointed Head of the Middle East, never any internal or external audit had any remarks on the accuracy and integrity of his accounting practices. "And these audits are done annually!" he shouts. Good point Maurice, I think but obviously don't say. Indeed nowhere in our records have we got any remarks from internal or external audit about malpractice in our Dubai office. He further mentions that the company just doesn't understand what 'doing business' in the Middle East means. He then asks to see the evidence against the allegations and I decline on that request.

The rest runs smoothly. Not that I take any consideration out of how people react. Sometimes, managers and staff, dismissed for severe and proven reasons, elevate themselves to the world's best actors.
Maurice only starts to get very nervous when he hears from Honoré that the termination is with immediate effect and as such he won't have a work permit anymore. That means that he will be an illegal immigrant in the UAE. So in the coming days, he'd better jump on a flight back to his home base in France or Canada. The coming days will indeed prove how strong his network is with the Dubai administration. Can he manage to stay here in the Emirates?
We'll find out. In any case, my job is done here.

When we walk together to the hotel lobby and shake hands for the last time, I can't however resist the temptation to ask him a few more questions.
     "In fact Maurice, do you know why Conrad isn't here?"
     "How should I know?" he replies.
     "When did you last meet Conrad?"

"I understand that I am not part of the company anymore; that I am not anymore a manager at CCG. So I can easily say Henry, that's none of your business. And by the way, if Conrad – who knows everything about my business here – is hiding away and has refused to defend me in Head Office, if he decided for whatever reason not to kill any of these false allegations, than he can f*** off too."

I am tempted to read out of these words that he didn't see Conrad yesterday. I am tempted to believe that Conrad is not involved in any of these fraudulent practices.

At the same time Maurice drove away from the hotel's long palm tree-bordered driveway, I realise that Conrad didn't call me at all. He must have landed in Heathrow hours ago.

While I wait at the front courtyard of the hotel for Kathy to return my call, I get another opportunity to admire the world's tallest building. It's amazing but what I – firstly vaguely – see is even more amazing. I notice a number of men hanging on simple ropes at, I guess, the 40th or 50th floor on the outside of the Burj. Oh my God, these are window cleaners just doing their job, but in a very, very old fashioned way and very unsafely. Is there no hoist or any better equipment than simple ropes? Kathy returns my call and I learn that Conrad didn't show up at the meeting in Heathrow. When I go back to the boardroom to wrap-up with Honoré, he is on his mobile and seems to be very nervous.

"That was Claudine. Conrad's PA. She was called half an hour ago by Conrad's wife. Conrad is taken to hospital by the London emergency services. Their assessment is a heart attack." Honoré tells me.

"We haven't seen the end of this story yet, Honoré. But that is very sad, very sad for Conrad. Unfortunately, our job isn't finished. I'll go and book a cab for us to go to the office and to inform staff over there. Can you in the meantime arrange dinner for us for tonight? Do book the outside restaurant here in the hotel. I want a first row table overlooking the lake. At 8:30 please."

Tonight needs to be real relaxing time. We'll enjoy the Dubai fountains event twice tonight; at 9 and at 10.

Con te partiro; with some good sea food, shrimps or crab, and a few Bombay Sapphires. I will need to see this heavenly show again before I descend back to the world of the homo sapiens. I just mentally need this to compensate for my earlier paranoia attacks as I learnt from our two security guys that nowhere was there any recording device in the meeting room, not in the yoghurt, not in the plastic flowers, not in the fruit punch. They checked it all and spoke to the hotel's Security Manager. In fact all this was a mistake from the catering department; it was ordered for the other meeting room on the ground floor.

Homines quod volunt credunt. (People believe what they want to believe.)

~ ~ ~ ~ ~ ~ ~ ~ ~

CHAPTER 15

McLinsey & Company

> *"The intuitive mind is a sacred gift, and the rational mind its faithful servant. We have created a society that honours the servant and has forgotten the gift".-<u>Albert Einstein</u>*

The restructuring of Aldessa ended up being extremely expensive and, given the slow pace, the integration saw some significant delays versus the initial forecast. City analysts raised some concerns but CEO Gary Mavis knew very well how to play them and managed to minimise the impact on the share price.

At the same time, the investigations in the Dubai office are still going on. During my visit with Honoré to the Dubai office, staff realised that this was a serious issue. We got more and more evidence of conspiracy and the local Finance Manager, the IT Manager, a Key Account

Manager and Maurice's secretary, got fired. They were all involved in the fraudulent practices. At the same time, Head Office legal department had launched a criminal complaint against Maurice. Every day, I get around 10 mails from the E&O lawyers on the Dubai issue. I also get the feeling they charge the company per mail; in any case, I have in the meantime seen at least 30 different names of lawyers on this case. And yes, any word produced will be charged.

The Aldessa integration, the Dubai investigation and the nervousness in the Head Office on Gary's succession, made 2010 a very hectic year. Indeed, in 2010 it was time for him to retire and CCG lost one of the most longstanding and most successful CEOs of the FTSE50. In recognition for his outstanding career, he got knighted in March 2010 as Commander of the Order of the British Empire. Not too many CEOs get this honour; half of them are leaders of large corporations in the financial industry. For their contribution to the wellbeing of the British population? I reckon the Indignados have no seat in that appointment committee.

Apart from his memorable leaving party, Gary's retirement was a key event in my life.

And 2010 brought some more memorable events.

On the first day of the year, Mr. Herman Van Rompuy takes up the newly created role of President of the European Council. At his maiden appearance he was countered by Member of European Parliament Nigel Farage, who said the President has "the charisma of a damp rag". Was this black humour or simply ludicrous coarseness of a representative of the English political upper-class?

And very early in the year, a massive earthquake in Haiti kills 230,000 people; one of the deadliest ever. This was succeeded in February by an 8.8 magnitude earthquake in Chilli; one of the largest in recorded history. Still in Chilli, hundreds of television stations broadcast live, for more than one billion viewers all over the world, the successful liberation of 33 miners who had been trapped for 69 days.

In the economic and financial world, 2010 was the beginning of the potential end of the Euro currency. The Eurozone and the IMF agreed for a first – but not last – bailout of over 100 billion Euros for Greece; soon after money was put on the table to rescue Ireland. And as you know, Greece got more, and more, and more. I personally always thought the solution for the Greece vs Europe debacle was not that difficult. Europe, under the leadership of the superpower called Germany, should just agree to buy Crete. This could then be followed by acquiring Mallorca from Spain and if you want, also Italy could put Sardinia on e-Bay. Problem solved, isn't it? And we could make all these islands the first and full pure European territories. With the Euro as a real currency; not a Greek Euro or an Italian Euro. A "Euro" Euro. And these territories would have no local legislation; only European laws would govern. To keep it simple, I suggest we make them all talk English. That way, we may even get David Cameron to support the Euro. One day.

A disastrous year 2010 was for BP; and even worse for the marine and wildlife in and around the Gulf of Mexico when the Deepwater Horizon oil platform explodes and millions of litres of crude oil get spilled.
But at the end, and despite all the financial and natural disasters, 2010 was the one-and-only year that will ever stay engraved in your memory as the year…to test your memory! Say it out loud, now all together, the name of that thing that caused days of disruption of all European and many transatlantic flights, the name of that fantastic volcano in Iceland

is...? I personally was fortunate that day. I was at Charles de Gaulle airport on my way to Madrid. Obviously the flight got cancelled but I could get myself on time on a train to Brussels; back home two days earlier than expected. So what did you say the name of the volcano is? Eyjasomething?
And only a few days before that complete standstill of European air traffic, a plane crashed in western Russia; killing 96 passengers. One of the unfortunates was the Polish President Lech Kaczynski.

And Conrad. How is Conrad doing in 2010? We hear he is recovering well but still has a long way to go and certainly won't be back in the coming months. I have never managed to find out from Kathy or Gary what their intentions were for that Heathrow meeting with him.

In the year prior to Gary's retirement, internal succession planning was the key discussion theme in the company's boardroom. Some of the members of the executive team had lost their interest in the operational success of the business; their sole focus was on getting into the CEO chair. Informally shortlisted were two Brits and one Frenchman. And the contemporary version of the Battle of Waterloo ended in Andy Coppersmith getting into that so alluring CEO chair.

Andy-James Coppersmith, at that time aged forty-two, was a product of London School of Economics, of Ernst & Young and of Kraft Foods. He joined CCG in the role of European Operations Director and moved quickly into the executive committee as Group Corporate Development Director.
Andy's management style was very different to the charismatic approach from Gary Davis. For Andy, leadership is ensuring that objectives are achieved through strict setting and controlling of policies, procedures and guidelines. Emotionless and with very limited attention to the human capital. Where he absolutely fails to engage

employees, it must be said that he manages the external stakeholders pretty well.

In 2011, he was spotted late at night leaving the Goose and Carrot pub, a famous transgender club in Croydon, in half-length black tight leather pants, a blond real hair wig with spiral curls and 'must-have' Louboutin high-heel shoes. A tabloid reporter headlined in a small press article, "CEO Andy or Anny?" The journalist probably didn't dare to go into detail, nor did he mention Andy's surname, nor any reference to CCG; he was probably too much afraid of being sued by an army of corporate lawyers. But, fortunately, this was all in the early days of the *News of the World* scandal and Andy managed to get out very well of this potentially career-ending – but shall we call it innocent – pub visit. I am sure our E&O senior partners were already seeing dollar signs when reading the article and started drafting internal memorandums headed 'alleged pub visit'.

While Andy was the instigator of the internal succession debate in the boardroom, and while he introduced engagement surveys and writes in the annual report about the drive of her – sorry his – employees, his current approach to internal career development is exactly the opposite. Out of the blue came two externally recruited senior managers who got a seat at the executive committee table.

Rafael Ferreira is one of them; he is an Italian/Brazilian top marketer coming from Unilever. Apart from his technical and managerial capabilities, Rafael is key to building the company's innovation pipeline. He is highly respected for his understanding of consumer needs and he seems to have the support and respect from his senior team. I give Andy the credit of being willing to recruit senior leaders with a management style opposite to his own. And opposite they are. Rafael spends his holidays with his kids in Canada, fishing salmon, or he canoes the Amazon River and sleeps in tents. Andy's travel is always in five or six-star hotels in the most vibrant cities of the world. And as you need to live and demonstrate your personal branding, Rafael drives the Range Rover Discovery; Andy drives a white Porsche Panamera 4S.

Another new leader at the executive table is Albert Van Beenen. Albert is a 40-year old Dutch man, very charming and very articulate. He started his career in the early days at Coca-Cola and comes with exhaustive retail knowledge and channel marketing experience, mostly gained at REWE and Red Bull. Of course he also has INSEAD and Harvard on his resume. He comes with real global experience; he and his family have been working and living in Australia, Bulgaria, Vietnam, South Korea and recently Chicago. Albert is now the driving force for building our sales growth agenda and I already feel that he's going to bring change at full speed. He's yet another leader that crossed my path whereby I massively appreciate his level of energy.

In terms of management style, he is very close to Andy. He's about facts and figures – cold figures. It's about processes. Albert is the typical manager who can't take intuitive decisions. Decisions – in his view – don't need to be taken by managers. Business decisions do not come out of the human brain; they result from the correct application of predefined processes. Holidays are an unknown concept to Albert; he works day and night. And in terms of car, Albert drives a pink Mini Cooper. No comment.

Albert is now in his second week at CCG. He informs me that next week Thursday we will terminate two of my colleagues, two of his direct reports. Together we build the rationale for this decision; his decision he stresses. I make it clear to him that I expect openness and honesty in our new professional relationship. He struggles building a strong rationale, and as such it was clear to me that the lead for these terminations was taken by Andy. It was Andy who had instructed Albert for these actions. That is as clear as crystal; but Albert hates me hinting at that. According to him, it is him taking this decision; nobody else.

Whatever, next week Thursday we'll both meet Randy Ingham and Tom Clifton in the Sofitel at Heathrow Terminal 5. They will be generously compensated for their redundancy and therefore he suggests that, "not fitting the new strategy" should suffice as a message. I will be doing most of the talking as Albert has only half an hour before catching his flight to Hong Kong.

Albert also asks me to look at the termination figures for Adele; Albert will decide on this in the coming weeks. My reply is strong and very unsupportive. Additionally, I know that Andy will never agree on this and therefore this is just a waste of time. He insists.

A day later, I am enjoying – well that's a big word, in the company canteen – the traditional Shepherd's Pie. I am sharing a small round table with Randy Ingham who tells me about his first experience with Albert. Randy has the feeling that Albert is planning to terminate him in the coming months. I keep quiet but I get a strong 'déjà vu' experience.

Years ago, at ES Pharmaceuticals and as a result of a worldwide restructuring programme, I had to fire my best friend, Chris. On a Friday morning, I called him to schedule a meeting the same day at 4 pm in my office. In the same call, I also invited him for lunch together that same day. On the terrace of a local restaurant, we had delicious 'moules frites' and talked about anything but business. At four o'clock I told him about his termination.

Some will call this beyond all ethical standards and very unprofessional behaviour. Chris, who has very high business ethics, is still a very good friend and he expressed many times his gratitude for the way I handled his redundancy.

Back to today. Just when I finish the lunch with Randy Ingham, Andy calls me for a short progress update on the planning of the senior redundancies. I initially don't mention Adele, but I feel he wants to hear more and therefore I carefully refer to my talks with Albert on Adele as a potential next victim. It's clear that that's exactly what he was fishing for; but in the same call he indicates that we shouldn't further consider that route. Andy is a smart leader, he had set up a trap for Albert to test if he would blindly follow his suggestions.

With this threesome at the top, all the other members of the executive committee are silenced. The impact of the three new leaders on the organisational culture is of the same magnitude as the Haiti earthquake. With Gary Davis, CCG had grown into a major global FMCG player with a 'family-style' respect for its employees. From a human resources perspective, that was our unique selling proposition; that was our employer brand. And this had a clear and direct result on how our employees interacted with our customers. Today the style and culture undergo massive changes. The current threesome sees CCG as a toy to play with; it's a pack of modelling clay and they squeeze and twist it until it gets a Unilever, a Nestlé, a Reckitt Benckiser, a Kraft Foods, a Danone, a Philip Morris or a Coca-Cola format. CCG's mission today is nothing other than to copy these big players. And to copy their underlying goal: short term profit delivery. That's where it goes wrong; with all of them.

I know that earlier in this book I criticised the influence of communism in business. But objectively, also the other extreme of blind and short-term capitalism isn't the solution. What does short term profit deliver? Apart of being –short term- beneficial to the shareholder? What does it deliver to the customer service? To the product quality? To customer loyalty and inflow? And thus, most of all, to the longer term existence of the business? If all your profit goes to the shareholders, what is left for innovation, for research, and for customers? Luckily we see some new trends evolving; even in major businesses. Look at Facebook. In 2012, Zuckerberg made it very clear in his letter to prospective shareholders. He clearly stated that what he cares about is his product, service and 'social mission' to connect people. The financial success of the business is only secondary to that. But no-one read his letter. Greed overtook their need for detailed information gathering. And so they bought shares at more than double the fair value. The buyers (institutional as well as the man in the street) can only blame themselves. Another example is –surprisingly- P&G that declares in its current purpose statement that consumers come first and that shareholder value will 'naturally follow'. The ranking in J&J's credo is as follows: customers first, then employees and the community and –not using the word "last", the shareholders.

Reflecting profoundly on absurd shareholder pressures, I –and you- end up automatically with asking how we came to today's dichotomy: the real world versus the 'expectations' world. We make our monies in real dollars or Euros through our customers paying for our products or services. But we run our businesses (and even worse, our management incentive plans) through reporting and targeting 'expected' dollar or Euro values based on the analysts' consensus of our expected performance. Or basically, we trade in a real world but manage our business in a greedy 'hypothetical' world. It's perhaps high time for the public listed companies to have a closer look at family owned businesses; that trade and manage in the 'real' world. And that absolutely put customers first while yes, of course, they do aim for sustainable profits. There is a lot that the management teams of public listed companies can learn from businesses like Lego, Hermès Group, Dr. Oetker, IKEA, BCD Holdings, Robert Bosch, Henkel, and so many more.

But some will keep running the investors' controlled rat-wheel.

So, while the CCG Board is kneading the clay – of course they can multi-task – they re-read their management books from the business schools that they attended. But they are very sociable, honestly. They invite many friends to the game and they are very willing to share the pack of CCG-clay. Initially, they started with some friends from Boston Consulting Group. Then, we got Hay management on board. Today, we permanently have around 10 consultants from McLinsey – you know who I mean – in our Head Office. We also have four junior consultants travelling around the world, to tell our experienced market leaders how to run a business.

And with the threesome and the consultants come the inevitable buzzwords. It kicked-in very late at CCG, but the bullshit bingo game is now present in all departmental management meetings.

> The management paradigm has now shifted towards a cross-functional aligned low-risk high-yield strategy, supported by a client-centred conceptualisation of bottom-up world-class idea generation. The core competencies of our engaged virtual and multi-disciplinary foresight teams, linked with our mindshare technology applications, will fast track a change catalyst to leverage consumer needs valuation. We will then Pareto-ize the benchmarking results and transpose in attribution models so as to champion the premiumisation of our mid-segment portfolio and to counter the demand shift.

I found it extremely painful; but fortunately for them, today's leaders don't have emotions. So they also don't feel the pain.

Albert's leading speech at the recent senior management conference in Heathrow was similar to the above waterfall of bullshit buzzwords. At the end of his speech, I think he got this from Al Pacino or from Barack

Obama, he walks to the centre of the stage and looks slowly at everyone individually in the audience. With a big smile, he jumps up in the air. Nearly half a metre high; his loose hanging Burlington sweater falls off his shoulders. And with a loud voice, he shouts,

"Yes we can! Yes we can! Say it all, yes we can!".

Silence; there is not one reaction from the audience.

"Yes we can! Come on, shout it. Yes we can!".

Apart from the soft noise produced by the sliding doors opened by two managers leaving the room and apart from one coughing; there is absolute silence in the room. Endless silence. But Albert keeps his charming smile.

"Come on guys. We are going to play hardball. Yes we can!"

One, out of 30 managers –who all find this an annoying performance- produces a silent, "Yes we can." One. Just one.

Rafael, who is co-leading this session, goes to stage and shouts loudly "Yes I can!" and takes over the lead. Shortly after, he calls for a break.

During the coffee break, I talk to Albert. The 'machine called Albert' doesn't seem to feel the pain caused by the embarrassment. He believes the session went very well.
"I have captured all the elements that I wanted to bring. The new market segmentation is now launched and we are 10 minutes ahead of our schedule. It's going excellently." He sips from his café latte and continues. "We'll skip the afternoon break and you instruct

McLinsey to prepare another workgroup exercise on responding to the consumer demand volatility."

He had not even noticed that there was zero buy-in in the room. But that's not a surprise to me; with Andy and the new leaders at the steering wheel, there is no room for feelings. Only facts and figures count; and the computer on the company's dashboard measures everything. The new leaders come from the school that brainwashed them with the pretended truism; 'If you can't measure it, you can't manage it'. To me, this statement is only true for situations where cause and effect are knowable and where there are no unpredictable influencing factors. You will probably agree that specifically on human behaviour (and that's not only staff but for instance also customers), their actions don't always have a linear cause and effect pattern; nor is it always predictable. Thus not fully measurable. But manageable. So I advised our new leaders to also consider another unchallenged truism; one from Albert Einstein.

> "Not everything that counts can be counted and not everything that can be counted, counts."

The result of this advice was as expected and intended. I didn't get invited to be a member of the leadership team preparing the next management conference; that's planned to be in Barcelona.

I am convinced now that in the months to come I'll spend massive time on listening to the mooning of my colleagues and on trying to keep them engaged as much as possible. Even if my own engagement level is not what it should be. But that's not such a big problem. Everything is under control at CCG. And the control mechanism is called 'consultants'. We keep measuring everything and when we dislike the outcome; then the consultants will throw another reporting tool at us.

And these results will once again be benchmarked versus a comparator group of companies. And so we'll find out that we'll do better than some others and less well versus the so-called top notch companies. So the consultants then advise to apply some elements of the strategy and tactics of those outperforming peers. Whether that fits our corporate culture, consumer strategy or general success factors doesn't matter. The view is to blindly copy what the others do. That's the only thing consultants generally bring to the table – apart from their excessive invoice. They implement approaches from company A in company B. Two years later, they do a refreshment exercise at company A where they then will advise them to implement the tactics from company B. And so they are the driving force on spreading knowledge. Isn't that nice, isn't that kind? I think they should get a Nobel prize for dedicating all their time on making the business world a better world.

I perhaps shouldn't be so cynical about them. But I am not the only one though with this view. Where I call it 'spreading knowledge' some others call it differently. For instance, Freek Vermeulen, a highly respected Associate Professor of Strategic & International Management at London Business School, says in his book *'Business Exposed'*, that business consultants are also guilty of spreading around the world bad or incompatible management practices. (5)

"Management practices, just like viruses, spread by hopping from one firm to the next. Most often, just like viruses, they get a bit of third-party help. In the case of management practices, that third party is often a consultant. And that is because management consultants are a bit like rats. Or, to put it more kindly, pigeons (referred to by the former London mayor Ken Livingstone as "rats with wings"). They spread diseases. ... As I have said before, a virus – like the flu – survives by spreading to a new host, preferably before the old one dies. Often, there are some creatures (e.g. rats) that facilitate the spread among the creatures of another species (e.g. humans). That's much of what management consultants do, even knowingly: picking up practices in one industry or country and recommending and applying them in others. Just like viruses or bacteria, some of these practices are not very helpful, to say the least (although, as explained, the harmful effects may only manifest themselves in the long run); others may have been useful in the original setting (e.g. industry) but completely inappropriate in the new one."

It looks as if I am moving into a stage like Marcel in the old days at Les Papeteries. I see business consultants coming and going. And none of them have a feeling for our business, they just want to measure everything. Just like the new top executives. They are all ripping the heart out of this fantastic business and replacing the heartbeat by downloading spreadsheets. At a speed of 120 download 'beats' per minute. That's not healthy. And at a similar speed, they produce the most trendy management buzzwords.

~ ~ ~ ~ ~ ~ ~ ~ ~

THE FACTS 2

Bullshit Bingo

From the early 1980s onwards, many FTSE100 or NASDAQ CEOs have had to live with the practice that once a year they would be depicted in a newspaper as a "fat cat". This occurs mainly when journalists have been reading the remuneration section of the company's annual report. It is also triggered when new legislation is being prepared on boardroom pay practices, or when an executive director is sent home with a 6 or 7 figure golden handshake. Debating the appropriateness of these pay levels is not the subject of this chapter. It is far too contentious a topic, now even more than late last century, and therefore I leave this with pleasure to the specialists at Mercer or Towers Watson.

I don't mind however having a discussion on the "fat cats" also becoming "old cats". This is not a statement about age. I only made the link recently, when my wife came back home from the pharmacy after visiting the vet with our oldest cat. The insert in the box of drugs explained that these would make our cat more relaxed and would also reduce its "excessive vocalisation". And that's where I am making the link with today's executive leaders and their tendency to over-vocalise buzzwords; more than to lead.

There seem to be two reasons for older cats to vocalise excessively. One is the feeling of loneliness and the other is the loss of their cognitive functions. In comparison, we know that it can be very lonely at the top. However, it is unlikely that the loss of cognitive functions applies so much to successful leaders. This leaves the question – what is then the cause of their addiction to business jargon? There is unfortunately very little research on this. Trying to find an academic or scientific answer to the causal roots of this behaviour is therefore not possible. This means that I have had to revert to deducing potential –but not proven- causes, based on the many papers and blogs published advising leaders to stop their "excessive buzzwords vocalisation" practice. Most publications related to management lingo emphasise the useless and even counterproductive character of buzzwords. This is supported by some brief research (slightly over 100 observations) I conducted myself recently. Surfing the web via Google for the words "buzzwords", "corporate speak", and "business lingo", I found that the content and tonality was:

a) 55% : advising against its use, saying it is counterproductive,
b) 34% : neutral, just explaining the phenomenon, or providing a list; some are a game (buzzword bingo)
c) 11% : positive and supportive, emphasising the advantages, and seeing it as effective.

To dig deeper, I think it's always good to consult a guru; this time not a management guru but a respected authority on language and communication, an author with a passion for clarity in communication. And thus I turn to George Orwell.

In his contribution to bloggingprweb, Chris Pilbeam refers nicely to Orwell:

"'Never use a metaphor, simile, or other figure of speech which you are used to seeing in print."

It's 65 years since George Orwell, creator of Animal Farm and one of the 20th century's greatest authors, offered writers this advice at the end of his essay "Politics and the English Language". And although the clichés George was thinking of probably seem quaint rather than common nowadays, his advice still holds true: avoid the buzzword.

Why? He wasn't just throwing a writer's tantrum. Orwell realized that buzzwords become so familiar to people that they create no emotional response whatsoever. And that's a big deal: when your reader isn't reacting emotionally to what you're saying, they're not paying attention and they're certainly not taking the action you're suggesting." (6)

Another interesting contribution comes from Mike Figliuolo, Managing Director, on his website www.thoughtleadersllc.com .

"The only way I know to roll back the tide of all the meaningless jargon in our world is to say what you really mean. Words spoken from the heart and the gut are clear, concise, meaningful, and genuine. They help ground you and your team. They signal that you are willing to take a stand for something you believe in instead of watering down your beliefs with complicated words so you will not offend someone or so your simple thoughts will sound more important. It is imperative that you realize such approaches have exactly the opposite effect. Using buzzwords makes you sound less intelligent. Filling your leadership philosophy with obscure or difficult to define concepts diminishes peoples' trust in you. Both behaviors are counterproductive and hinder you from reaching your goal of becoming an authentic leader." (7)

On Signal vs. Noise, a weblog by 37signals, LLC, the following view is put forward:

"These buzzwords are often a mask. People who use them are covering up their ideas — or the lack thereof. They are overcompensating. They don't have anything substantial to say so they try to use impressive sounding words instead. But people who abuse buzzwords don't sound smart. They sound like they are trying to sound smart. Big difference. People who really get it aren't impressed by this sort of jargon. They smell BS. They can read between the lines and see what's really there; fear. Fear of clarity. Fear there isn't actually anything worthwhile to convey." (8)

I would also like to mention an interesting experiment, commonly known as the "Doctor Fox lecture". The experiment was led by Donald Naftilin in the early 70s. At the University of Southern California, Dr Myron L. Fox was presenting to a highly educated audience, mainly comprising psychiatrists and psychologists, most of them active in the area of mental health education. They were all invited to a type of train-the-trainer conference. At the end of Dr Fox's half hour presentation and Q&A session, the audience was asked to evaluate the presentation on aspects including "Did he stimulate your thinking?", "Did he give enough examples to clarify his material?" and "Did he present in a well organised form?". The results were that 95% of attendees rated this presentation as stimulating and similar overwhelmingly positive ratings were given to the other assessed elements of the lecture.

However, the so called Dr Fox was in fact an actor and had no knowledge of the paradigm on which he was presenting. The researchers had instructed him to deliver the lecture with an excessive use of double talk and neologisms. They had also coached him to adopt a lively demeanour, to convey warmth and to intersperse his nonsensical comments with humour. The conclusion that the researchers made was that Dr Fox's nonverbal behaviour completely masked a meaningless, jargon-filled and confused presentation.

While I agree that jargon and buzzwords are not exactly the same, for the sake of this chapter, the experiment indicates that "what" you say is less important than how. It's all about the way in which you bring your message and how you market yourself. In the above experiment, Dr Fox was introduced to the audience as a remarkable and highly respected authority in the field of his lecture, Professor from another university, author of two books and many scientific publications.

There is also the noteworthy research from Dr Bentley, anthropologist at Durham University. It doesn't directly explain the root cause but does shine a light on the potential reason for use of buzzwords. In his study "Random Drift versus Selection in Academic Vocabulary: An Evolutionary Analysis of Published Keywords" (9), Dr Bentley researched the use of keywords in the academic and scientific worlds. He came to the conclusion that academics that use trendy buzzwords enhance their reputation as their work will be cited more often by peers. And in those worlds, being cited is pure free marketing and the best tool for extra funding.

Somewhat closer to answering the question of why we use buzzwords, is this extract from Finance Wiki:

"A number of buzzwords are used in the world of finance. In general terms, a buzzword is a word or a phrase used in a particular field like finance or information technology (and for almost all the fields of human activities like management, administration, technology and so on), and the user uses the buzzword to give a stylish and trendy tinge to that particular word or phrase and the meaning conveyed through that word or phrase. The purpose to use a buzzword may be varied: from impressing the laypersons to convey a meaning in an indirect or subtle way."

Another useful quote for this brief research comes from Jennifer Chatman, Management Professor at the University of California. "Jargon masks real meaning", she says, adding "People use it as a substitute for thinking hard and clearly about their goals and the direction that they want to give others". (10)

And Cathy Vandewater on Vault.com (11) phrases it as follows:

"But beyond being obnoxious to everyone else, why is jargon so bad? Frankly, it's very the opposite of sounding informed. Common knowledge dictates that if you know what you're talking about, you'll talk about it. You won't fall back on vague catch phrases. Which is kind of ironic and unfortunate, considering most people pull out the jargon to sound smart, in-the-know, and high level. The truth is, though, that at best, business-speak sounds a little lame. At worst, it can seem purposefully dishonest."

It is fair to say that there is currently a growing belief and understanding that being genuine and honest are key drivers for success in leadership. With that in mind, a 2010 study from the Universities of Basel and of New York seriously challenges the excessive and inappropriate use of management buzzwords. In this study, participants rated sentences that were written in simple, unambiguous and compelling language as more truthful than the more complex and vague or multifaceted sentences.

The academics gave the following three reasons to explain why concrete language is more powerful in indicating truth:

1. As our mind processes concrete statements quickly, you automatically associate quick and easy with true.
2. It is easier to create mental pictures of concrete statements and "easier" makes it "more true".
3. When something can be easily pictured, it just seems more likely, more believable

In the spirit of this study and thus in simple words, the key finding is: If someone has to think too hard about what you are saying, they're less likely to believe it. Unless it's brought by a true —or fake, à la Doctor Fox- authority.

If we transpose these findings to the management world, would that mean that managers use fashionable business words as a way of self-marketing? Do people talk about you and admire you when you master the art of business lingo? In the language of Twitter, do you create more "followers" by showing off with your knowledge of trendy buzzwords? Of business lingo, corporate speak, corporate "slanguage", or –as it's called on urbandictionary.com- "vaginal words"? All this terminology alone adds to the confusion.

It even confused Lord Alan Sugar at a Q&A session at London Business School. This is what happened. A student raised the following question:

"Hello Sir Alan. My name is Alex, I work in Human Resources. I was just wondering how much importance you place on softer skills in business. Influencing skills, team working etc."

Lord Sugar, a bit confused, "Sorry on what?"

"The softer skills"

"What are the softer skills? Excuse my ignorance. I am an old-fashioned bloke from Hackney."

"Things like team working, influencing skills, stakeholder management, that sort of things", Alex repeats.

"Yeah. I think these are new words made up to keep people busy if you ask me. Sorry I got no answer to that really. Management is management. …. You can if you like create things to do in an organisation if you haven't enough other things to do."

Apart from his words, Alan Sugar also clearly demonstrated, through his non-verbal behaviour, his antipathy for what he in another interview called "consultant speak". It is a relief to see Alan Sugar –yes a somewhat old-fashioned, but very successful manager - talk like a human being.

Out of the above views and some more research on this topic, I make following conclusions on the corporate use of trendy and/or innovative business buzzwords.

Scientific literature does not provide one singular and overriding root cause; many reasons are listed for the use of buzzwords in corporate environments. Here are my own conclusions as to the key reasons:
- Reputation enhancement and self-marketing. The user is of the belief that these trendy buzzwords will generate them more

"followers". They believe that it demonstrates their level of intelligence and proves they are "up to date" with latest innovative practices, strategies and trends.
- Closely linked to the above, a desire to be stylish/trendy. Growing and fast tracked (junior) managers feel that the use of these buzzwords will strengthen the view of more senior executives on their capabilities.
- Copying behaviour. In some environments (like consulting businesses) it is seen that corporate speak is just the business language. It is how all others talk; so why shouldn't I do the same.

We find this specific language in print as well as in verbal communication. The real "excessive" usage is more observed in verbal communications (mainly business presentations and strategy setting meetings). For written forms of communication, the "excess" is mainly observed in job application letters.

In terms of business functions in large scale operations, the use of corporate speak is mostly seen in the marketing, sales and human resources functions. It's also largely practiced in finance and information systems whereby much of the terminology used can also be categorised as jargon. The practice is less observed in the following functions: manufacturing, transport & logistics, legal and general administration.

In terms of type of organisations, it will be no surprise that the top users are the management consulting firms (advising in all areas but mainly in general strategy, sales, and IT), FMCG industries and the academic world. It has not yet fully embraced the world of civil servants, although there seems to be a growing trend in the US.

Of course, millions of business buzzwords have been generated over the recent decades and more will reach us through email and presentations in the coming years, despite the growing antipathy towards this type of corporate speak.
I felt that this chapter would be incomplete without a buzzword list and with some occasionally amusing clarifications; some gratefully stolen from bloggers and bullshit bingo-players.

I'll leave it up to you to assess if this section is really "value adding". If you would like to comment on this, I suggest "we take that offline". I do realise that listing these examples may be counterproductive to my intention to ban all bullshit business speak from the corporate floor; but that may be more of a dream than a "big hairy audacious goal".

So here is my corporate speak alphabet. I am confident you have them all on your Bullshit Bingo cards. Please note this is not a scientific work.

Acquisition
Demonstration of the corporate food chain, whereby larger eats smaller and then excretes all non-essential nutrients.

Bangalored
You have just heard it via the trade union – not via senior management – your department, and therefore also your job, will soon be outsourced to India. The consultants convinced your Board that it's much cheaper over there. You can only pray –to the Holy cows– that you get a decent redundancy payment out of it.

Centres of Excellence
Yet another invention from the consulting firms; like "best practice". What is "best" and what is "excellent"? Certainly beats centres of failure. Most companies have a nice set of both.

Don't f••• the payroll
Blunt advice to avoid romantic and sexual relationships with co-workers. I learned this one from one of my previous bosses. Rachel, Kate, Corinne and Rebecca will know who I mean.

Employee Engagement Survey
A survey tool the COO heard about at the last industry leaders' dinner, and now wants to introduce one asap throughout the full business. It's intended to be used to show off the results at the next board meeting, in the social responsibility section of the annual report and at that next industry dinner. It's assumed it will measure the likelihood of the staff not resigning from the business. You could also say it measures employee happiness; but that's too basic. Another technique used to assess employee engagement is to just talk to your staff. But that's far too basic….

Fast track
A corporate ladder consisting of wounded or deceased bodies of co-workers, trampled by colleagues excessively using buzzwords on their way to heaven. (Note: "corporate" in "corporate ladder" is from the Latin "corpus", meaning "body.")

Going forward
Usually serves to add two meaningless filter words before you present your next slide. Frequently followed by the presenter sipping from his Starbucks while beaming the next slide.

(Big) Hairy Audacious Goal
A strategic vision statement, created to focus the business on a single medium-long term organisation-wide goal which is audacious, very likely to be externally questioned, but internally not regarded as impossible.

It is what it is
An expression used by people when they are attempting to be insightful but either have no clue what to say next, are incapable of coming up with something meaningful, or would prefer to change the subject altogether.

JDI
Just do it. When your boss is under pressure, it easily becomes a JF***ingDI.

Knowledge Management
It started as document imaging. Then it gave way to document management, which in turn moved to content management. It now has evolved into Knowledge Management. It's an organisation's ability to "manage" its "knowledge." Primarily this is done by pumping as much company information as possible into databases and developing a system that keeps track of it all. Supposedly, this allows everyone in the organisation to take advantage of the collective knowledge of the company.

Leapfrog
To surpass your competition, usually by engaging in one gigantic, hopelessly ambitious leap of faith that is almost certain to end in ruin and despair. Bring a parachute, golden or other.

Move the needle
This one has nothing to do with heroin; it's a favourite of venture capitalists. If something doesn't move the needle, meaning that it doesn't generate a reaction (like, positive cash flow), they don't like it much. So when pitching VCs (Venture Capitalists), make clear that you intend to move the needle. Or you could just say, specifically, how your plan and product are superior to those of your competitors.

Negative growth
To positivise –just to use another buzzword– a bad outcome. As in "We have seen last quarter negative growth in our core markets in Europe and Asia but our market share has doubled in Turkmenistan to 0.5%.

On the same page
A recognition of being in agreement. Commonly used by the boss at the end of a meeting where most teammates were disagreeing. If you are all physically on one A4 page, than you have probably ended up in a teambuilding session. Smell (☺) the dynamics.

Peel the onion
To conduct a layer-by-layer analysis of a complex problem, and in the process, reduce yourself to tears.

Q1
A slick and immensely creative way to say "first quarter".

RACI Matrix
Returns **A** **C**onsultant a good **I**ncome. It's a way of defining roles in a team or organisation. I am **R**esponsible for the work but can't make decisions. She is **A**ccountable but is entirely reliant on others. You'll **C**onsult but you won't be doing anything useful. And he's just waiting to be **I**nformed.

Stakeholder Management
The art of acquiring enough opinions from people, groups, or leaders within a company to deflect blame if, at the end, a project doesn't meet the expected deliverables.

That being said
I just said something that was probably either really complimentary or full of praise, but now I'm going to use a transition statement that implies that I'm going to get really, really real for a minute.

Upskill

To "upskill" is not different to "to learn". Basically it's about acquiring more skills; or also to put your skills at a higher level. In that context, it most likely originates from the word "upskirt".

Vubicle

Not a spaceship. It's nothing more and nothing less than a cubicle with a window; so a cubicle with a view. In most organisations, this place is strictly reserved for fast tracked junior managers. Once they move successfully up the ladder, they may eventually also get a door. Old-fashioned businesses then tend to call that spot "an office".

With all due respect…

This is the most subtle way to say "I disagree".

Xerox subsidy

The practice of using the company's photocopier, printer, or fax machine for personal reasons.

Y

Yeah; the first letter in the alphabet that doesn't deliver a commonly accepted buzzword.

Z

Zame as Y. Unless you want to be instructed in zero based budgeting, zero accidents policy, zero defects policy, zero whatsoever.

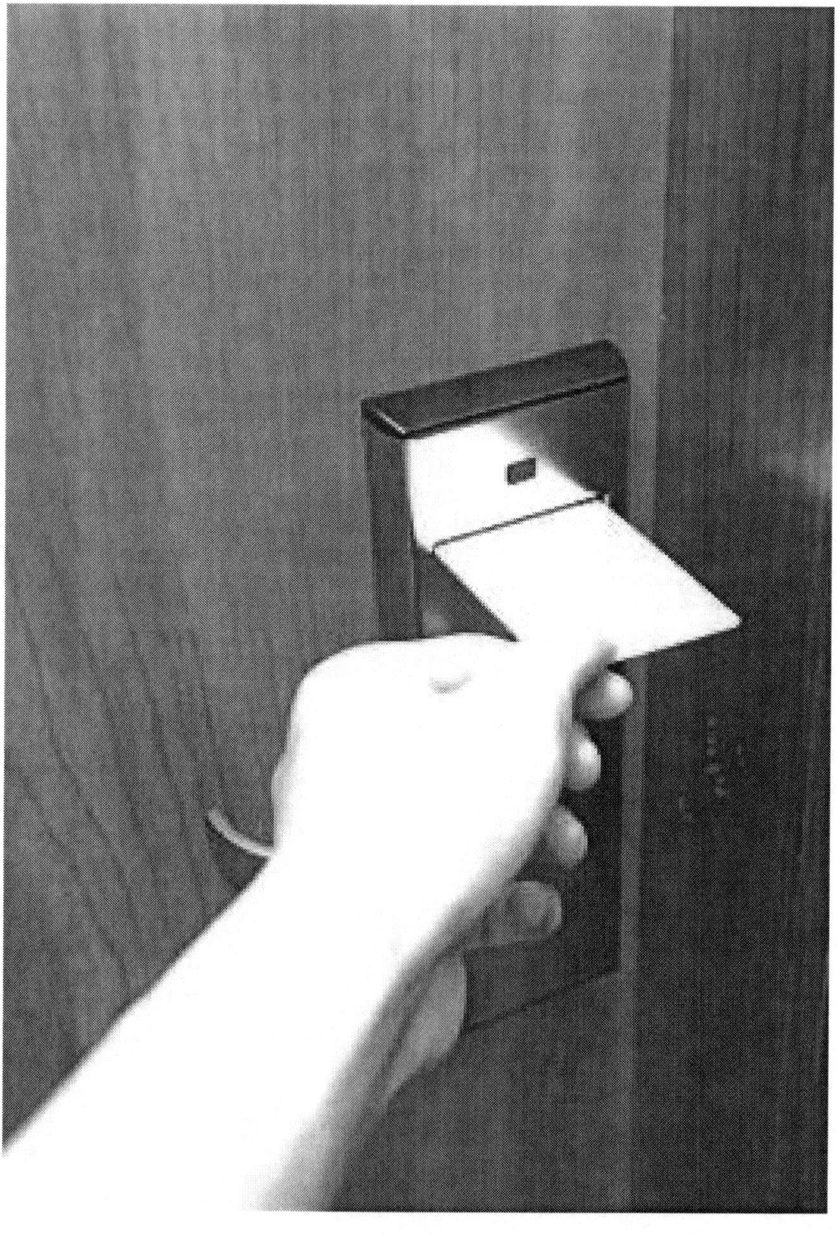

CHAPTER 16

Family alienation.

> "Imagine life as a game in which you are juggling five balls in the air. You name them - work, family, health, friends, and spirit - and you're keeping all of these in the air. You will soon understand that work is a rubber ball. If you drop it, it will bounce back. But the other four balls - family, health, friends, and spirit are made of glass. If you drop one of these, they will be irrevocably scuffed, marked, nicked, damaged, or even shattered. They will never be the same. You must understand that and strive for balance in your life."
> -Brian Dyson

That next management conference took place in Hotel W in Barcelona. This fantastic building in the form of a sailing ship – a bit of a miniature of the Burj Al Arab in Dubai – has a modern yet very comfortable interior. I don't exaggerate when saying I know lots about hotel interior decorations. I can in detail describe you the immense lobby of the Shangri La in Singapore. And I can do the same for the executive rooms in every Sheraton Tower in the world. The work desks in every Crowne Plaza room are of dark wood and rest on a shiny metal leg. The bathroom marble of room 1424 in the Marriott Royal in Bristol is brown and of Italian origin. Same for room 1425; both come with a corner bathtub. 1425 has courtyard view whereas 1424 and 1419 are overlooking College Green and Park Street. The reception desk of the Holiday Inn Oxford Circus in London is on the left hand side; for the welcome desk of the Marriott Grant in Moscow go right. Same for the Le Meridien in Casablanca.

But...don't ask me the colour of the carpet in the dining room at home. The walls of our second bedroom are painted in light blue, or is it light green? The old hunting cabinet in our dining room has three or four doors? Our lawn mower is a Honda, or is it Toro? It seems that Sonja has ordered a new wooden garden shed; according to her she asked me twice but didn't get a reply. I have no clue on when my son's summer holidays are starting; I have now forgotten to call my sister three years in a row on her birthday. My friend Dirk went through a divorce and needed some advice, but I wasn't home and he didn't get a reply to his last email. Jo, another friend started his accounting firm in Antwerp but I wasn't at the opening ceremony; I was in Dakar. His lovely wife Vera gave birth to their son Winnie. I met him first when he was 18 months old. With my friend Ronny, I had arranged to go to the Ghent annual boat show. I cancelled so as to get on my Sunday flight to Hong Kong and further to Taipei.

At Brussels airport, two lines away from me, a young couple with a child were waiving at me while queuing at the security check. Do I know them? Who are they? Weeks later my wife told me that our neighbours had politely informed her that they saw me at the airport; but "I was too busy to react".

In July 2009 I flew on a Monday morning to Madrid and arrived around lunchtime in our offices in the city centre. The meeting had started at 2 pm and at 2.20 pm my wife sent me a text message. "Call urgently." I changed all my plans for that day and for the week and arrived back in Brussels in the late evening. Just before midnight, I took my place next to my mother's bed in hospital. She died three hours later.

In those years, it looked as if I was fully sucked into my job, neglecting friends and family in full. And even worse; not at all realising that this was wrong. Absolutely wrong. Not even realising that a job is only a stage in life; a temporary stage in a temporary life.

But is that so wrong? I was working very hard for the benefit of the family, wasn't I? And I wasn't completely isolated or de-socialised. Not at all.

I had created a new network of friends. Peter, who lives in Leuven and works for a large construction firm, I see him almost every week in the Brussels airlines lounge in terminal-B. I know his daughters are studying very well. His wife got elected last year at local town elections. And he's going to be assigned next year to Anchorage in Alaska for a six-month period.
Simonne, the front desk manager at the SN lounge, is very interested in my holidays to Qatar; she is planning to go too. And the bartender at the Louis C Jacob hotel in Hamburg is talking to the banks to look at acquiring himself a small hotel in South Germany. And Paula, the waitress at the breakfast restaurant of the Crowne Plaza in Marlow is preparing for the wedding party of her youngest daughter.

Hold it! That lizard is a bit bigger than the fly —from chapter 1- on your garden terrace. This needs action taking! But good to see you are still reading outside in the fresh air. Shall I top-up your glass of wine?

And Sylvie, who emigrated ten years ago from Lyon to the UK; next week she will organise a drink for her colleagues at the Marriott.

And Viku, the Moldavian cab driver of Streamline taxis in Bristol is going to visit his parents in May. Waleed, my favourite private chauffeur of AAA cars in Maidenhead has just returned from his Eid Al-Fitr holidays in Jeddah. Ted, our company driver in Miami, is doing some extra job in the Cheese Factory restaurant in town so as to get some savings for his planned holidays to Bratislava next year. His daughter is working there at the American Embassy.

Sarah, the red-haired Scottish flight attendant in the cabin of the small Learjet BMI plane, is promoted and will next month start on long haul flights to the States. Paul, the French waiter in the bar at the Frankfurt city-centre Steigenberger Hotel will resign next week; he has secured a job at the Courtyard Hotel in Montpellier; closer to home. But please don't tell the Steigenberger management yet.

And Sharon, the Head of Customer Service at the 6th floor Club Welcome Desk of the Shangri-La in Singapore; She, she is ever so beautiful.

You see; I am not getting alienated.

In October 2011, just after that fantastic one week Indian summer in Europe, I travelled to Paris to investigate a potential issue of sexual harassment. You read about it so often in the tabloid press and it's also a great theme for business jokes, but now it happened in one of my divisions. On the Thalys train to Paris, I was reading in the newspaper about Steve Jobs – God has his soul – and his visionary leadership. While reading the article, I received a call from my PA Nathalie to inform me that the Sofitel Arc de Triomphe Hotel was overbooked and she asked if I was OK to stay in the Ambassador Hotel on Boulevard Haussmann.

That evening, while checking in at the Ambassador, I met Angelique. Last time we met was more than 20 years ago. You see, I meet friends everywhere.

It may sound perverted, but I recognised her immediately. Angelique was the one with the C-cup at the psychology exams in Antwerp. Over the years, she had moved to a D-cup (at least) and was clearly still very proud of her sexy body. Half of her slightly tanned breasts bulged out of her tight white shirt, three buttons were loose and her blue lace bra was slightly visible. She looked like the modern version of a waitress from somewhere on the beer festivals in Germany.

Last I heard about her was that she allegedly was working in a hotel in Paris; but that's not true though. She was in the hotel as a guest; she was in Paris for business together with her boss, a Commander of the NATO Allied Joint Forces in Naples. She already had some commitments for that night but the day after we could have dinner together. And so we did. I had forgotten though that tomorrow night would be a Friday night, so I needed to inform my wife that "the meeting would take much longer and I'd only be back on Saturday morning".
I had booked a table at the Fermette Marboeuf, nearby to the Champs-Elysées. I still find this one of the most romantic places in Paris; le Marbeuf does not only offer excellent French cuisine, it also offers a

most admirable interior of Art Nouveau splendour. The stained glass vault is of an indescribable beauty. So was Angelique that night.

Apart from a very relaxing night and the two of us sharing our walkabouts and experiences of the last 20 years, we accidently ended up in a conversation with the couple at the table next to us. I talked a bit about the latest trends in management – what else can I talk about? – and Angelique chatted casually about shopping and travelling in Italy. The lady with short black hair, I guess in her mid-forties, was relatively quiet and only talked about little things. We had the impression that she was in politics or a senior civil service manager.

At the cloakroom, the waiter told us who our table companions were that night. The man was one of the most renowned financial professors and the woman was none other than a former minister of justice. Rachida Dati was the French Minister of Justice till 2009 when she was recklessly sent away by her initial sponsor, Sarkozy. Currently, she resides in the European Parliament.

It was a great night in Paris. We both enjoyed the dinner and since then we always call each other when one of us is in Paris or Rome; we are now good friends. And good friends you only have when you are not alienated. But let me be clear, that night in Paris nothing indecent happened.

Apart from the fact that I had forgotten that this Friday, October 7th, is my wife's birthday.

Why was I in Paris that night?

~ ~ ~ ~ ~ ~ ~ ~ ~

THE FACTS 3

Give it up, baby give it up…

Life is not eternal; that's a fact. Climbing the corporate ladder also, one day, comes to an end. For the most fortunate, this happens after reaching the top. Frequently, people halt – unwillingly – half or three quarters of the way up. And sometimes, people just get off the ladder. In the most unfortunate situations, people pass away whilst building their career and their business. Over recent years, we have also seen more and more leaders deciding to bring an end to their careers themselves. Regrettably, this often occurs for health reasons. Family reasons are also frequently cited. The latter seem to be mentioned where it is perceived to be a more appropriate and acceptable reason than the real, underlying one.

The anthology below is added to this work as a moment for reflection.

The Irish Times, June 12, 2012. Just three weeks after being appointed as **Horse Racing Ireland**'s new director of communications, Michael O'Hagan has resigned with immediate effect. The 51-year-old, who has also resigned as chief executive of Irish Thoroughbred Marketing, said last evening he was leaving both posts for "purely personal reasons". O'Hagan said: "I've been in this job for 11 years and while I've loved it, there is an awful lot of travelling and I simply want to spend some time at home. "I've given a lot of time to this industry and now I think I should give more time to my family. It's time for a change. I was asked to take up a new position and I felt it was right to make a decision now rather than six months down the line."

Foodanddrinkdigital.com, August 9, 2010. Brenda C. Barnes will step down permanently from the positions of Chairman and Chief Executive Officer so she can continue to focus on improving her health. The company announced that Barnes has resigned from **Sara Lee**'s Board of Directors and will not stand for re-election at the company's 2010 annual stockholders meeting in October. Barnes had been on medical leave since May 14, 2010 after suffering a stroke.

Marketwatch.com (WSJ), January 28, 2011. **Marina Bay Sands** CEO Resigns for Family Reasons. The chief executive of Las Vegas Sands Corp.'s new casino in Singapore plans to resign, according to an internal memo, the latest in a series of management shuffles and hitches in the company's lucrative Asian operations. Marina Bay Sands Chief Executive Tom Arasi will resign from his post effective Feb. 1 for personal reasons, according to an internal email reviewed Friday. His resignation comes only 18 months after he commenced the role and less than one year after the Singapore integrated resort opened its doors to the public. "At this point, I have decided to pause, take a breather and spend more time with my daughter and other family," Mr. Arasi said in the memo addressed "Dear colleagues" that circulated Friday. He didn't respond to phone and email requests for comment.

Electronicsfeed.com, May 14, 2012. Peter Bauer, CEO of **Infineon Technologies AG,** will resign his post at the end of the current fiscal year due to health reasons. Peter Bauer suffers from osteoporosis. During the last several years he already endured numerous fractures of the vertebrae. Recently, his condition significantly worsened and, after due consideration, he informed the Supervisory Board of his decision to leave.

Stltoday.com, January 24, 2012. The last big name from the old days at Anheuser-Busch is leaving Pestalozzi Street. Dave Peacock, who went from August Busch IV's right-hand man to Carlos Brito's U.S. point man, resigned from **Anheuser-Busch InBev** Monday, a move some see as one of the final steps of the brewery's transition to new ownership. The 43-year-old – a second-generation A-B employee who met his wife on his first day of work there – says the parting was his idea, and amicable. He'll remain an adviser to the company, but he wants to do something else while he's still young enough to do so. "I've been really blessed," Peacock said. "When you grow up in St. Louis and your dad works for the brewery, you never even dream you're going to have a shot at the job I had. But it's time to try something different."

As well as the sad story of Steve Jobs' death, there are unfortunately many more examples of people passing on, having either reached the top of the career ladder or while they are still climbing it. Charlie Bell, aged 60, CEO of McDonald's Corp died from an apparent heart attack in 2004; Roberto Goizueta, aged 65, CEO of The Coca-Cola Company, passed away in 1997; Steve Appleton, aged 51, CEO of Micron Technology didn't survive his plane crash of 2012. And this is just a very short list; you will know yourself of friends and colleagues who died while building their careers.

The statistics of the International Labor Organisation (ILO) state that every year, 2.3 million workers die as a result of accidents or work-related diseases. The ILO also estimates that in Europe, the overall cost of work related accidents and diseases, including stress-related ones, is around 2.6 to 3.8 per cent of Europe's GDP.

Another well known, though very different, story is that of Jerry del Missier. In June 2012, Barclays bank announced being pleased to appoint Jerry as their new Chief Operating Officer. Not even one full month into his role, he resigned under the pressures of the Libor investigations related to the manipulation of inter-bank interest rates. Together with his CEO, Bob Diamond, these are just two of the many senior leaders in the banking industry that have had to step off the career ladder. In many cases this resulted from alleged and/or proven fraud. None of these initially highly respected leaders would ever have expected to end their careers in such a way. This also happens to other senior executives for reasons other than fraud; general company underperformance is one of them. Examples here include some senior managers at Nokia, like Colin Giles, Nokia's Senior Vice President of Sales, who was only appointed a member of the Leadership team a year before leaving. In 2010, Yong Nam, the CEO of LG, resigned because of the poor performance of LG in the mobile phone universe. In the meantime, LG has been overtaken by Apple as the third largest mobile phone manufacturer; with Nokia still at premier position; Samsung being the number two. In a 2006 shock announcement, Volkswagen informed the world that its VW brand CEO, Bernd Pischetsrieder, would step down. His career was ended suddenly, due to a disagreement with both the unions and his boss on restructuring the business. Didier Lombard stepped down in 2010 as CEO of France Telecom amid criticism over his alleged role in a wave of staff suicides. Missing the forecasted revenue targets, Brian Dunn, CEO of the electronics retailer Best Buy, was pushed to resignation in 2012. Yahoo!'s CEO, Scott Thompson, who had padded his resumé with an embellished college degree, was also "kindly asked" to leave. It's widely known that this issue was instigated by one of the key shareholders. A massive oil spill in the Gulf of Mexico brought an unplanned end to the career of Tony Hayward, former Chief Executive of BP, mid 2010. Early in 2012, Bill Weldon stepped down as CEO of Johnson&Johnson amidst a series of product recalls and FDA investigations. Bill Weldon had been successfully climbing the career ladder in J&J since 1971.

Heavy is the head that wears the crown. Overnight, massive career respect and praise can turn into a slaughtering nightmare.

And many are the examples of similar stories of less senior managers; although most of these "junior" career ending stories don't hit the press. Nevertheless, being more junior doesn't make the event less painful for the person affected.

There has also been a relatively new trend where senior leaders pro-actively undertake measures to cope with the challenges of business life or to definitively say farewell to the corporate pressures. More and more senior leaders don't shy away from revealing their real reason for initiating a major change in professional life; whether it is an inability to cope with the challenges or the inner desire for a life-changing journey.

Again, some examples.

The CEO of a San Francisco consulting firm is very open about her approach to working hours and particularly to her approach towards the invasive modern communication tools. Staff and customers know that she doesn't check emails after normal working hours. "When I'm on, I'm on, and when I'm off, I'm off" is her saying.

A highly respected and very successful trader on the London Stock Exchange made a fantastic career in "the City", but decided to end his years of commuting to London to stay home in his village, hoping –not even being guaranteed- to secure a job as a local teacher. What was guaranteed was that this job would not even pay one tenth of his previous earnings.

Or the remarkable story of the ex-CEO of one of the biggest car manufacturing plants in Belgium; remarkable for his candour and integrity in sharing his experiences with the world. He describes his experience of stepping back as "Waking up out of an emotional coma. Stepping down is not appreciated in today's world; it looks that only upwards steps are tolerated. Whatever the future may bring, I will certainly spend more time with my family. I won't make that mistake once again."

I also like to refer here to part of the speech of Anna Quindlen, the American author who won the Pulitzer Prize for Commentary in 1992. In her speech to the graduating class of a Pennsylvania university, she shared the following advice.

"You will walk out of here this afternoon with only one thing that no one else has. There will be hundreds of people out there with your same degree; there will be thousands of people doing what you want to do for a living. But you will be the only person alive who has sole custody of your life. Your particular life. Your entire life. Not just your life at a desk or your life on a bus, or in a car, or at the computer. Not just the life of your mind, but the life of your heart. Not just your bank account but your soul. Get a life. A real life, not a manic pursuit of the next promotion, the bigger paycheck, the larger house."

I would like to leave you and your reflections with a final quote from Lily Tomlin, American stand-up comedian, writer, actor and producer; probably most known from her appearance (together with Dolly Parton and Jane Fonda) in the movie "Nine to Five":

"The trouble with the rat race is that even if you win, you're still a rat."

~ ~ ~ ~ ~ ~ ~ ~ ~

CHAPTER 17

Twelve windows.

"You don't know a ladder has splinters until you slide down it." -Bum Phillips

I am again on my way to Paris.

It's early November, raining but very mild when I arrive in Brussels-South for the connection to the Thalys high-speed train at 11.13 am. As always I am far too early and so I go for a coffee and a croissant to the pub opposite the train station entrance on the Place Victor Horta.
The place – I don't recall the name of the bistro/pub – but it has an outside covered area and is full of Thalys staff who come here in groups, having a beer and a few cigarettes in between two train journeys.

The coffee is strong but the croissant is deliciously fresh.

At the round table next to me sits a man with small spectacles, a black leather jacket, black Boss trousers and light blue socks. On the floor next to him stands a black pilot case. I can't see the other side of his face but I assume he is wearing a Bluetooth earpiece and is on the phone to someone. He is talking French and relatively loud but most of what I hear him saying doesn't make any sense.
He turns his face to me; now I can see he doesn't have an earpiece in – so he is not connected to the world via his Blackberry on the table and so he's not on the phone talking to anyone.

He has a somewhat strange appearance. His leather jacket is not the most fashionable and it's partly decoloured while the left jacket sack is torn. His hair, surprisingly black for a man who I guess to be 55-ish, hasn't seen any shampoo or conditioner over the last days. On first sight though, he is however wearing a nice clean white shirt and a double nodded light blue tie. Like his socks. He has a remarkable large grey moustache; of the David Icke type, the renowned English author.

"Ces taxis roulent toute la journée et personne n'a jamais vérifié un reçu."

He then picks up his phone from the table, brings it to his right ear and is now quiet for a minute till he puts the phone back on the table and concentrates on observing the two middle-aged women who are joining the taxi queue. He sips from his glass of beer, takes the bottle of Chimay Bleue and pours the last drops into his glass.

Chimay Bleue is a dark Belgian Trappist beer; initially brewed as a Christmas beer. Its powerful aroma comes with a relatively dry taste with a caramel note.

"Aucune de ces gouttes de pluie n'atteindra jamais la mer, elles s'écrasent d'une façon monotone sur tous ces gens qui marchent dans la rue. Rien se termine vraiment là où il faudrait."

He turns again to me and says,

"Je vais à Paris."

I in fact thought he opened a conversation with me but he wasn't. He looked at me but wasn't talking to me; he was talking to God knows who. Or was he though talking to me?

"Grande acquisition, très stratégique. Ça va changer notre 'footprint' dans le monde. Les conséquences seront majeures pour le monde entier."

And then he turns his eyes to the sky and the clouds.

"Douze fenêtres."

I raise my eyebrows and order another coffee.

"Le train ne s'arrêtera pas avant Paris. Là, je prends le taxi pour le quinzième arrondissement."

Now that makes sense.

The Polish waitress brings me my second cup of coffee with the traditional one portion packed Belgian cinnamon-gingery cookie called 'speculoos'. The Americans call it a 'Dutch windmill cookie'. She doesn't look Polish at all, she is small, has short black hair and a very small wasp style waist. Her middle finger is ornamented with a very large square-shaped ring with a black stone – dark grey marbled. Her eyes have a very similar colour. She emigrated 10 years ago from Tarnowo, together with her parents and two younger brothers. She has now been working for more than five years in the bistro at Brussels South. She's very fluent in French and English, and Polish of course. Like so many in the Brussels horeca industry, she doesn't speak a word of Dutch.

I paid her the two Euros and 10 cents for the coffee. She then walks to the strange man next to me and puts her right hand softly on his left shoulder. I can't hear what she is saying but his response is clear. Well clear; at least it is loud.

"Ils ont dit çà cent fois; demain ils vont le répéter et rien ne va changer jusqu'au moment où quelqu'un va se plonger dans la comptabilité. Les mois de septembre, octobre et novembre…."

Silence follows. The waitress replies, "Yes, I know".

"….Et puis. Ils vont tous voir que c'est une erreur incontournable. Mais Monsieur Leclerq va continuer, comme si rien ne peut l'arrêter."

Apart from the raindrops that never reach the sea and the "twelve windows", you could at the end just assume that he is a bit worried about an upcoming acquisition which he's going to Paris for. He has serious concerns on the financials. Or do I just wrongly read that all in his words? And is he really 'gaga'?

Then the waitress turns back to me and I look her straight in her eyes. Without saying anything, she reads in my eyes that I am a bit troubled with this man.

She gives me the story.

Pascal lives in Marche-en-Famenne, an hour from Brussels. He has spent his entire career at Belgacom, the semi-privatised Belgian phone operator. He nicely grew his career step by step and made it up to senior team leader of the international accounts department. Only two hierarchical levels separated him from an executive board position. He had been working hard, very hard. Pascal was a real workaholic and was very demanding to get the most out of his team. He himself has worked most weekends and never took his full holiday entitlement. Sometimes during holidays he went abroad for some general management courses, leaving his wife and son at home or dropping them for a week in Ostend at the coast. He missed his son's graduation day; because of an urgent and very important business meeting.

While at Belgacom, he regularly visited the bistro for a quick lunch with some of his colleagues. Most of the time, he ordered a cheese-ham toastie, a lasagne or a panini and always two Chimay Bleue.

Two years ago, after a period of six months' sick-leave, he was advised to take a step back on the corporate ladder. This wasn't a 'remotion', a self-initiated decision to demote in order to regain energy for next steps in life. This was a 'take it or leave it'. He was succeeded by a guy with a Leuven university degree in economics and a master-after-master degree at a Madrid university. Pascal couldn't cope anymore with the workload and with the strategic changes and – according to his colleagues – he started making significant errors in his relationship management with key accounts and with superiors. In October last year, Pascal was terminated after close to 30 years of service.

Since then, he has come to the bistro almost every Thursday; still carrying his briefcase from when he was really in business. It is said that on Thursday afternoons he has a therapy session with his psychiatrist somewhere in Brussels. His old team and colleagues also still come from time to time to the bistro; but never on Thursdays.

"The poor man," the waitress says. "I pray for him every evening after he's here. The poor man."

She then walks back inside with my empty cup of coffee on her Hoegaarden-branded serving plate.

It's time for me to go back to the railway station to get the 11.13 am Thalys to Paris.
Once in Gare du Nord, at the end of the platforms, I will walk to the right and join the queue to grab a taxi to the 15th district. Funny, that's the same district Pascal was rambling about. I am on my way to discuss with our legal advisor and with the local management teams the integration of two businesses following last year's acquisition.

"Je te vois à Paris, Pascal," I say. "Bonne chance!"

No reply.

~ ~ ~ ~ ~ ~ ~ ~ ~

CHAPTER 18

Clifton bridge.

> *"When I was younger, I could remember anything, whether it had happened or not; but my faculties are decaying now and soon I shall be so I cannot remember any but the things that never happened. It is sad to go to pieces like this but we all have to do it."*
> -Mark Twain

It's Thursday late evening; to be precise, a quarter past midnight. Address: Marriott Bristol. That's the time and place of the crime scene.

There are still 15 emails that require my attention before tomorrow morning. From 8:30 am I'll be in a Risk Committee meeting all day till four when I'll be leaving for the airport. I still have to read the reports from the headhunter on the six interviewed candidates and reduce this to a shortlist of three. To not make tomorrow a complete waste of time, I should read the 16 pages of listed risks. I also need to reply to Deloitte on the tax issue in Australia. To the Finance Director, I committed to advise before the end of the week on the cross charging issue of the two Spanish expatriates in Germany.

My mobile rings, I see it's a call from the US. I refuse to take the call – they should call me at a decent time – and I continue to write on the Employee Development section for the corporate plan.

Two minutes later, I receive an email from the US operations. And at the same time a text message.

"Henry, please call me immediately. Ben Sterling was involved in a terrible accident on the Interstate and passed away on his way to the hospital."

Here comes the Bristol crime act. With a hard smash, I close my laptop. Without disconnecting it from the mains, I take the machine with my two hands off the desk and throw it wildly against the wall of the hotel room. It hits the unfortunate pastel painting of the Clifton Bridge and the broken glass rips parts of the greenish wallpaper. I turn around, walk to the window, experience that I can't open it, and for a few minutes long, I am swearing and shouting as hard as I can. In the building opposite the hotel, I count 12 windows. I am turning mad. I get out of breath and throw myself on the bed.

Henry W Derrick crashed.

He, the untouchable, the unconquerable, he the one who can cope with everything, he who adores the Rolling Stones' song *I have the whole world, in my hands,* he who is more flexible than pizza dough. He, who has now reached his limits.

Because of my shouting, it is not a surprise that a few minutes later the Night Shift Manager knocks on my door. Luckily we know each other a bit and so he doesn't kick me out of the hotel. I convince him that I am OK; whatever 'OK' means. But I need something to calm down and so I ask him to bring me a few gin and tonics. He refuses; coffee, water or coke I can get but no alcohol.

Ten minutes later, I am in a night shop buying a small bottle of gin and a large bottle of tonic. And a Cadbury's chocolate bar with nuts.
Back in my room, I am somewhat calming down. I haven't touched the Gordon's yet, but the walk in the cold and fresh air has done me good in cooling down.

I feel sorry but there isn't any blood in my veins, any chemical stimulus in my brain that can make me do the call to the US. I also neglect the outstanding emails and the corporate plan. Anyway, most likely also my hard disk has crashed. That's two crashes then for the cost of one.

The first G&T is consumed ad vundum and I pour myself a new glass immediately, take a seat on the bed and finish it in two gulps. I grab my mobile to set the alarm for tomorrow morning and notice that this morning the alarm was set for 4.45 am. I remember I started working this morning in my hotel room at 5 am.
And then, then I decide not to set an alarm at all. Strange, scrolling on the mobile to 'alarm off' gives me a good feeling; a feeling of freedom. I have another last gin and tonic and go to bed.

It's seven in the morning when I wake up. The mirror tells me everything; I look terrible. And so does the Dell computer and the Clifton Bridge on the floor. The bridge now looks more like 'The Scream' from Edvard Munch. While I walk to the bathroom, I make a wise decision and decide not to go into the regular early morning overdrive. This morning, I'll take it easy; I'll take my time and start with a very relaxing hot bath.

In the corner bath, my thoughts do not solely go to what happened to me last night but obviously also to what happened to Ben Sterling. Ben is one of our most talented UK Finance Managers. His parents are running a small but successful wholesaler operation and Ben was engaged in that business from the early days. I forced the US operations to consider Ben for the vacancy of Financial Controller; I had to push hard on them but I was convinced that Ben was a very suitable internal candidate. Last Monday, I think he flew in on Sunday, starting his new job. Yesterday, he had scheduled meetings with real estate agents for renting a house. Ben and I had long discussions on this subject as he insisted on having a five-bedroom house so that there was a spare study and a room for when his parents would come to visit him. Unfortunately, that was not within our policy. At the end of the school year, his two sons and his wife – who was not really supportive of his new job – would join him in New Jersey.
I reckon that they will now never ever go to New Jersey.

I get out of bath and while I brush my teeth, I prepare another bathing session with fresh but hot water. I think I must have fallen asleep as when I get out of bath – for the second time this morning – it's close to nine am. The Risk Committee meeting must have started already and I don't feel sorry for not being there. I however feel an obligation to call my PA and I need to ask her to book me on an earlier flight home today; I know there is one around midday.
Before I even can call her, my mobile tells me that I have eleven missed calls. Three are from the US General Manager, one from my boss, one from the Group HR Director, one from the company Medical Director, one from Deloitte – that's probably on the Oz tax issue, one from my PA Nathalie and three unknown numbers. I also have seven new text messages. Just the volume of all these notifications and a few automated meeting and task reminders, make me feel sick. I make one call. I very quickly tell Nathalie that I am not feeling well, will not come

to the office today, ask her to rebook the flight and instruct her to tell everybody that I am not available today. Then, I go back to bed; I am not even in the mood for breakfast. I am not hungry but also I have a desire to not see or hear anybody at the moment.

"Leave me alone!" I am ready to shout but luckily I can hold that impulse.

On the plane back home, I mentally walk again through the happenings of the last 12 hours. I am of course not yet at a stage to think about solutions, not even about root causes; it's only listing happenings and events.

Back at home, my wife is very happy to see me so early on a Friday afternoon. Now she has time to tell me that the washing machine has broken down, that we need to go to the vets with the oldest cat, that the tax authorities want to see me on my last year's tax declaration and that tomorrow night my parents-in-law will come for dinner. For the second time that day, I need to hold the desire to shout:

"Leave me alone!"

After I told her what had happened last night, she forced me to go to see the local doctor. To my surprise, he spent almost a full hour of his time with me and apart from prescribing some drugs, he gave me some good initial advice. He insisted that I visit him again in a week's time.
Most of the weekend I stayed in bed; but on Saturday and Sunday afternoon, Sonja and I went for a walk in the woods. We hadn't done that for years in Belgium; it was really refreshing but at the same time made me feel desire for our holiday house in France.

Two years ago, we bought a fantastic old 18th century watermill in the south of France; a good hour's drive north of Montpellier. It's in a nice, tranquil small but steep valley, surrounded by pine woods. While the house has all the comfort and didn't need any refurbishments, it has no TV, no landline, no internet and the Blackberry doesn't pick up any signal. The closest neighbours are at a 10 minutes' drive; our only contact with the outside world is a small portable radio. The only living beings close to us are the birds, the squirrels and the small trout in the mountain river longing our plot. We bought the place for its quietness, tranquillity and peaceful location. A kind of 'away from the busy world'. Perhaps an early signal of 'leave me alone'?

Buying the house indicates that even two years ago there was something gnawing inside me and if I had better understood that signal from my body, we perhaps could have taken action much earlier. But rat-racer Henry didn't pick up the signal; why should he? I was so successful, CCG had grown enormously and I had grown together with the company – unlike many of my colleagues from the early days who had been made redundant as a result of so many acquisitions. I was the survivor and many senior and junior managers relied on me to continue the company's success story. I was in my late forties and in a position no-one could ever have predicted. Not even Miss Ingrid – who had rated my leek painting so highly – not Mr. Schelkens, not even Professor Van Calster.

Now comes the key question for Henry.

And for you?

Why didn't I pick up the many signals over the last years? Although I was very solid in my job and kept receiving the recognition every human being needs, in hindsight, a lot of my motivation, my eagerness and engagement had disappeared slowly over the last years. Very annoying is my physical inability to keep working 15 or 16 hours a day. I can't anymore. Certainly over the last months, I have experienced that returning back to my hotel room around 8 pm only leaves me for that day with the appetite for a quick bite and then as soon as possible to bed. Contrary to the past, I decline most dinner invitations. Working till midnight had become a thing only for once or maximum twice a week; I couldn't do it anymore all week long. Preparing for the week ahead of me on a Sunday afternoon had turned from common practice into an exception; it even happened from time to time that my body forced me to lay down after lunch and have a two hours Sunday nap. What a red flashlight!

And during the week, Albert likes me to join him on his in-market business reviews. Two weeks ago, we did within one week, Dubai, Israel and Casablanca; the week after next is planned for Cambodia, Laos and Vietnam; that'll be without me this time.

But even more worrying for me were the mental signs. In all the project groups where I'd had a seat – many times the lead – I felt my input was getting more and more limited. So was the drive to make the project a success, to show off with the work we had done. On many occasions, many projects just became a 'tick in the box' exercise. I had blamed many managers in the past for this behaviour; it unfortunately is a bit typical for large organisations, and now I seemed to be doing exactly the same. I had the feeling that so many initiatives were just set up for the external world, for window-dressing. I am still today convinced that this is the case, but it annoyed me massively, more than ever. As a young rat-racer, I played the game, as I saw the corporate and personal benefits for doing so. I knew the board liked that stuff, but today I can't find the drive to keep playing these stupid games. Let's be honest, does the shareholder give a shit about us reducing our CO_2 emissions, about buying forests in Brazil to compensate for it? About enforcing child labour policies on the subcontractors of our subcontractors? About winning – or buying – the trophy of best employer in Mali? About our business ethics policy? About whatever? Shareholders are interested in the share price and dividends; that's it. All this corporate social responsibility stuff is only invented to ensure the executive members of the audit committee have a job. Or do you think investors have that high business ethics themselves? So why do all those pension funds then invest for instance in the energy sector, including nuclear energy. Or even in the profitable weapon industry? Or in banking? Is there any business today more corrupt than the financial industry?

That is unless the world is now really ready for what Richard Branson calls 'philanthrocapitalism'. In his exciting book *Screw Business as Usual*, he pleads strongly for leaders of businesses – small or large – to do the right things for this planet. He doesn't mean just from an ecological aspect but also social in terms of fighting poverty, homelessness, fighting shortage of natural resources, fighting the economical negative spiral that has been created by the businesses themselves. Branson intensely advocates businesses that are doing 'good' for the community of the village called 'the planet', will also do 'good business'. Sounds logical to me. But is the world ready for it?

Sorry, I digress again. Typical, I can't keep my mind focussed on key topics. I have the feeling there is so much to do, so many issues are unsolved. I think I just can't cope with the workload and am unable for the first time in my career to find an efficient solution to it.

On top of that also comes the massive change programme at CCG; every Director and Senior Manager is working extremely hard on defining the new strategy. Since Gary Mavis retired, nothing from the past should be maintained; it all needs to be changed. Now that Graham Hill has also retired, his successor Albert – the new kid on the block – of course likes to take the lead on that change programme. And no surprise, I find it very hard to support all those change initiatives. Irrespective of that and as said before, I do massively admire and envy the energy level of Albert and of many other colleagues. I have the feeling that many of them are at the steering wheel of their Ferrari while I am close to a standstill on my bike. And only now I notice that I have flat tubes and an un-oiled chain. My mental and physical battery is empty. At the horizon, I see the Ferraris taking a new direction; I am losing them and I come to the conclusion:

"I will not make another step on the career ladder."

Did you hear that? Did you hear me saying, "I will not make another step on the career ladder." That's me saying that – me, Henry, the gold member of the rat-race club!
At this stage it's a bit unclear if this is just an observation or a personal decision. I think it is both.

So it's the disagreement with the new strategy and vision, the volume and pace of change and the increasing volume of work in general. But in fairness, on many occasions, I was advised to get some additional resources; every time I declined the offer. "Me, Henry, I can cope with it. No problem."

And then, there were the numerous human disasters – like Ben Sterling's sudden death, that had an unexpectedly serious impact on my morale and on the way I was looking upon the work-life balance. It's the chicken and the egg story, isn't it? Was I more apt and emotionally more open than ever before, or did these happenings change my emotional willingness to reflect on real important things in life?

Alex Janssens, our Belgian General Manager for Italy had just turned 50 when, at Leuven hospital, he got the tragic news; it's cancer. Despite the hard message, it was amazing how Alex coped with that; one week later he was back in the Rome office. Short weeks though, as the Mondays and Fridays were reserved for chemotherapy in Belgium. Two months later, the verdict was fatal; the cancer had reached the liver. Alex passed away in June 2010.

I rarely spoke to my neighbour Ludo. He is working weekend shifts at the Belgian railways, so we only very occasionally met each other. Ludo's sons are professional athletes and when he can, he joins them on training camps and competitions. In August 2010, he was cycling alongside his sons who were training on the Greek island Kos in preparation for a triathlon somewhere in the US. Behind the backs of his sons, a car hit and killed Ludo.

In Ivory Coast, Jean-Baptiste, one of our sales reps, got killed during the civil war. This happened at the company premises, despite the clear instruction of our General Manager Paul that no-one should come to work. But Jean-Baptiste was so proud of his job and the company that he wanted to safeguard the company's products in the warehouse. On his own, he wanted to combat an army of rebels; a fight he lost with his life.

Karim, one of our District Managers in Cairo – who happens to be the one who drove me through town during my last visit, got shot at one of the demonstrations during the Arabic Spring. He survived but lost both legs and will never work again.

In October 2010, a very capable and promising young manager – aged 36 – informed me that he would be absent from work for private medical reasons sometime in the next two months. He is shortlisted for a bone marrow transplant and as soon as a donor is identified, he'll have to rush to hospital. It took almost four months to find a suitable donor; he was so excited as it was an excellent match. However, something went lethally wrong; he died in February 2011.

And yesterday, my best and most loyal friend, the oldest cat, was diagnosed with a severe lung infection and with a fatal injection, he departed this life on earth.

Of course, I also lost some good friends and colleagues at the early stage of my career; only at that time – however sad the news was – my reaction would have been, "These things happen; let's move on."
Now, that's absolutely different today. Nowadays, moving on, however small the hurdle is, has become a big challenge.

The doctor also prescribed two weeks' absolute rest; I accepted this sound advice. For the first time in my career, I'll be two weeks off sick. So what?

~ ~ ~ ~ ~ ~ ~ ~ ~

THE FACTS 4

Brain elasticity

In 1960, Europe counted three young people for every elderly person – young being defined as under 15 and elderly as being aged 65 or over. In contrast, the current Eurostat prediction is that in 2060, there will be more than two elderly people for every youngster.

In the US, using the same definitions, researchers predict that the numbers of elderly people will more than double over the first 50 years of the 21st Century,. Same story in Australia, where the Australian

Bureau of Statistics calculated that the number of people aged between 65and 84 would grow from 2.4 million to 6.4 million between 2007 and 2056

The United Nations accurately predicted that the world population would reach seven billion by late 2011. They have further predicted that it will increase to over nine billion by 2050 and will exceed ten billion by 2100. "Furthermore, the implications of population ageing cannot be dismissed. In the more developed regions, the population aged 60 or over is increasing at the fastest pace ever (growing at 2.4 per cent annually before 2050 and 0.7 per cent annually from 2050 to 2100) and is expected to increase by more than 50 per cent over the next four decades, rising from 274 million in 2011 to 418 million in 2050 and to 433 million in 2100. Compared with the more developed world, the population of the less developed regions is ageing rapidly. Over the next three decades, the population aged 60 or over in the developing world is projected to increase at rates far surpassing 3 per cent per year and its numbers are expected to rise from 510 million in 2011 to 1.6 billion in 2050 and to 2.4 billion in 2100."

"Globally, the number of persons aged 60 or over is expected to more than triple by 2100, increasing from 784 million in 2011 to 2 billion in 2050 and 2.8 billion in 2100."(9)

Despite the immense impact that these changes in our population make up will have on all our daily lives in the very near future, the figures do not seem to surprise us anymore. The issue is frequently featured in the press and on television

Obviously related to all of this are the dependency ratio figures expressing the number of "active" people over the "non-active" people;

the latter generally defined as the age-groups below 15 and over 64. These figures show such an alarming trend so that politicians all over the world need to get into action and decide on measures no-one of their voters are waiting for. Sarkozy overcame the "invincible" French unions and moved the age for receipt of state pension from 60 to 62. His successor Hollande, only elected through the 'blank votes' from the extreme right, is already planning a partial reversal of that decision. He'll be lonely in Europe. Poland moves to 67 by 2040, which may prove to be late compared to the rest of Europe. The Dutch move to 67 by 2025 and the Germans will also move gradually to the same age by 2029. Similarly, the UK moves to 67 by 2028. However, in early 2012, the Coalition Government confirmed it was planning to link the pensionable age to life expectancy figures; thus making it likely that the UK will move towards 70. Ireland goes to 68 by 2028 and Italy by 2050; to be more accurate, Italians will get a state pension at the age of 68 and 4 months. Belgium is currently sticking to the age of 65 but has begun to reduce the widespread opportunities for early retirement.

While all these moves are prompted by the enormous public deficits, they are of course also influenced by the ongoing increase in life expectancy and by the coincidental effects of the 1950-1960s baby boom.

On top of that, we are in an era of declining fertility. The CIA factsheet (2012 estimates) refers to a general fertility rate of below 2 births per woman in all European countries (apart from France at 2.08 and Ireland 2.01). In most African countries this figure is above 4.00; with Niger heading the ranking with a staggering 7.52 births per woman. However with very high infant mortality figures.

A variety of organisations are having to consider the effects of the "greying globe" beyond the areas of pensions and retirement
New studies and initiatives are taking place in many areas: effects on social security, –other than pension, effects on healthcare provision and cost, transportation, housing, workforce and labour planning, changing consumer profiles, and so on. And on education: how many trained geriatric nurses will be needed in ten or twenty years' time? Regarding ageing consumers, back in 1983, the United Nations had recommended that governments implemented some form of protection for elderly consumers, that governments:

"Restrain the intensive promotion and other marketing techniques primarily aimed at exploiting the meagre resources of the elderly." (12)

With the statutory pension age moving gradually towards 70, let's look deeper at the issue of the ageing workforce. US business leaders call it the "Silver Tsunami". Below is a brief overview of some interesting initiatives, plus research and examples that encourage reflection upon how serious is this issue.

In 2011, Flemish people elected the word "stoeproken" as the most popular word of the year. "Stoeproken" is best translated as "sidewalk smoking" and its popularity is very logical given the introduction of the smoking ban in Belgian pubs and bars in 2011. (In the UK, the phenomenon itself had years before also given birth to another fantastic new word: "smirting", as a combination of smoking and flirting outside on the pavement). In the same Flemish survey, the most popular word in the category of business/economics was the word "citroenloopbaan". Literally translated, this means "lemon career". It refers to the bitter and sour feelings the –typically Generation X– employees have about their careers. Many feel squeezed like a lemon might be; but the word also refers to the shape of the fruit itself. At the beginning of their career, there are very few opportunities to secure a job; even for highly educated graduates. Then follows a stage of very hard graft, a feeling of high "squeezing" pressure to earn as much as possible before they end up in unemployment or in (very) early retirement between the ages of 45-55-. They only have 20 to 35 years to make a living and to prepare for the remaining, say, 35 years during which they will need to rely on their savings and some minor state pension support.

Switching continents, an early 2012 study by PwC Canada suggests that this famous Generation X (people born between 1961 and 1981) is being "squeezed at both ends" by younger workers who are aggressively trying to move up the ranks at work and by the "Boomers" who are staying in senior roles longer due to delayed retirement.

The European Working Conditions Survey has monitored the extent to which people believe they would be able to do the same job by the age of 60.

"On average, well over a half (59%) of European workers responded positively to the question. Positive answers increase with age (73% of men and 70% of women aged over 50). A quarter of workers in Europe think they would not be able to do the same job when they are 60 years old and less than a fifth (16%) of all workers report they would not want to. There are important differences between countries. Over 70% of workers in Germany and the Netherlands feel they would be able to do their job at 60 compared with 26% of workers in Slovenia. The percentage of workers believing they would be able to do their job at the age of 60 corresponds closely with the actual percentage of older workers in their country's workforce. Out of the 10 Member States with the lowest percentage of workers expecting to be able to do their job at age 60, seven are also in the bottom 10 in terms of the proportion of workers aged 50 and older in the workforce. The percentage of workers believing they would be able to do their job at age 60 is also close to the actual percentage of older workers in their country's workforce." (13)

Digging deeper into the EWCS figures, we see significant differences when asking self-employed men (70% responding they can do the same job at age 60) and male employees (57%).

The EWCS, sponsored by the European Foundation for the Improvement of Living and Working Conditions, makes the following conclusions:

"Autonomy plays a protective role and work intensity a deterrent role. Workers in low strain and active jobs report higher levels of sustainability than others. Work–life balance is important and positively associated with sustainability of jobs. Working time duration seems to have a limited impact; levels of reported job sustainability remain the same in the case of long working hours. Being able to take some time off as well as having some autonomy in relation to taking breaks, etc. are positive resources. Experience of discrimination, violence, abuse, bullying or harassment are associated with lesser levels of job sustainability. Less physically demanding working conditions are associated with higher prevalence of job sustainability. Social support from colleagues and managers plays the expected role. High support is associated with a higher proportion of positive answers to this question. Job insecurity is associated with lower levels of job sustainability. Not having monotonous tasks is assessed positively in terms of job sustainability as well as cognitive dimensions of work. The highest levels of workplace innovation are associated with higher reporting of job sustainability. Intrinsic rewards are associated with higher levels of job sustainability." (14)

In general, I regard it as a positive trend that individuals are prepared to or even want to work until later in life. However, this will no doubt be heavily influenced by the economic climate, so that in reality, there is a fine line between people being "willing to" and "having to" work until they are older.

It's also good to see that on the employers' side, positive trends are evolving. These trends show that the business environment recognises the challenges for "older" employees. Irrespective of the success of these initiatives, their existence and endeavours are already contributing to the "well-being" of many people.

A good example is the Australian job search website "www.olderworkers.com.au" that only offers job opportunities with age-friendly employers and focuses on applicants aged 45 plus. A similar one is "www.adage.com.au"; also in Australia.

In Germany, the production line at the BMW's Dingolfing plant has been converted into a dedicated plant for workers aged 50 plus. The plant has been converted with massive attention to ergonomics and has been designed by automotive engineers with the help of doctors specialised in treating older workers. Even the production line itself has been slowed down to around one third of the normal pace, to account for the workforce's general slowing down in later life. The place is now nicknamed "Altstadt", the German word for Old Town. BMW's efforts to keep experienced and skilled workers in work, rather than lose them to early retirement, should not surprise us as BMW estimates that by 2020, 45 percent of their workers will be aged 50 and over. A.T Kearney Consulting awarded the plant the "Zukunftspreis" in the renowned competition for "Factory of the Year".

Similar age related initiatives have been taken by other major companies like Siemens, France3, Renault, Eli Lilly, Procter&Gamble, Asda, IKEA and Tesco, as well as many other small and medium sized companies in the profit and non-profit making sectors.

One of the Tesco's initiatives is, according to some, reaching a level of absurdity; even if it perfectly underlines the differences between youngsters and older shop workers. In 2007, the retailer developed a guide for older workers to enable them to understand the teenage slang used by their younger colleagues. That's a slammin' idea.

A general acceptance of the ageing workforce is also confirmed in a study by the French Ministry of Employment. Whereas in 2001, French employers considered workers to be "old" at age 55, by the time of the 2010 study, this age had increased to 58.5.

"The number of employers who are concerned about the negative consequences of an increase in the average age of their workforce has fallen in recent years. In 2001, a third of employers (33%) felt such an increase would have negative effects on labour productivity whereas less than 15% felt the same way in 2008. In addition, only 39% of employers in 2008 associated the ageing of their workforce with an increase in labour costs compared with 47% nine years earlier." (15) (*free translation*)

In conclusion, with the state pension age moving towards 70, but with a confirmed willingness by employees to work longer and with industry implementing measures to support the ageing workforce, it all seems to come nicely together. Flexible legislators, flexible employers and more adaptive workers –forget the unions in this context- have found mutual interest.

And what about our ageing brain? Its flexibility? And our general coping elasticity?

Here comes the worrying part; I'll refer to two recent studies.

The first one is a 2009 project from the University of Virginia Cognitive Aging Laboratory, published in the March 2009 issue of the journal *Neurobiology of Aging*. Over a seven-year period, 2,000 healthy participants, aged between 18 and 60, were tested on their cognitive capabilities. The overall conclusion can be seen as frightening and depressing. Top performances in some of the tests were accomplished at the age of 22. A notable decline in certain measures of abstract reasoning, brain speed and in puzzle-solving became apparent at 27. The researchers found that average memory declines can be detected by about age 37. On a slightly more positive note, improvement of vocabulary and general knowledge actually seem to increase at least until the age of 60. While the research with the same participants is planned to continue much longer so as to confirm trends, Timothy Salthouse, the study's lead investigator, states:

"These patterns suggest that some types of mental flexibility decrease relatively early in adulthood, but that how much knowledge one has, and the effectiveness of integrating it with one's abilities, may increase throughout all of adulthood if there are no pathological diseases." (16)

An even more recent study was published in the January 2012 edition of the BMJ (formerly the British Medical Journal). Around 7,000 London-based civil servants were assessed from the mid-1980s onwards. Researchers from France and England concluded that cognitive skills, such as memory and reasoning, are already typically declining among people as early as the age of 45. According to the authors:

"The age at which cognitive decline begins is important because behavioral or pharmacological interventions designed to alter cognitive aging trajectories are more likely to work if they are applied when individuals first begin to experience decline." (17)

With the above in mind, it is a small step towards looking deeper into Alzheimer's figures. Alzheimer's is a progressive neurological disease

of the brain leading to the irreversible loss of neurons and the loss of intellectual abilities, including memory and reasoning, which becomes severe enough to impede social or occupational functioning.
The American Alzheimer's Association estimates that 5.3 million Americans have the disease.

"The Alzheimer's Association estimates that there are 500,000 Americans younger than 65 with Alzheimer's and other dementias. Of these, approximately 40 percent are estimated to have Alzheimer's." (18)

In the European Union, there are around five million people with dementia, of whom 60 to 70 percent have Alzheimer's. Scientists fear that these numbers will double in the next twenty- five years if the disease cannot be successfully treated or prevented. According to the UK Department of Health, the current number of 670,000 people with dementia is expected to double in the coming 30 years. Globally, it is estimated that in forty years' time, there will be over 100 million people with dementia. With an expected global total population of 9 billion by that time, that would be over 1%. As the disease is strongly age related, and with people expected to work much longer than today, it can be assumed that employers will be facing circa 5% of their elderly workers suffering from a form of dementia.

In the Encyclopaedia of Mental Disorders, Rebecca J. Frey, Ph.D., writes:

"Health care professionals use the term "insidious" to describe Alzheimer's, which means that it is very gradual in onset. Many times people recognize the first symptoms of the disorder in a friend or family member only in hindsight. In addition, the present generation of people old enough to be at risk for Alzheimer's is the first generation in history to know what the diagnosis means; there are therefore very powerful emotional reasons for attributing the early signs of AD to normal aging, job stress, adjusting to retirement, and other less troubling factors." (19)

In conclusion, despite economic needs and despite governments' and employers' efforts, the following decades will show how well the human body (which to some extent can be supported through ergonomic initiatives), and moreover the human brain will cope with the continued occupational requirements. Science indicates that the cognitive capability decline kicks in much earlier than the average statutory pension age.

Scientific research on the mental stage of the ageing population in general will be a hot topic in the coming decades. This is indicated by the 2012 "Award for Medical Research" by the Metlife Foundation; handed to the Antwerp University Professor Christine Van Broeckhoven for her ongoing research on detecting the early symptoms of Alzheimer's. In the UK, the Prime Minister launched an initiative in March 2012 which aims to deliver major improvements to dementia care and research. The year before, the White House launched a $156 million programme dedicated solely to combating Alzheimer's disease.

Employers and employees will need to find an answer as to how to bridge the gap between the early stages of cognitive decline to the date of retirement. I predict that in this and the coming decades, the management of an ageing workforce will become a key task for managers and leaders; so critical that it will hit many Boardroom tables. Certainly, it will become a key topic in human resources policies and procedures.

CHAPTER 19

Into solution mode.

"Being the richest man in the cemetery doesn't matter to me. Going to bed at night saying we've done something wonderful, that's what matters to me."-
<u>Steve Jobs</u>

On my way back from the doctor, I listen to some music in my car; it's one of my favourite songs: *Objects in the rear view mirror may appear closer than they are*. I have always been a fan of Meatloaf's music – mainly for the bombastic piano performances. It approaches the 'goose bumps' feeling that I also get from listening to *Also sprach Zarathustra*. Agreed, it's a slightly different style.

Today, I get dragged by the lyrics of the song and specifically by that one sentence; this is so basic and so straightforward.

"And if life is just a highway, then the soul is just a car."

I replay it many times and forget to stop at the butcher shop. At the next crossroads, I make a U-turn and drive back to the shop. What was it that I was asked to bring home; was it pork or lamp chops? And something else too; but what?

While I am queuing in the shop and at the same time torturing my memory to remind me what I had to buy, I get a call from one of the lawyers at E&O. I decide not to take the call. Only 20 seconds later, a call from Jo-Anne in Hamburg. I know what this will be about so I'll take the call; there are anyway still four customers to be served before it's my turn. And I know she'll just be asking my OK on the salary proposal for the new Marketing Manager for Bratislava. I also know she will have done in-depth research on the appropriate reward positioning – so I am pretty sure that I'll agree with whatever figure she will propose.

So I pick-up the phone but don't give her the opportunity to say a word.

"On your question Jo-Anne, I agree with the figures. But I also have a question for you. Is it pork chops or lamb chops?"
"It's pork," she replies.
"Super, thanks. Speak to you soon."

While I am about to push the red button of my Blackberry, I hear her adding, "And don't forget the red onions."

That is exactly what it was; Sonja had asked me to also buy some red onions. How did Jo-Anne know this? Is it that secret art of telepathy that only women master?
It's now my turn to be served at the butcher shop and the first thing I ask for are six red onions.

"That we don't have, Sir; you'll find that in the grocery shop next door."

Back in my car and before starting the engine, I go into reflection mode.

"So the medical doctor called it a burn-out," I say to myself.

It's March 25th, 2011. I reflect. Although I am still sitting in my car, my mind brings me to the fifth floor of our Head Office. I am walking through the long, dark and chilly corridor towards the Executive meeting rooms; at the very end of which is the boardroom. Thick greenish carpet, left and right soundproofed doors with stained glass. On the wall are large pictures of all the previous members of the Executive Committee and of the Board. All pictures have a wide cherry wooden frame with gold decorated ornaments. This is CCG's hall of fame.

I reflect.

I don't want to end up in this hall of fame. No way! Nor do I want to end up like the young deer in the butcher shop. Hanging against the wall with my neck nailed or screwed in a dark oak board. (You may now finally have an answer as to the idiosyncratic picture on the back cover.)

I reflect. I decide.

I decide to resign.

~ ~ ~ ~ ~ ~ ~ ~ ~

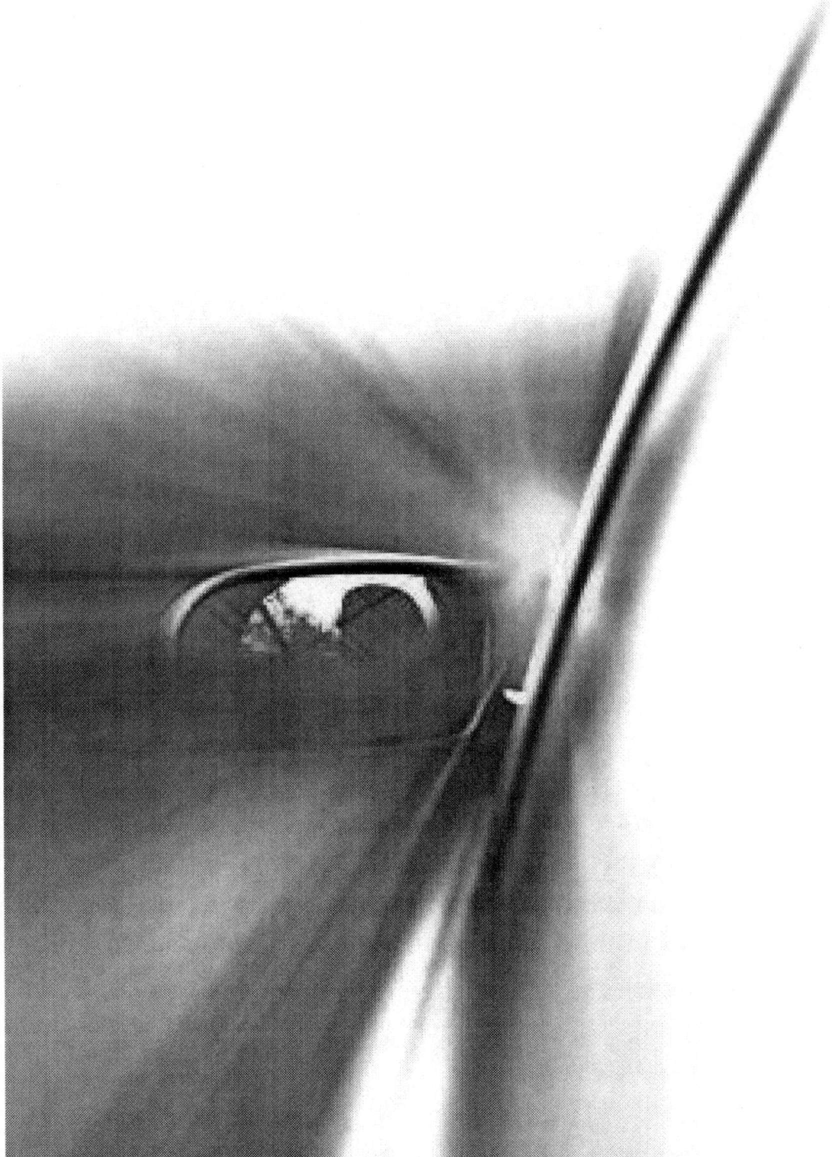

CHAPTER 20

The fat lady doesn't sing.

"If a train station is where the train stops, then what's a workstation?" -<u>Unknown</u>

The 'new' CCG management has maintained one practice from the 'old' one; they never accept a resignation. Once you have joined the CCG family, you never leave before retirement age; you never divorce the family. Of course the company cannot neglect the binding laws that allow any employee to resign – subject to contractual or legal notice. But the company can indeed at any time try to convince you not to leave or make a counter offer.

This is the company's proposed deal. I work my notice till the end of September and I'll add an additional three months to that so that the leaving date would be end of December 2011. The rationale was that they really wanted my support to make the company's transition a success story and to ensure we achieve in these hectic times the operational results. I was also required to keep this resignation strictly confidential; it should only be known to the CEO, Albert and Kathy. In compensation for my accord, a small leaving gratuity would be prepared and proposed at a later stage.

Not really sure that he can cope with that, but rat-racer Henry accepts the offer to stay another nine months. It is agreed though that he'll do less long-haul travel.

The certainty that this hectic life will come to an end in December, boosted my energy level and I felt indeed driven to help the company with the reorganisation of the top level Sales structure. I also felt relieved and freed-up from the obligations that come with playing the corporate game. When I disagreed with a decision, I could now freely say, "I disagree" rather than the common "interesting".
Our new structure proposal was ready for implementation mid-April 2011 and we announced this globally on April 26th. In contradiction to the confidentiality, Albert found it necessary to also announce – now eight months ahead of the agreed leaving date – my departure. And so it happened. By that, I felt even more relieved; it was now known to the business that the future of CCG would be without Henry. But that however also came with some disadvantages. Although it was a good learning point, it quickly became clear to me that even a Senior Director can lose all his powers once it's known to the younger rat-racers that he won't have a big impact anymore on their climbing journey.
There was, for instance, young and eager Charlotte; she's not gold in the rat-race club, she's platinum; at least. I was shortlisting candidates for a senior General Manager job. Without a call or email to me or any contact with the recruiting Regional HR Manager, she approached

Albert directly. Albert was – rightly – not interested in her application but I called her on the same day of her direct approach to my boss. My message was that I wanted to see her the week after next to discuss her application. In the meantime, I expected her to draft a fully-fledged business plan for the market but without talking to anybody in the business. Her application for this 'very senior role' needed to be treated extremely confidentially.

When I received her business plan proposal, I went back to her – without reading any of the 30 PowerPoint slides – and asked her to dig a bit deeper into the profit pressures for the bottom segment brands and also to elaborate on the consumer needs for the age group below 25. I gave her a bit more time to do so as 'unfortunately' I had to cancel our initial meeting. A new appointment date was scheduled for two weeks later. I knew that on that date she had an industry meeting but sadly I couldn't do another day in that week. In the early morning of our meeting date, I cancelled the appointment with the message that I had secured another much better internal candidate.

In retrospect, that was not nice of me. I mishandled Charlotte for Henry's fight against the club that he praised so much over the last 20 years. Revenge is an ugly thing.

Late in June I schedule an appointment with Kathy, the Group HR Director, to hear if there is any more news on drafting an agreement on my leaving terms. As I had agreed to destroy my initial letter of resignation, we had nothing on paper at this moment; all was based on mutual trust. I accept that Kathy is also extremely busy and agree to meet again and to get clarity late August after both our holidays.

In that August meeting, she explains that the company isn't ready yet to commit to an exact leaving date. This story really starts to look like a Ring of Möbius; it's unclear where it started but even much more uncertain where it will end.

The week after, Kathy calls me while I am in a meeting with our advisors from E&O on an outstanding issue on the Middle East fraud. She informs me that she has resigned from the company to join British Airways; she will leave by the end of December.

Things are getting clearer now, the company just can't afford for the number one and the number two in HR to leave at the same time. She also tells me the following,

"We still agree and accept your resignation, as long as you do your six months' notice, starting from 1st September and as such leave at the end of February next year."

"You must be kidding!" is my impulsive reaction.

"It's good to hear you are with our legal advisors from E&O at the moment. Talk to Marc Rich, who is aware of my situation and of your request to leave the company," she replies.

"It's not a request, Kathy, it's a decision. And if you want to go the legal route via your lawyers, then I'll get my legal advisors to talk to them."

It ain't over till the fat lady sings. Even Bradley Wiggins said so, two days before his 2012 Tour de France victory.

In the weeks after, Kathy and I have frequent and sometimes intense discussions on the issue. But we highly respect each other and so we find a midway solution; I will indeed continue to work till end February. Everything will be put on paper once E&O have advised on the legalities and Deloitte on eventual tax issues on closing my employment file at CCG.

We are now early January. The first two lots of advice from Deloitte are outrageously wrong; E&O hasn't advised yet. Kathy has disappeared and there isn't a successor yet. While there still isn't anything on paper, Albert makes an attempt to keep me till end of June. That's where we come to an end of my patience. The same day that my legal advisors write to the company, they get a call in the evening from E&O saying that the company is preparing a settlement agreement. A draft version will be with us next week. Apart from some minor issues in the draft, we agree on the content. The week after (in the meantime it's now mid-February) I sign the agreement in the office of my legal advisors. The scanned agreement is sent to E&O on the same day of me signing; the original is sent by TNT. The company will sign once they receive the original version. On the same day, one hour after the signed agreement was sent by email, I am driving back home and I get a call from my advisors.

"You won't believe this, Henry, but E&O wants to make another change to their proposed agreement."

"But Thierry (my advisor), I have signed a final version; final is final, isn't it? I have signed the document as they proposed and produced. And what's the modification they still want to make?"

"That isn't clear yet. Marc Rich was not available but they'll send us a new final version after the weekend. Of course I don't need to tell you that the document is only final and binding once all parties have signed. So let's wait and see what they come up with," Thierry replies.

That final version didn't come on the Monday; we are now legally in limbo as we are, yes we are Thursday 1st of March 2012.
Although I had already said farewell to Nathalie – and all other close colleagues – I call Nathalie and ask her to book me a flight back to the office for Monday morning next week; I also inform Albert that things aren't progressing as it should and so I'll be back at work on Monday. His reply:

"That's excellent. You can help me massively as we have an issue in Paris office that needs sorting urgently. You are the only one who has the background knowledge to deal with this. Could you go to Paris on Monday?

Rather than replying, "F*** off," Henry goes into another strategy – honestly don't know why – and gratefully accepts the request. A bit of tourism on the company's expenses; why not? Most of the stress, the game playing and lots of the work volume are gone. And I am almost gone as my successor is in place. I still disagree on the strategy but I am not concerned anymore. So I call Nathalie again to cancel the flight to London and to get me instead on the Thalys to Paris. I'll do Monday and Tuesday in Paris, travel back slowly on Wednesday to Brussels and work from home on Thursday and Friday. What's the problem? And of course, in the meantime they keep paying me.

The issue in Paris is quickly solved and so I have indeed the time on Tuesday to visit the Notre Dame and the museum on the Quai D'Orsay. I reckon that over the last 10 years, I have probably been to Paris 60-70 times but never had time to visit the Cathedral. On Wednesday, opposite the Gard du Nord, I take the time to have a coffee on the terrace of La Maison Blanche. I have 25 minutes before the train to Brussels will depart. Knowing that the area is a bit of a dangerous place for pick-pockets, I put my travel bag on the chair next to me and push it firmly against my hip so that I can feel it while I am having my coffee and make a few calls. I call Mike and Nick on the outstanding bonus issue for the management in the UK; both are very surprised to get a call from me as they both thought I had left the business last week. Anyway, it must have been during the call with Mike that my bag got stolen without me noticing anything; really not anything. No-one had seen anything; the only thing the waiter remembers is that an African man was taking a seat on the terrace, three seats away from me and when the waiter returned, the man was gone; without ordering any drinks. Another client on the terrace had indeed seen someone running away – with a black leather bag, but that guest didn't make the link with a theft. I had lost everything except for my mobile and my wallet.

On the train back home, I get a call from Jan, our Business Development Director. He needs my advice on an issue in Turkey. In principle we could easily sort out the issue over the phone but I agree with Jan to come and visit him next week Monday in his new office.....in Paris. So Tuesday I can do the Louvre. And Monday morning I'll do the antique fair on Porte Clignancourt. Thursday and Friday we can then again work from home. On that Friday, I get a courtesy call from one of my colleagues in Hamburg; he's just asking how I am feeling now that I have left CCG. Richard tells me that they are still struggling on the inter-company cross-charging for the Spanish expats in Germany. As I am still in service, I agree to get involved again and to sort this now for once and for all. I suggest I'll come over to Hamburg for this; I always like to go to Hamburg. It's a nice city and mostly very fine colleagues. So that's a journey for week after next, probably for Monday/Tuesday and the rest of the week 'work from home'.

It's amazing how comfortable and stress-free I feel in this completely new rhythm; I can be so laidback now. It even seems to be noticeable to others. Sofie, the Brussels airlines head stewardess on the flight to Hamburg – we have met a few times on this journey, tells me I am looking very relaxed. In fact she means "much better than the months before".

Yes, I very much like this new work pattern; I adore it. There are very few big business decisions to be taken, that's now for my successor. I am in fact only working half-time and as such absolutely overpaid for what I add to the business. And I can keep doing so while almost everywhere I go, I am offered a farewell dinner. Yes I think that I feel relaxed but in reality I am not. This is not the right way of leaving a company –that I have loved so much– and so I push my advisors to get the case sorted immediately.

On such a farewell dinner event in Serbia, I get a call from Thierry, my lawyer.

"Henry, it took them around six weeks to review the agreement but we have just now received the ultimate version; ready for you to sign. Apart from two corrected spelling errors, they haven't changed anything. Only the leaving date is now set at 30th April. I would assume you can agree with that?"

"Well, I suggest you go back to them and propose to make that leaving date the end of December 2012," I reply.

"What?" Thierry replies with a big, very big question mark in his intonation.

"I am joking, Thierry. Although I do like the new lifestyle offered by the company, it's now really time to begin a new life. I'll come to your office next Monday to sign."

Early May I got my final payslip in the mail at home. Five minutes later I was on the phone to payroll. They confirmed there was an error and a small overpayment. Yes you read this right, I complained on an overpayment. That's probably human ethics overtaking business ethics. According to payroll, it was a mistake in the social security calculations prepared by Deloitte.

"Begin a new life," I seem to have said to Thierry.

With all the emotions and commotions of the last year, I have not really focussed in detail on 'the new life'. Everybody is asking me about my plans for the future, and my standard answer is, "I have one big plan and that is not to make any plans for the coming 12 months."

Out of most reactions, I can read either a certain level of jealousy or a level of disappointment. A Senior Director at the 'young' age of 50 who resigns and has no alternative job; not even a plan for another job; that's considered to be an odd concept.

And that all in 2012; in the midst of the economic crisis. What a special year.

Peter Crouch got overlooked for the Euro 2012 despite his stunning volley against Manchester City earlier in the year. In the Eurozone, things are getting worse. Greece gets another €130billion while the Spanish banks need around 60bn Euro. In the Middle-East, things are calming down; apart from Syria where Kofi Annan resigns as peace envoy. In Oslo, Anders Breivik was sentenced to 21 years in prison while in New-York a pastel version of *'The Scream'* by Norwegian artist Edvard Munch was sold for US$ 120million; a new world record. Furthermore in the artistic world, the reunited Spice Girls took a black cab to drive to the Eurosong contest in Baku. Or was it to the Olympics closing extravaganza in London? Victoria managed a smile or two.
And what happened in the air? China's first manned spacecraft docked with their own space station. The crew included the first Chines female astronaut. A little bit further in the Universe, NASA drops the 6-wheel rover 'Curiosity' on Mars! Just before landing In Brussels, while you hear the automated voice in the cockpit saying "100-50-40-30…", Henry enjoys a glass of Cava to celebrate his last corporate flight. In the UK, a helicopter swoops over the London capital; James Bond opens the door and Queen Elisabeth II parachutes to the Olympic stadium.

"I can feel it coming in the air tonight, oh Lord. And I've been waiting for this moment for all my life, oh Lord. Can you feel it coming in the air tonight, oh Lord, oh Lord."

It's seen as even more outlandish when I share some of my initial thoughts for my future. These are: buy and run a small hotel, go into politics and aim for a seat at European Parliament, go back to the early days and be an underpaid tourist guide, or become a driving instructor. And assessed as even more extraordinary is getting initiated in wood-turning and wood-carving and produce religious artworks. I may also go and work in the local town's nature and environmental protection department; as a rat-catcher. Poor joke. Or just stop working, definitively. Another wild and absolutely undeveloped thought is to become an author and publish novels, or management books, or why not a combination of both. It's also not excluded that I could become one of the one million HR consultants that populate this globe.

I do know my wife's favourite out of the above list; she would just love me to stop working. I am not sure on that. I don't consider myself to be a man to do the washing and ironing on Monday, gardening on Tuesday, shopping on Thursday and cleaning on Friday. What about Wednesday? you ask. That's football, man! Wherever my next journey will bring me, Wednesdays are reserved for football. Full stop; no debate. And if there is no interesting game on Wednesdays, then I could relax on the sofa, with a beer and a cigar and play Angry Birds on my laptop.

Or every morning reading the newspaper, then go to the pub for a few beers, then late lunch, then have an afternoon nap and wake-up just on time for "Blokken" on Flemish television. On Nederland 1 that is "Lingo", on France3 it's "Des chiffres et des lettres". In Germany I would get out of bed for "Gottschalk Live" and in the UK for "Put your money where your mouth is". Then dinner and finally back to the pub till late night.

No, thank you. I don't see that as an interesting filling of my time; unless I plan to become senile before age 60. I may though indeed stop working in large-scale corporate environments. As you definitely will have noticed, I am less attracted by the politics in today's companies in the FTSE50, CAC40, Bel20, DAX, or similar.

Now a decision to fully stop working – I mean in a sense of withdrawing from an environment where you are paid for your efforts and capabilities – that requires some financial considerations. It may be a nice dream from my wife – who stopped working herself four years ago, but is it financially sustainable? Is it at all doable at age 50? Knowing that statutory pension age will probably soon move to 67 or beyond, that means the coming 17 to 20 years with no income at all. And with life expectancy figures somewhere in the 80s; the next stage of yet another 20 years again at zero income or very, very little pension? OK, we have been living over the last 10-15 years at relatively low spend and have been saving well. But the returns on these bank savings these days don't even cover the inflation rate. So that's yet another zero income. OK, we have some properties that we could sell off at a later stage but no-one has a clue on their future value. OK, we have some stock options and a few deliver good dividends; these will probably pay for heating and electricity. OK, hopefully I will enjoy the benefits of a company pension plan at age 65; that'll keep us going for a few years. But apart from that, it looks that we'll be eating our savings and shares day by day. That doesn't look good and certainly doesn't leave room for one day ending up in an expensive care home.

On the other hand, let's look at this in a very simple way. Very basic; you know I like that. On average, people start working between age 20 and 25. On average, people stop working between age 60 and 65. Say that this is 45 years of income generation. If I stop working now; I have only done around 30 years; so I'll be missing one third of "income generation time".

But out of the recently published statistics by the International Labor Organisation, my last annual earnings were five times over the country's average. Let's take a very safe margin here as you know that these kinds of statistics are rarely very accurate. So say that over the full career, it was 'only' double the average.
So, I have generated 1/3 less of the time but at a level at least double the others.
That makes me conclude that there are no financial needs that would force me to keep working beyond today. I know that maths has never been my core strength, but that seems right though, doesn't it? Challenge me if you have a different view. But please don't come with the socialist arguments on moral obligations with respect to solidarity. Don't tell me I need to keep contributing to the system. I may have earned double the average, but rest assured, I have also contributed more, much more than double to the social security and tax system. Enough is enough, because as I have said before, what will my return be on that? Zero state pension?

OK, my wife and I also realise that if I keep working in senior jobs in corporate life for another five or 10 years, we can easily afford that yacht in Monaco or a sea-front house in Florida, or the mountain chalet with indoor pool in Switzerland and still go twice a year to New Zealand on holidays. Sounds attractive; but we don't need it. And dinner every week in a Michelin star restaurant; no thank you. I prefer my wife's beef and onion pie. And obviously first, the delicious tomato soup.

I don't know; I may be wrong on the maths. We'll see. Whatever. And if I am absolutely wrong on the figures, then we still have three options. The first one is that our son André, by that time a very successful businessman, will financially support us. But forget that; we even don't want to consider that.

So that leaves two other options. One is to decide not to carry on with life beyond our financial expiration date. I know that's a shocking statement but you know in the meantime that I strongly believe in freedom of choice. Based on my solicitor's advice, I can't elaborate further on this. Last option, as alluded to above, is to just wait and see how the government and the social security system is going to help us when we go bankrupt. I expect them as a gratitude to my massive contributions during my career, to put us in a luxury day-care home somewhere in the lovely Ardennes. Here we will get the penthouse suite. The private elevator will mount me to the roof-top terrace; the heaters are on and the butler will bring me a gin and tonic, an ashtray and a good Cuban cigar. This every day at 10 am and 4 pm. To ensure we don't get bored, they'll send us on holidays to Portugal twice a year. During the weekends, we'll have a private chauffeur to tour the lovely area. And Sonja will have a personal shopper twice a year to visit the Galeries Lafayette in Paris.

In your dreams Henry. We'll see.

But currently I have that irresistible desire to stick to one of my philosophies. Initially, I wanted to market this book under the title "3 x 25". That stands in fact for how I see the basic life cycle of a human being in the developed world. Hereby, I define the first stage of life of 25 years as learning and developing. This stage gets succeeded by 25 years of hard working, continued learning, building a family and creating earnings. Then, in my philosophy comes a third stage of well-deserved 25 years of rest. Given current life expectancy figures, you may probably want to critique this view. OK then, let's make it 3 times 30; I can live with that. But don't ask me to support the current overstretching lifecycle of say 25-50-10. That would be an investment of 75 for a return of 10. That doesn't sound to me like a wise investment. You may also say that I am blind to current economic issues and to the national pension deficits everywhere. Again, I agree. But what we need to understand is that all of that has been created by ourselves, by our excessive consumption and living standards. A little bit less luxury (and that's our plan) may do wonders. So forget Sonja's private shopper. But Henry insists on the butler and the cigar. We'll see.

"Prediction is very difficult, especially if it's about the future"; this is a great quote from Niels Bohr, a Danish physicist.

Honestly, I don't know yet where life will take us. You may find out when we next meet and exchange business cards. Henry may surprise you. You may get one-headed Henry W Derrick, Vice-President at Siemens, or SABMiller, or InBev. Or McLinsey! Or – oh, I would love that so much – HR Director Deloitte. Unlikely though. But if the cheap, self-printed and slightly wrinkled business card were to state "Henry – Religious Artworks", I still hope you'll shake him by the hand and offer him a beer. Chimay Bleue please.

And dinner. In a cosy Italian restaurant. No black pepper.

~ ~ ~ ~ ~ ~ ~ ~ ~

CHAPTER 21

The management basics.

"I don't go by the rule book... I lead from the heart, not the head." -Princess Diana

Now, six months after having departed corporate life, I have defined for myself a new mission: challenge the rat-racers and their blindfolded climbing of the corporate ladder. Sauced with a bit of humour and lots of invites to self-reflection, I regularly "infotain" at company and industry events. Just for fun, not as a proper job, as in fact I am still in that phase that my wife prefers most; just enjoying life. You will however, not find me in the pub every day and I am still totally unskilled in ironing.

"Good afternoon. I am really angry today, so I do apologise upfront if I get a bit emotional in this session. I know, emotions don't belong to business life. But it's all the fault of your Finance Director. Normally I book my flights to these events myself; business class of course. Gives me a lot of airmiles. But this time your Finance Manager booked my flight through easyJet.

Of course I ended up in a middle seat squeezed between two junior marketers on their way back home from a conference in Brussels. They turned me crazy. I got two hours of discussion on the best positioning of the products on the shelf in a grocery store. For one it was at eye-height and supported with a digital display – proven by studies of Manchester Business School. For the other one, the only importance to catch the consumer's attention was a floor mat. Scientific research done by the University of Pennsylvania had proven that consumers first look to the floor and that's when they take their impulse purchase decision. So you need a branded floor mat. While the two guys continue arguing, I am reading the Harvard Business Review. The article refers to a 2012 study from the HEC Paris. In their research, they found that a brand got longer looks and was more likely to be chosen when it was placed in the centre of the shelf. I got fed up and suggested to the guys that we should go back to the old sandwich man on the street; with two cardboard posters over his body. On the back it should read "look up" and on the front "look down".

They didn't appreciate my intervention. Those marketers.

"Wir leben Auto's" (Opel),
"Sure we can" (TNT),
"Think different" (Apple),
"Let your fingers do the walking" (Yellow Pages).

So I am not feeling so good after this flight. Again, sorry if I am a bit a 'pis vinaigre'. You understand that, yes? 'Pis vinaigre'? 'Pis' is like 'peeing' and 'vinaigre' is that sour liquid thing that the English like to poor over their French fries. Yes, vinegar. So, in short, I pee vinegar as I feel very sour. Because of your Finance Director.

Life would be much easier with just one language, wouldn't it? I am in for consolidation, standardisation and centralisation. One global language and yes, it should be English. Same for one currency; the Euro of course. Globally. Globally, that means including the UK. And one religion. I opt for Islam. My wife (then it would be 'wives' in plural) isn't supportive to the thought; she doesn't like the burka.

Yes, I would also standardise clothing in business life. We should all go – men and women – for the burka. Wouldn't that be a life-changing thing? For the first time in corporate life, it wouldn't be about 'who you are' but about 'what you say'!
Next step would be about what you do; but that's perhaps a step too far.

And what do we managers do in fact? We 'managers'? What do we do? Eight hours a day? What do I say, eight? That's not enough, real managers work 12-14 hours a day. And at least half of the weekend. If you don't do that than you are not today's manager. And certainly not the manager of the future.

But what do we do all day long? After we've had a shower, brush our teeth, skip breakfast and drive to the office. What do we do then?

I'll help you. Let's go back 20, 30, 40 years. For some here in the room it looks like 100 years. Let's go back to kindergarten. What did we do then after we had filled our dipper, Mum washed and dressed us, we threw our Kraft's Betterfood biscuits on the floor and Dad drove us to kindergarten. What did we do then?

We played. And Miss Ingrid told us what to do and what not to do. And today we do what the CEO asks us to do. And we played with Lego blocks on the floor mat. Not branded by the way. And when my friend next to me stole my plastic Dinosaurs, I poured my fruit juice over his pink plush Tinky Winky and thieved his Matchbox Mercedes. And today in the management meeting, when the Supply Chain Director tells you that he is going to offer 'your' John a better paid job in his department, then you react. And then you'll convince his personal assistant to come and work for you. And behind his back, you'll try to convince the Operations Director that anyway Supply Chain should be your responsibility, not his.

At 10.30 am at kindergarten, Miss Ingrid put us all nicely in a circle; each of us on our peeing pot. And we were quiet and looked at each other. That's not different to today's board meeting. We sit there nicely aligned around the oval meeting table and look at each other. And from time to time we produce shit. Management bullshit.

Then we had 15 minutes of singing or making music or whatever terrible noise. That's today's team meeting. That's when we talk to our people, or shout; nothing else other than trendy buzzwords. And not more than 15 minutes because we don't have more time for our teams.

Next we had again some free playing. While little fat Ken slapped me in my face because I had so called thieved his wooden toy blocks, I returned him by putting my right food on his cardboard castle. Got you! He started crying and got Miss Ingrid's attention. He then pointed at me. The bastard. And when Miss Ingrid walked towards me, luckily Tracey prompted her to her piece of art: "Look Miss, I have made the highest tower ever with these wooden blocks."
"Well done Tracey." But Tracey had first stolen the blocks from Ken.

And how is that today? Latest estimates and next year operational planning. "I am ready Miss CEO. I bought three new machines, they are ready and we are fully prepared for overtime. But Ken's product development teams are nowhere. I'll have to lay-off 45 people if he doesn't come up with anything." And then Ken complains to Miss CEO about Roberto – the Marketing VP – who hasn't given any final specs yet. And Roberto says proudly, "Look here CEO, I have 30 new products in our innovation pipeline; that's more than ever." And then the CEO says, "Well done, Roberto."

And when we all went back home to Mum for lunch at 12:00 pm, we nowadays go back to our private cubicle. We have a sandwich and some crisps and rather than playing a bit with Mum and our sister, we now play Facebook. Or LinkedIn. Many just play Solitaire. And also the CEO goes back to his office with one or two of his direct reports. For a so-called business lunch. And of course as he's the boss, he's ever ambitious and target-driven. He's again on an acquisition trail and wants to kill the competition. So they play Pacman. Or an interactive game of Minesweeper. Or Stratego.

After lunch we go back to kindergarten for a few more hours. More game playing. And we listen to Miss Ingrid reading out of some books. She reads and let us from time to time fill in missing words. That's today's brainstorming session on the creation of our mission charter and values. The boss – or an appointed consultant – leads and we fill in with what we believe we stand for. And although you have been working more than 10 years for this company, at the end of the session you'll know what your company's values are. At least on paper.

And when we aren't calm enough, then Miss Ingrid puts us back in a circle and tells us the rules of the game. No shouting, no cheating, no lying, no hair pulling and no fighting.

Yes indeed, that's today when we get in our mailbox our corporate policies. Procedures. Standards. Guidelines. That's when we once a year get a refreshment session on policies and standards.

Product recall policy. Conflict of Interest Guidelines. Dealings with Public Officials standards. Financial reporting integrity standards. Stock Ownership Commitment Policy. Code of business ethics. Policy on related party transactions. The zero-gift acceptance policy. Disclosure Controls and Procedures Policy. Guide to scientific exchange and other non-promotional activities. Media Interaction and Public Appearances policy. And, the Policy on Policy Review.

It's all about corporate governance; no shouting, no cheating, no lying, no hair pulling and no fighting. Unless it's to the benefit of the company.

There are also the seven million specific Human Resources policies.

Whistle blowing policy. Performance Development guidelines. Vacation days policy. Uniformed services leave policy. Anti-discrimination and harassment procedures. Smoke-free workplace policy. Progressive discipline warning policy. Employee screening standards. The casual dress code policy for customer interacting workers. Breast feeding accommodation policy. And then, watch this you unhealthy rat-racers – your family may need it soon – the Funeral and Bereavement policy.

Once a year at Kindergarten we went to the local indoor playground. That's your today's annual management conference.

Oh, and also, in the afternoon at Kindergarten we all slept together. I won't make a comparison here with corporate life. But don't forget that it's proven that adult men think about sex every 12 seconds. Also

in the boardroom. By the way, in a study in the US, 37 per cent of office workers who slept with their superiors said to have been rewarded with a career boost.
A Belgian stand-up comedian expressed it this way: "To succeed, you need to suck-seed".

And in the early afternoon we went back home. And today, in the late evening we go back home.

So what is 'management'? Let's ask the consultants. Because that's what we managers do; isn't it? Well there it is. We have it! The definition of a manager could be "an individual in an organisation who is entitled to bring in consultants". Those consultants justify their existence by bringing change. The manager takes the credit for that change. He then gets rewarded through a promotion. The others who need to execute the change idea – once again get tired and frustrated. So the manager brings in a consultant to work on employee engagement. The consultant ensures that the engagement score increases, and thus the manager can now say that he is also a great leader. And thus he gets promoted; again.

Seriously now."

Then I go a bit deeper with the audience back to the fundaments of management and business. Back to the basics as defined by Taylor in the early 20th century. Taylor is in fact through his scientific research, the inventor of business consulting. According to him, management "is an art of knowing what to do, when to do and to see it is done in the best and cheapest way".

In general, the purpose of a business – small or global – is to produce an added value to customers who are willing to pay a price for it, higher than the cost of that product or service to the seller. That is the case today; that's what it was centuries ago and what it will be in the 25th century.

But for that, you don't need managers. The butcher at the corner achieves that without managers. As does the pub-owner, and the notary.

We managers were only created in the 19th century during the industrial revolution. When machines were also invented and the machines brought mass production. Rather than Jack and Jill producing something in their backyards, environments were created with hundreds of Jacks and Jills. And the leader of the gang, the owner, created a layer in between him and those who add value. That's were management is born.

I like the definition of F. John Reh, yet another business consultant. It's very basic but it's clear: "Management is both art and science. It is the art of making people more effective than they would have been without you. The science is in how you do that." And the answer is through planning, organising, directing and controlling. Reh explains further, "Four workers can make six units in an eight-hour shift without a manager. If I hire you to manage them and they still make six units a day, what is the benefit to my business of having hired you? On the other hand, if they now make eight units per day, you, the manager, have value."

So it's about effectiveness to the organisation; about what you and your job add to the business.

Here is some more of my speech.

"And there is nothing so easy in business life, ladies and gentlemen, as evaluating your managerial effectiveness. It's so basic, so basic that unfortunately no-one applies it. And honestly, you don't need a team engagement survey for that; you don't need a 360° for that or any other tool to enrich consultants. What you need is to ask yourself on a regular basis three basic questions:
1. What have I added to the business this week?
2. What have I contributed this week to the financial wellbeing of the business?

It's that simple. But, challenging though if you dare to ask yourself those questions not every week but on a daily basis. And for the real heroes; try it at the end of every hour! It only takes five seconds. Now, that's only two questions you will say. Correct. Here is the third –and to use another buzzword – "mission critical" question:

3. What have I added this week to my personal and family wellbeing?

Now most consultants and management gurus may agree with question 1 and 2, but raise their eyebrows at question 3. But why, honestly? Here comes yet another buzzword: "the holistic view". You should really have a holistic view on yourself. You are not just the Accounting Manager, or the Sales Director or the Quality Engineer, or the Risk Manager. You are John, Marleen, Fred or Cindy.
Yeah, I have done this on purpose here; this ordering of man, woman, man, woman; like zipping traffic on a motorway ahead of a lane closure. Also just to reflect the stupidity of the mandatory listing of men and woman like on the electoral lists in Belgium. What a load of bollocks this so-called positive discrimination is. What's going to be the future on this? It's probably going to grow towards further anti-discrimination listings so that in future electoral list will look like this.

First a gay, catholic, non-unionised, black youngster. Second a middle aged, Muslim woman in a wheelchair. And third on the list an atheist, blind paedophile, obviously male. And fourth an elderly, unemployed hooker of Asian origin? Give me a break; all that non-discrimination nonsense. It is even going so insane that Scotland Yard is banning the word "blacklist" in fear of discrimination claims. Consequently, also "whitelist" – for acceptable contacts – is thrown in the dustbin; the internal advice is now to only use the terminology red and green list! Give me a break!

Sorry, I am digressing again and realise I am skating on thin ice. But it's about foolish non-discrimination and exactly where you shouldn't discriminate or differentiate is on yourself. You are not the Accounting Manager and – of secondary rank – John. You are John. You are Marleen. You are not someone before 6 pm and somebody else after 6pm. You are who you are.

And that for me is the most critical basic of management. Apart from some technical capabilities that we all have learned, you also have a non-professional heart, a soul, a mindset. You have spiritual beliefs; you have a philosophical look of life. Be holistic and be yourself. And being a successful manager is about acting that way; being genuine and being yourself.

Additional to being authentic, providing trust, interest, challenges and development to your teams, that's what makes you a leader. With some sourced knowledge of the industry and the market, with innovation and strategic capabilities and with – again – genuine communication capabilities, that's what makes you a visionary leader.

Thank you."

~ ~ ~ ~ ~ ~ ~ ~ ~

THE FACTS 5

The real management basics

Finding a consensus on what "management" really stands for is almost as difficult as finding a solution for the Palestinian / Israeli conflict. When you Google the word "management", you get over 4.5 billion results. That's much more than for each of the words sex, drugs or alcohol, but less than for "love" or for "money".

Nevertheless, it's always good to start off by looking at some definitions from respectable sources.

This is how the Cambridge Business Dictionary defines "management": (20)
- "the activity or job of being in charge of a company, organization, department, or team of employees
- the group of people who control a company or organisation
- the activity of controlling something, or of using or dealing with something in a way that is effective"

From the same source, these are the descriptors for the verb "manage":
- "to be in charge of and control a company, department, project, team, etc.
- to be able to use something, for example time or money, in an effective way
- to be responsible for investing money for investors". (Note: the latter as a definition under the heading Finance / Stock Market).

The Longman Dictionary of Contemporary English gives the following definition: (21)
- "the activity of controlling and organizing the work that a company or organization does
- the people who are in charge of a company or organization
- the way that people control and organize different situations that happen in their lives or their work".

Another source is Dictionary.com. Their (abbreviated) definition of the noun "management" is as follows (22):
- "the act or manner of managing; handling, direction, or control.
- skill in managing; executive ability.
- the person or persons controlling and directing the affairs of a business, institution, etc.
- executives collectively, considered as a class (distinguished from labour)".

Etymologically, the verb "manage" is believed to originate from the mid-16th Century from the Italian "maneggiare", which means "to handle". Especially used in the sense of "to handle a horse"; it is influenced by the French word "manège"; standing for "horsemanship". It is assumed that this meaning was extended from the 1570s onwards to other objects and to business. In the early 18th Century, "management" in the sense of "the act of managing" was being used in the sense of a governing body; initially of a theatre.

Based on further research into literature, it can be said that management as a function mainly comprises planning, budgeting, controlling, organising and reporting.

Employees and teams will follow the manager for many reasons, whether they be their technical capabilities or managerial competencies. Another generic and unquestioned reason for staff to follow the boss is the obvious impact the manager has on the individual's pay and employment. The manager instructs, controls and pays (except in those environments where pay is purely collectively regulated, without any performance criteria).

In the 1950s and 60s, the term "leadership" was introduced to the commercial world, initially to give a new brand name to the same activity as management, but later on to describe additional and different characteristics. It began with James MacGregor Burns in the 1970s referring to "transactional leadership" (say management) and "transformational leadership". The transformational theory, according to Burns, yields several pros which are: it appeals to the moral side of developing social values and individual purpose, asks the most fundamental question of what the ultimate goal of leadership is and why one should be a leader.

Employees and teams will follow the leader for their visionary and influential leadership rather than just for their positional power. The influence that a leader may have on pay and employment has less relevance than in the case of the manager. Of course also the leader recognises, stimulates and rewards performance. However the form of reward is generally not just financial but encompasses longer term rewards such as enhanced career prospects, international experience, project work and so on. The leader tends to reward more through tools which deliver longer term employee engagement.

Many authors state that management and leadership are not mutually exclusive; others will say they are very distinct concepts; it all depends from what angle you look at the activity. The common agreement -in both concepts- is that there needs to be another party (staff, the team) to interact with. The different concepts and views come from looking at the "how"; how you run the team and what your aim is for the team's result. As such, the word "leader" very rarely appears in job titles that are still pre-reserved for Director, Chief, President, Manager, for example. But the term "Leiter" is however still common in German speaking environments.

Academic researchers, bloggers, management gurus and many others have created hundreds of lists that provide an overview on how management differentiates from leadership in terms of "running a team". These –frequently contradictory- lists show how blurred the debate is.

The table on the next page gives an abbreviated and amalgamated overview.

MANAGER	LEADER
Shorter term view; to be done today, this month, etc.	*Long term perspective, much more visionary.*
Plans and budgets.	*Creates strategy and direction.*
Gets things done through instructions and control.	*Gets things done through inspirational trust.*
Emphasises bottom line. Allocation of resources.	*Looks at longer term horizon. Prioritisation of investments.*
Get the task done (status quo is OK).	*Challenges, stretches.*
Acts as a boss.	*Coaches, facilitates.*
Asks about how and when.	*Challenges on what and why.*
Pays.	*Rewards.*

Some authors would add the McGregor's theory X and Y types, as well as the Blake and Mouton grid in terms of being "task" or "people" oriented, to this list. The latter leadership grid is seen as a bit old-fashioned but still remains attractive given its efficiency and simplicity. We need, however, to be careful in adding these theories to the comparative list as it could lead us into the endless and controversial debate on "soft skills". While it is commonly agreed that leaders –as opposed to managers- give greater emphasis on human needs, and that true leaders have a genuine interest in people, really successful leaders never keep their eye off what needs to be achieved. The attainment of pre-defined goals is key for leaders, but their targets are achieved "with" the teams rather than "through" them.

A 2012 poll on LinkedIn sought votes on the following five most underrated leadership skills. These are the results: (total voters 192)
1. managing expectations and performance   19%
2. negotiation skills   6%
3. implementing strategy, i.e. goal-getting   7%
4. winning buy-in from staff   25%
5. creating a winning culture at work   43%

There is also the question of whether leadership is a born or learned capability. It's a frequently discussed and debated issue, but personally I am not sure how relevant the question is. "Inborn", many top level, mainly political, leaders will say. In fact it isn't; or at least it's a combination of born and developed abilities. Research on identical twins suggests that leadership capabilities are one third born and two thirds made. However, it's important to note that the born capabilities are in a certain sense a prerequisite to enable the further development of other leadership skills.

In general, the attributes that we have or haven't got from Mother Nature and that can make us a successful leader are: willingness to take risks, assertiveness, intelligence, extraversion and empathy. Regarding intelligence, it's not so much the pure IQ that counts but the

social intelligence; the capability to analyse and understand processes and groups.
This clearly brings us towards Daniel Goleman's theory on Emotional Intelligence. (23)

"I have found, however, that the most effective leaders are alike in one crucial way. They all have a high degree of what has come to be known as *emotional intelligence*. It's not that IQ and technical skills are irrelevant. They do matter, but mainly as "threshold capabilities"; that is, they are the entry-level requirements for executive positions. But my research, along with other recent studies, clearly shows that emotional intelligence is the sine qua non of leadership. Without it, a person can have the best training in the world, an incisive, analytical mind, and an endless supply of smart ideas, but he still won't make a great leader."

As an aide memoire, emotional intelligence includes self-awareness, self-regulation, motivation, empathy and social skills.

Building further on this —and to come to the point of the management basics- I have further researched studies from many different sources. Whether it's called "management" or "leadership" is less relevant for the below overview; this summary is aiming for a description of the basic characteristics and capabilities required to successfully manage/lead/run a group of individuals in a commercial environment. The reader may say "there's nothing new in here"; and that's intentional. It's about the fundamentals, the basics.

- Having a clear plan, objectives or mission; attainment of your objectives is your first –but not only– mission. The "what" is your priority; not the "how" –except for integrity. Towards your goal(s), have –and demonstrate– robust belief, strong commitment and persuasive ambition.
- Having a genuine interest in people. Dale Carnegie lists this as one of the most important aspects of leadership. It's also one of the "11 Simple Rules" from Dave Packard (HP) as proclaimed in one of his management conferences in 1958. "Have a sincere desire to like, respect and be helpful to others".
- Feeling responsible –and acting accordingly– to all those with a stake in your business; shareholders, employees, customers, government and society at large.
- Balancing control and trust in respect of leading your staff and ensuring –with all your actions– that your followers trust you. Integrity is key to this. You don't always need to seek agreement on the decisions you take, but your staff and stakeholders need to trust what you decide.
- Communicating clearly, openly and in a straightforward manner. Know when to communicate factually and when emotionally, but always with passion. You don't communicate because you just like to hear your own voice, you communicate to convey a message. Make it a clear and unambiguous message without excessive use of business jargon.
- Maximising your resources. The Frederick W Taylor theory (theory regarding squeezing resources may be a bit discredited today, but in a commercial environment, cost management is fundamental. Non-contributing resources need to be cut

immediately. Contributing resources need to be rewarded –in all their forms- immediately.
- Having an understanding that you can make mistakes. "Have a dream, get on with it and if you fail, then fail fast, learn fast and fix fast", as said by Kevin Roberts, CEO Saatchi & Saatchi and the inventor of Lovemarks.
- Being conscious of time constraints. Planning, prioritising and trustful delegation are critical success factors. Be careful: creating time management spreadsheets may waste you more time than you ultimately gain. Also be clear to others on your level of tolerance for unanticipated interruptions.
- Being conscious there is also life outside the Boardroom. Plan social and family time.

And I would like to add one more. This one doesn't come out of literature but out of personal experience in dealing with many leaders. It's one that for me differentiates good leaders from very successful ones. It's having the capability and willingness to "let go" from time to time. Leadership is frequently linked to perseverance, to not giving up, until the defined goal is reached. And there is no doubt that pushing has helped managers to develop their careers. Many managers however keep pushing to achieve every set target, but that risks burning down their reservoirs of energy. Whether you are endlessly chasing a client, fighting for a change programme or pushing hard and long for an innovative project, it impacts upon your internal battery life. Sometimes "letting go" is the best way of recharging these batteries. I frequently coached leaders on "going for the fights you can win" and on defining those you would like to win. Achieving a good balance on the "must win" and "like to win"-scale, is yet another attribute of successful leaders.

As already demonstrated earlier in this chapter, the subjects of management and leadership generate differing views; it's not a physical science. Peter Drucker's view is this:

"Effective leadership is not about making speeches or being liked; leadership is defined by results not attributes.

But he also wrote the following; hinting on attributes:

"The leaders who work most effectively, it seems to me, never say "I." And that's not because they have trained themselves not to say "I." They don't think "I." They think "we"; they think "team." They understand their job to be to make the team function. They accept responsibility and don't sidestep it, but "we" gets the credit…. This is what creates trust, what enables you to get the task done."

Ultimately, creating trust is probably the most critical attribute. In a 2005-2008 study, Gallup asked 10,000 randomly chosen employees what they really need from leaders. Gallup learned that "followers" are looking firstly for trust, Also commonly cited were compassion (in the sense of caring), stability and hope. Important to note here is that stability in this context doesn't mean that leaders shouldn't provide change. Here it means to provide a form of certainty, in the sense of a guaranteed pay cheque at the end of the month but also in the sense of providing transparency, and knowing that they can count on the leader in times of need. In my view this aspect is not so different from "trust".

Suitable to the overall theme of this book and to conclude this chapter, is the following quote from Stephen Covey. Dr Covey is one of Time Magazine's 25 Most Influential Americans and is of course the author of many bestselling management books.

"Management is efficiency in climbing the ladder of success; leadership determines whether the ladder is leaning against the right wall."

CHAPTER 22

Athens, Georgia, USA.

"If you're climbing the ladder of life, you go rung by rung, one step at a time. Don't look too far up, set your goals high but take one step at a time. Sometimes you don't think you're progressing until you step back and see how high you've really gone" -<u>Donny Osmond</u>

Soon, it will be one year ago that I left corporate life. I must admit; there have been occasions where I missed it somewhat. Not really the business meetings, the corporate plans, nor the comments like "great progress, better than ever but still below plan". What I have been missing from time to time is the chats with colleagues and the intellectual debates. It's strange but I am in a certain sense also missing the speed of life. I now realise that the speed of actions and the continuous moving from one place in the world to another, doesn't give your body lots of opportunities to complain. Today, now that I have time for sports, my body has also found time to resist. After only three squash games, I got an inflammation of the Achilles tendon. Both feet. So I started cycling, fell of my bike and broke two bones in my right hand.

I have also been missing those things that I hated before; airport queues, dusty hotel rooms, life-threatening taxi journeys, etc. Not waking up anymore at 6.30 am with Chris Moyles is another great loss; I am missing the BBC Radio1 breakfast show. Mostly, I am missing a new game that I play at breakfast in hotels. It's not the "That's an indiscrete question" game but another one I started testing a few years ago. I serve myself some croissants at the buffet , two slices of Gravlax smoked salmon, a teaspoon of fresh-cut onions, four cherry tomatoes and eight capers. Yes eight, not nine not seven, exactly eight. Once seated at the table, I spread the two slices of salmon on my plate; preferable an oval or rectangular plate so that I can put one slice on both sides. I decorate the slices with the chopped onions, and when available, I also spread a plentiful amount of dill over the salmon; so much that it looks like the grass of a football field. The four cherry tomatoes are put at the back end of each slice of salmon; these are the imaginative goalposts. Then the four capers are put on one slice; in the form of the four dots on a dice. Same for the other slice of salmon. Then I imagine that these eight capers are football players, two teams playing a Champions League game. And then, preferably when the waitress walks by or tops up the coffee, I start to comment the football game like a reporter on Sky Sports TV. Loud. Well not really loud but also not just mumbling; loud enough for her and my neighbours to hear.

"Peter Crouch; faaaantastic; wow; this must be the goal of the year. Amazing. 59 minutes; the ball comes up. He takes one touch; it's a scissor kick, top left-hand corner. This is an absolute quality goal. His number eight this season but probably the most extra-ordinary goal of his career!"

A well-dressed, probably well-educated and good earning business man, playing football with his eight capers in the hotel's breakfast room. It creates some attention and raises many eyebrows. I find it funny; you'll find it probably ridiculous. Or worse, lunatic.

Whatever. I am missing all those travel experiences and those cross-cultural encounters. That's perhaps logical when you move overnight from excessive travel to almost full abandonment. Indeed not full, as Sonja and I have travelled a bit over the last months but it wasn't three or four flights a week. We have done Malaga, the Dead Sea in Jordan and short city-trips to Budapest and Prague. Currently we are in Athens; not the Greek capital – you must be crazy to go there nowadays, but Athens in Georgia, US, near Atlanta. While Sonja will fly back to Belgium next week, I'll stay here for another few months. People are great here and I get plenty of time and rest for working on my next novel.

My new life as an author is in good shape. Obviously I have also read an immense number of novels; learning from others, they call that in business life. You know, this thing here in your hands may one day become a great success. You never know, I may make it to the nominees list of the John Blogs "Awkward Management Fiction Award" for the world's bestselling author of Antwerp South.

"Dinner will be at seven, Henry."

"Thanks Lucy," I reply and add, "but tonight I will skip the lobster."

"The City View restaurant tonight also serves fresh seabed oysters from British Columbia, if you want," she replies with a warm smile.

Soon, she'll bring me my traditional pre-dinner drinks; a G&T on the rocks. Then I reckon it will be turkey with French beans; no lobster and no oysters.

Lucy is a very charming young woman with Hispanic roots. We frequently chat when we meet in the lobby or in the bar. She has worked in the Stone Hills Hotel for two years now and is one of the most customer centric members of staff. I really believe that she can make a nice career in the hospitality industry. Lucy is hard working and does her job with passion; what else do you need? On top of that, she cares for her customers, a capability she brought with her from her previous jobs as a nurse in a children's hospital in Nashville.

And if this first novel becomes a success, then I want to make it with the next one to the front page of *Time* magazine. Insane or realistic? Doesn't matter. I have always learned that ambition is the prerequisite for success. Who knows, what about a big audacious goal turning into a self-fulfilling prophecy. It doesn't even need to be hairy; why is it hairy in fact?

Self-fulfilling prophecy; what a nice phrase. That reminds me of one of our many management team dinners at CCG, somewhere in a London boutique hotel. I was flirting with one of my female colleagues. I don't remember the exact words I said at the dinner table to Audrey, but it must have been something along the lines of:

"The next step forward? I don't know guys. The next step is probably Audrey and I taking the next 13 steps to the bedroom floor tonight."

"Wishful thinking," Audrey replied while sipping from her glass of expensive Rioja and looking me cheekily – but also invitingly – straight in the eyes.

"Or a self-fulfilling prophecy," I countered her attack.

Sorry – I am digressing again; hopefully you are getting used to the results of my uncontrolled switching between my left and my right frontal hemispheres. It's exceptional, a doctor once told me, my competence to switch in nanoseconds from emotions to reasoning. I still don't know if that assessment of my brain's velocity meant an extraordinarily capability or just that I was turning nuts. For the sake of my self-esteem, shall we all agree it's the first?

Whatever, back to Audrey now. After all the other colleagues had gone to bed, we killed an excessive number of G&Ts in the bar together. Ellis, the bartender, was to English norms very generous on the G. I reckon that the last glasses had more gin than tonic. We were sitting opposite each other in two comfortable red velvet chairs. There was just a small Parisian round table between us. Every time she burst out laughing – probably because of my excellent jokes – she kicked my legs painfully with her pointed high heel shoes. Since that night, every next time that I had dinner with Audrey, I brought with me a pair of football shin pads. A few years later, she got me again though. That was in Puerto Rico after a visit to one of our local factories. The meeting with the local management team was a difficult one in the sense that staffing requirements … .

Henry stop this. Stop rambling. That evening in Puerto Rico, the two of us had a poolside dinner, so I was wearing Bermuda shorts; and no shin pads. Back home, Sonja learned that the bruises on my legs were so-called the result of us playing a half-hour football game against the factory technicians and electricians. We lost the game; 4-nil.

I can't share with you more details of what further on happened with me and Audrey that night in London. Yes, we did together – and both barefoot – the 13 wooden steps to the next floor. Once we arrived at Audrey's bedroom door; honestly I don't recall anymore. Really, I don't recall at all. I can only assume that at that critical moment, my brain again switched promptly from emotions to logical thinking. And so, I probably wished her a good night and went to my bedroom. I think. I don't know. Honestly.

But what I do remember is that night's dream. I rarely dream at night; sometimes I do at home but almost never in a hotel room. But as the night started a bit in an emotional atmosphere, probably my brain wanted to go on that way.

It's also not a surprise that the dream was just like in a David Hamilton movie, starting with Audrey dressed in a white long and very transparent robe. No underwear. Freudian shrinks will be able to explain this. In her right hand, she is holding a glass bottle of milk. It is a very sunny spring day, and vivid and attractive like a young foal, she promenades through the Bavarian meadow-land. An overflow of Dandelions colour the pasture yellow; it could have been a commercial for DHL. On the small sandy road alongside the pasture, the notary was following her slowly in his Studebaker car. Sitting next to him is Françis Brun, the French trade union leader, and in the back of the car are Andy Coppersmith and my son André. They are enjoying a gin and tonic. All of a sudden, the notary drives at full speed, then breaks at the end of the grass-land and parks the old-timer. He gets out of his car, spreads a blanket with light-brown and white squares on the soft grass and welcomes Audrey with a kiss. On the cheek.

Françis Brun walks to the boot of the car; I think, "Oh my God, not the gun again." Today, he seems to be in a less aggressive mood and returns with a large casserole full of delicious tomato soup. While Audrey is serving the soup in five smaller bowls, she decants a bit of the milk in her bowl. Half an hour later, the notary drives Audrey to a small boutique hotel nearby the village; regrettably the Scottish manager offers her some less transparent clothes. That doesn't hinder Audrey to keep smiling; she is oh so beautiful; whatever she wears. She's more sexy than any trainee in any Kiev hotel and also, I am sorry Angelique, she doesn't need a D-cup to make me dizzy.

In the bar of the village hotel, the Polish waitress serves her a Chimay Bleue beer. The notary is having a glass of Slovenian white wine and enjoys a Cohiba cigar. They relax while they are both watching "The Bodyguard" movie. In the early evening, she says farewell to the notary, leaves the hotel and goes shopping to the local tax-free shop. Here she buys an iPod and then leaves the old village. Walking back through the pasture from where she came – I don't know where she came from – she listens on the iPod to Andrea Botcelli's Con Te Partiro. I can hear the music and dream about exquisite cuisine at the borders of the Dubai fountains. A dream in a dream, can anybody tell me, is that at all possible? Or is it just a fraudulent thought?

While Audrey progresses through the meadow, she shakes hands with Mr Blancpain, with Kathy and George, with a Moldavian cab driver, with a BA first officer, with a Polish waitress whose middle finger is ornamented with a very large square-shaped ring with a black stone, and with Sylvie from the Marriott who offers her a picture of the Clifton Bridge.

With this dream, dear reader, this book will come to an end.

Halfway her journey on the meadow, Audrey starts climbing – with an everlasting smile – an imaginative ladder. For a split second, I thought she was climbing a stairway to a Brussels Airlines plane. But she wasn't; there are no stairs at all. There is just a warm and soft wind that helps her ascent. Close to a single low-hanging white cloud, she drops Andrea Bocelli, waves at me, and quickly draws something on the back of a Deloitte headed envelope. She throws me the envelope, artistically folded in the form of a sailplane. Unfolding the paper, I notice it's a leek painting. Her short hand written message at the bottom reads "What's your room number?" Then she disappears slowly in the heavenly white cloud and also disappears out of my corporate life.

At the same time, the notary drives by slowly. He offers me a lift and I take a seat in the back of the car; squeezed between CEO Andy and my son André. On our way to Munich airport, we have a big argument in the car. André insists that I join him in taking the first train back home. He needs my advice and support on an important personal investment project. On the other hand, Andy wants me to jump on a plane to Heathrow to chair on his behalf a meeting at the Marriott airport hotel on our corporate ethics programme. I am so proud of my son's plan to buy an old brewery in Antwerp and to reconvert it into a business hotel. But the meeting at Heathrow is also important as we have invested a lot of time and money in this programme.

I wake up when charming Lucy from the Stone Hills Hotel softly pushes my shoulder while I hear her saying, "Henry, you didn't finish the delicious turkey?"

This brings an abrupt end to my dream but I luckily remember the last part.

I see myself climbing a ladder – neither a corporate one nor an imaginative one like Audrey's, it's a real wooden ladder. I am climbing this ladder to clean the first floor windows of the hotel. The 12 windows from my son's brand new Antwerp hotel.

Any comments on this book are welcomed at the following address:

Henry W Derrick
Stone Hills Hospital – Dementia Care Center, Stone Hills 140
Athens, GA 30100
USA

Best regards,
Henry

~ ~ ~ ~ ~ ~ ~ ~ ~

Ausgang · Exit
Gepäckausgabe · Baggage claim
GO FOR GREEN
EXCHANGE

CHAPTER 23

In good shape.

A recent medical check-up at the Antwerp Centre for Occupational Health has proven that Henry is in a good shape. Blood pressure is OK. His resting heartbeat is at 62; which is excellent. Total lung capacity is around 5.3 litres; that's good for a smoker. There are no indications at all of early dementia or Alzheimer's. The only minor issue is a relatively high level of cholesterol.

Last month, Henry visited a friend who is a psychiatrist, in fact a well-known psycho-analyst. After him analysing the 'Audrey' dream and the 'breakfast salmon football game', the psychiatrist is however of the belief that Henry is completely nuts and should be sent with urgency to a mental care home. At least that is what he said, at three o'clock at night in a pub nearby The Royal Albert Hall in London. They both – emphasis on both, were as drunk as a skunk. Or should I better say – given it was a posh establishment, as drunk as a lord. That reminds me of that old joke about a young lad in court.

"Yes I confess Sir, at the time of thieving the four chickens I was as drunk as a judge."

"You probably mean as drunk as a Lord," the irritated judge replied.

"Yes my Lord," the guy said.

Today, Henry massively enjoys working in his son's hotel. Here you see that dreams – even of the weirdest mind – may come true. Cleaning windows, setting up the meeting room and doing some overall admin stuff. Last week, he stood in for the sick night porter. He even did a double shift and also helped serving breakfast. So this time, it was Henry asking a young female customer, "What's your room number please, Madame?" Of course with a suppressed hidden smile. And what he likes most of all is driving the business customers from the hotel to Brussels airport and secretly listening to them while they are phoning their head office.

"The second quarter results are OK but the second half of the year they will end-up below plan. I think we need to get us a new Sales Director; John just doesn't get the team aligned to our overall strategy."
And.

"It went well, very well. PwC believes the current owners are hiding around 0.9 million of tax risks. But that's peanuts against our opportunities to enhance the margins. I'll be back here on Monday and have a final walk through the employment costs."
And.

"No I don't think we should share this yet with the Legal department. It's too early. But I'll drop you tonight a fully detailed report."
And.

"Sweetie, I'll be late tonight. I missed the lunchtime flight. The meeting took too long. Can you take Sam tonight to music school? I'll also have to work Saturday so we better cancel our visit to your mum. No Sunday doesn't go as I am flying to Moscow in the late afternoon."

And Henry, he pretends not to speak or understand one word of Shakespeare's lovely language.

When you need Henry, go and find him at his son's hotel. If he is not there; then he'll be in his holiday house in France.
There, he'll be working on his next novel or writing blogs on 'management basics'. Or paving the steps to his private beach on the river bank. Or cutting trees. Or fishing trout. Or just relaxing in the sun; of course with a good Cuban cigar.

I am sure he'll offer you a gin and tonic; or a Pernod. He's as happy as a man can be.
As a young adult, he decided to prioritise on building a successful career. That was his choice at that time; thus it must have been the right choice. Today, he decides to relax. That's his choice; so it must be the right choice.

Never in his life has Henry visited Georgia. As such, it is advised not to send any mail to fictitious Stone Hills in Athens, Georgia.

The author of *'Rat-race to the Boardroom'* can be reached at: henry.w.derrick@gmail.com. He promises a reply; but be patient, it won't come at the speed of the corporate rat-race.

~ ~ ~ ~ ~ ~ ~ ~ ~

Acknowledgements

Every reasonable effort has been made to contact the copyright holders of materials reproduced in this book. If any have unintentionally been overlooked, we would be glad to hear from you and make good in next editions.

(1)	Center for Advanced Human Resource Studies, School of Industrial and Labor Relations, Cornell University, New York. http://www.ilr.cornell.edu/depts/CAHRS. Working Paper #94-08
(2)	Ram Charan, *What the CEO wants you to know*. Published by Crown Business. February 2001.
(3)	News Release, Academy of Finland, 28 February 2011. www.aka.fi. Academy of Finland © 2010
(4)	*Does Happiness Promote Career Success?* Journal of Career Assessment. February 2008 16: 101-116. www.jca.sagepub.com; Copyright © 2009, SAGE Publications.
(5)	Vermeulen, Freek. *Business exposed: the naked truth about what really goes on in the world of business. 2010*, Pearson Education
(6)	www.bloggingprweb.com/corporate-speak
(7)	© 2012 thoughtLEADERS, LLC: Leadership Training for the Real World
(8)	*Buzzwords say all the wrong thing*, by Matt. 25 September 2006 on 37signals.com
(9)	Bentley RA (2008) *Random Drift versus Selection in Academic Vocabulary: An Evolutionary Analysis of Published Keywords*. PLoS ONE 3(8): e3057. doi:10.1371/journal.pone.0003057
(10)	By Max Mallet, Brett Nelson and Chris Steiner, 26 Jan 2012 on www.Forbes.com, 2012 Forbes.com LLC™
(11)	*Bad Business Jargon: It Is What It Is*. Cathy Vandewater on Vault blogs. Published 31 January 2012
(12)	VIENNA INTERNATIONAL PLAN OF ACTION ON AGING. UNITED NATIONS NEW YORK – 1983

(13)	United Nations, Department of Economic and Social Affairs, Population, Division (2011). *World Population Prospects: The 2010 Revision, Highlights and Advance Tables. Working Paper No. ESA/P/WP.220*
(14)	Eurofound (2012), *Fifth European Working Conditions Survey*, Publications Office of the European Union, Luxembourg. doi:10.2806/34660. ISBN 978-92-897-1062-6
(15)	Defresnes M., Marioni P., and Thévenot C., *L'opinion des employeurs sur les seniors: les craintes liées au vieillissement s'atténuant*, Dares Analyses, No 55, September 2010
(16)	Journal 'Neurobiology of Aging' Vol. 30 No. 4 April 2009. *When does age-related cognitive decline begin?* Timothy A. Salthouse
(17)	*Timing of onset of cognitive decline: results from Whitehall II prospective cohort study.* Archana Singh-Manoux, Mika Kivimaki, M Maria Glymour, Alexis Elbaz, Claudine Berr, Klaus P Ebmeier, Jane E Ferrie, Aline Dugravot. British Medical Journal. BMJ Publishing Group Ltd. Jan 5, 2012.
(18)	*2010 Alzheimer's Disease Facts and Figures*, Alzheimer's & Dementia, Volume 6. ©2012 Alzheimer's Association. All rights reserved. Used with permission.
(19)	Encyclopedia of Mental Disorders; on www.minddisorders.com. Advameg, Inc.
(20)	Cambridge Business English Dictionary © Cambridge University Press
(21)	http://www.ldoceonline.com/dictionary/management. Longman Dictionary of Contemporary English, Copyright © 2012 Pearson Education Ltd.
(22)	http://dictionary.reference.com/browse/management; from Dictionary.com
(23)	Reprinted by permission of Harvard Business Review. Excerpt from *What makes a leader?* by Daniel Goleman; issue January 2004. Copyright © 2004 by the Harvard Business School Publishing Corporation; all rights reserved.